KB266215

ALL ABOUT JUNIOR TOEFL
[LISTENING]

Advanced Course

Bansok Junior

ALL ABOUT JUNIOR TOEFL LISTENING (Advanced Course)

1st edition : Printed in Jan. 25, 2009(1st impression)

Authors : Naomi Kim, Alan Hahn
Publisher : Mi-soon Ko
Editor in chief : Seung-ju Kang
Editors : Min-jung Kwon, Dam-hee Cho
Marketing Department : Keum-hee Kim, Chang-won Lee
Design : Joo-hee Moon
Publisher : Bansok Publishing Company
Address : 904-Ho, B-Dong, Woolim Blue9. 240-21, Yeomchang-dong, Gangseo-gu, Seoul, Korea
Registration No. : 9-33
Web site : www.bansok.co.kr
E-mail : bansok@bansok.co.kr
Phone : 02-2093-3399
Fax : 02-2093-3393

Copyright © 2009 Bansok Publishing Company
Reproduction in any manner, in whole or in part, in English or in other languages, is prohibited.
All rights reserved.

ISBN 978-89-7172-486-6   13740
Printed in Korea

ALL ABOUT JUNIOR TOEFL [LISTENING]

Advanced Course

Bansok Junior

PREFACE

iBT 토플이 국내에서 시행된 지 벌써 1년이 넘었습니다. 언어의 4가지 구성 영역인 Reading, Listening, Speaking, Writing 능력을 골고루 측정하는 iBT 토플은 언어 이해력과 논리력, 분석력, 표현력, 응용력 등을 종합적이고 총체적으로 평가하는 시험입니다. 영어를 학습함에 있어 어느 한쪽으로 치우침 없이 각 영역이 서로 균형 있게 조화를 이루는 학습의 중요성을 확산시킨 데에 iBT 토플의 역할이 크다고 할 수 있습니다.

4 영역의 통합형 문제의 등장으로, 토플 시험에서 리스닝 섹션이 차지하는 비중이 여느 때보다 크게 증가했습니다. 문제는 청취력은 짧은 시간 집중적으로 공부한다고 해서 실력이 부쩍 늘어나지는 않는다는 것입니다. 글로 써있을 때는 무슨 의미인지 쉽게 알 수 있는 내용도 원어민의 발음으로 들려주면 무슨 내용인지 도무지 모를 때가 많습니다. 청취력을 향상시키기 위해서는 무엇보다도 매일매일 영어 듣기 환경에 귀를 노출시키고 청취 절대시간을 늘리는 것이 중요합니다. 배경 음악처럼 영어 테이프나 라디오를 틀어 놓고 무의식 중에 귀를 영어에 노출시키는 것도 좋지만, 하루에 일정 시간 이상은 오로지 듣기에만 집중하여 청취 학습을 하는 습관을 들여야 합니다. 듣기 학습은 받아 쓰기와 따라 읽기를 병행하는 것이 최상의 방법입니다. 짧은 문장이라도 원어민이 말하는 것을 반복해서 들으며 받아 적는 연습을 하면 원어민의 발음과 문장의 리듬에 익숙해질 뿐만 아니라 놓치기 쉬운 세세한 발음까지 잡아 내어 문장이 어떻게 구성되는지를 자연스럽게 터득하게 되는 효과도 있습니다. 여러 번 들어도 잘 안 들리는 부분은 스크립트를 보고 원어민처럼 말할 수 있을 때까지 계속 따라 읽으며 외우는 것이 효과적입니다. 다음 단어가 저절로 나올 정도로 따라 읽어 표현이 입에 붙은 문장은 잘 잊혀지지 않습니다. 하지만 아무리 효과적이고 뛰어난 듣기 학습법을 알고 있어도 직접 이러한 방법을 활용하여 공부하지 않으면 아무런 소용이 없습니다. 듣기 공부는 하루도 빼놓지 않고 해야 한다는 것을 기억하고 실천하는 것이 토플 리스닝 시험에서 높은 점수를 받을 수 있는 가장 확실하고 빠른 길입니다.

iBT Listening 섹션 준비의 지침서가 될 본 교재는 기본적인 청취력 향상과 토플 리스닝 정복이라는 두 가지 기본 목표를 가지고 집필 되었습니다. 리스닝 섹션의 출제경향을 철저히 분석하여 각 문제 유형별로 최적의 전략과 학습방법을 제시하고 있습니다. 또한 실제 시험에 자주 출제되는 대화 상황과 강의 주제를 중심으로 지문을 제작하여 실전 시험과의 유사성을 높였으며, 학습 효과를 극대화 하기 위해 난이도가 높은 문제들을 뒤쪽에 배치하여 자연스럽게 난이도를 조금씩 높여가며 공부할 수 있도록 하였습니다. 4주 학습 완성을 목표로 구성된 학습 계획표에 맞추어 본 교재를 차근차근 공부해나가면 부쩍 향상된 청취 실력과 더불어 iBT 토플 시험에 완벽하게 준비된 자신감에 넘치는 자신의 모습을 발견할 수 있을 것입니다.

Naomi Kim, Alan Hahn

CONTENTS

Overview

각 문제 유형에 대한 소개와 분석이 들어 있으며
문제에 효과적으로 접근할 수 있는 핵심 전략이
제시되어 있다.

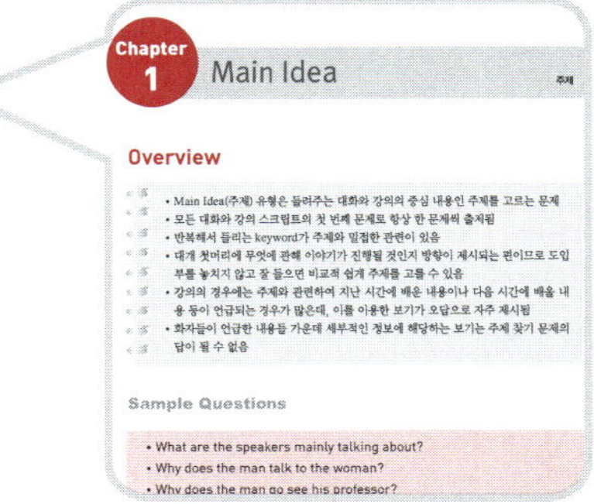

Preview

실제 문제를 풀어보며 앞서 제시된 전략을 적용
해보는 코너이다. 문제 접근법과 해결법이 문제
풀이 과정과 자세한 해설을 통해 구체적으로 설
명되어 있다.

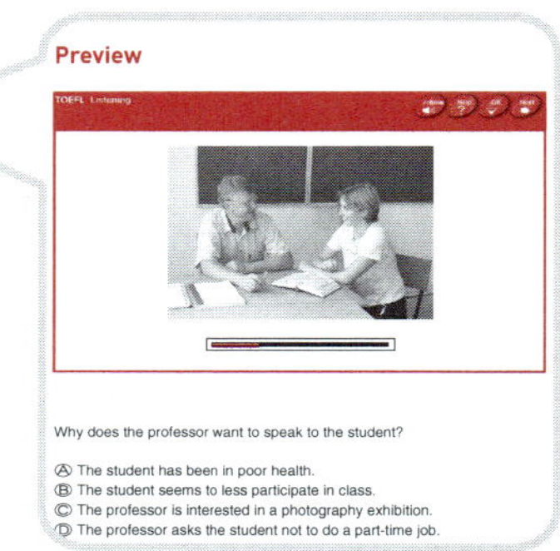

Office Hours/Service Encounters/Lectures

실전보다 짧은 길이의 다양한 스크립트를 듣고
문제를 풀어본다. 각 문제 유형을 단계적으로 공
략할 수 있도록 난이도가 조정되어 있다. 대화는
문항당 1 문제, 렉쳐는 문항당 2문제 이상이 출제
되어 있다.

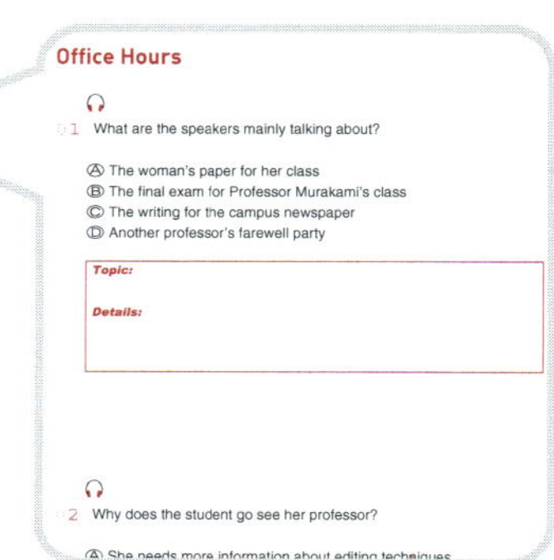

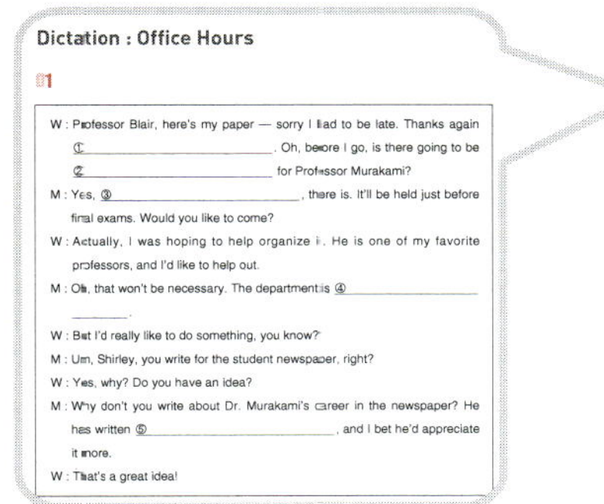

Dictation

Office Hours, Service Encounters, Lectures
의 모든 문제를 풀어본 후, 스크립트를 다시 들어
보면서 빈 칸에 받아 쓰기를 한다. 내용의 흐름을
다시 한 번 확인하고, 단어의 정확한 발음과 강
세, 끊어 읽기, 스펠링 등 청취의 기본 요소들을
점검한다.

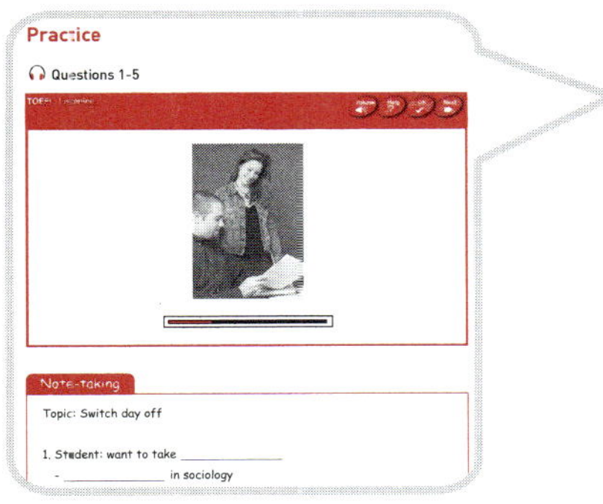

Practice

앞 코너에서 각 문제 유형을 집중적으로 학습한
후 Practice에서는 실전과 동일하게 제작된 문제
들을 풀어본다. 실전과 마찬가지로 하나의 스크
립트에 모든 문제 유형이 출제되어 있다.
스크립트를 들으면서 제시된 note-taking 박스
의 빈칸을 채워보고 문제를 풀 때 자신이 메모한
내용을 활용해보도록 한다.

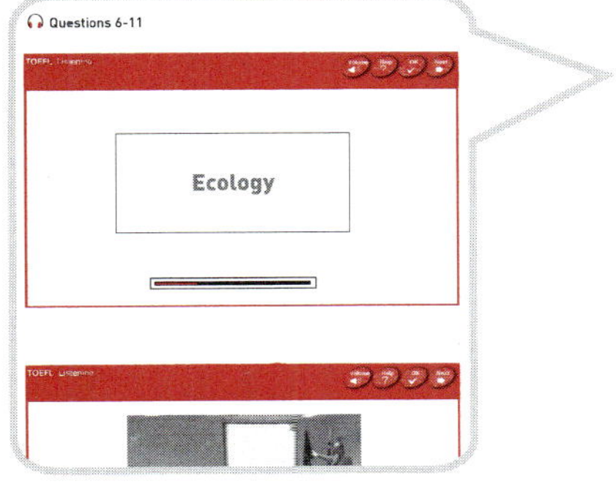

Actual Test

본교재의 모든 과정을 학습한 후 최신 iBT 출제
경향을 반영한 실전 난이도의 문제를 풀어보며
본인의 실력을 점검해본다.

iBT Listening 특징!

iBT Listening 섹션은 기존 CBT의 짧은 대화 지문이 없어지고 긴 대화 지문과 강의로만 이루어져 있다. 대화와 강의 모두 CBT에 비해 지문이 상당히 길어졌으며 실제 대화와 수업과 같이 말을 하다가 잠시 쉬는 부분이나, 머뭇거리는 부분 등 보다 현실감 있게 구성되어 있다. Listening 섹션의 주요 특징은 다음과 같다.

1. 2~3개의 파트로 구성된다.

한 개의 파트는 대화(conversation) 1개, 강의(lecture) 2개로 이루어져 있다. 따라서 시험이 2개 파트로 구성되어 있으면 총 2개의 대화와 4개의 강의가 출제되며, 시험이 3개 파트로 구성되어 있으면 총 3개의 대화와 6개의 강의가 출제된다.

2. 대화는 지문당 5개, 강의는 지문당 6개의 문제가 출제된다.

대화는 약 3분간 들려주고, 지문은 약 400~500자로 이루어져 있으며 각 지문당 5개의 관련 문제가 출제된다.

강의는 약 3~5분간 들려주고, 지문은 약 500~800자로 이루어져 있으며 각 지문당 6개의 관련 문제가 출제된다.

3. 대화는 Office Hours와 Service Encounters로 나뉘어져 있다.

Office Hours 대화에서는 학생과 교수가 대화를 나누고, Service Encounters 대화에서는 학생과 사서, 기숙사 직원과 같은 학교 직원이 대화를 나눈다.

4. 강의는 Monologue와 Discussion으로 나뉘어져 있다.

Monologue 강의에서는 교수가 혼자 강의 주제를 설명해나가고, Discussion에서는 학생과 교수의 질의 응답으로 강의가 진행된다.

5. Note-taking이 허용된다.

지문의 길이가 상당히 긴 편이므로 note-taking을 적극 활용하는 것이 좋다.

6. 대화와 강의 환경이 실제 상황과 유사하다.

CBT에서는 화자의 말이 딱딱 끊어지는 느낌이 나고 정형화되어 있었으나, iBT Listening에서는 화자가 말을 하며 머뭇거린다거나 말을 더듬는 등 대화와 강의 상황이 실제와 같이 보다 자연스럽게 이루어져 있다.

7. 다양한 영어권 국가의 발음과 억양을 들려준다.

미국식 화자의 음성 외에도 영국이나 호주식 화자의 음성을 들려준다.

8. 지문의 일부를 다시 듣고 푸는 문제가 출제된다.

화자의 태도나 말한 의도 및 목적을 묻는 문제(stance/function question)에는 헤드셋 표시가 나오고 지문의 해당 부분을 다시 한 번 들려준다.

9. 2점의 배점이 주어지는 문제도 출제된다.

대부분의 문제는 1점짜리 이지만 2점짜리 문제도 간혹 출제되며 배점이 따로 표시된다.

iBT Listening 구성

문제 유형		특 징
Basic Comprehension	Main Idea	지문의 주제 찾기
	Details	지문에 직접적으로 언급되어 있는 세부 정보를 찾기
Connecting Information	Inference	지문에 직접적으로 언급되어 있지는 않지만 지문에 흩어져 있는 정보를 바탕으로 논리적으로 추론할 수 있는 것을 고르거나 결론을 도출하기
	Connecting Information	지문에 정보가 어떻게 조직되어 있는지 내용상, 구조상의 전개방식을 이해하고 내용들 사이의 관계를 바탕으로 정보를 연결하기
Pragmatic Understanding	Stance/Function	지문에 제시되는 정보에 대한 화자의 입장과 태도를 파악하고 발화 목적과 의도를 알아내기

		화자	토픽
Conversation	Office Hours	학생과 교수	시험, 성적, 수업 참여도, 과제물, 수업 내용, 현장 학습, 전공 선택, 인턴, 진로 등
	Service Encounters	학생과 학교 직원	기숙사 생활, 도서 대출, 교재 구입, 수강 신청, 카페테리아 이용, 학비 납부 및 장학금 신청, 실습실 이용, 학교 행사, 동아리 활동 등
Lecture	Monologue	교수	history(역사학), literature(문학), economics(경제학), political science(정치학), psychology(심리학), film(영화), anthropology(인류학), archaeology(고고학), photography(사진), biology(생물학), astronomy(천문학), geology(지질학), paleontology(고생물학), urban planning(도시공학)
	Discussion	교수와 학생	

1. 어휘력을 기른다.

시험에 자주 등장하는 토플 수준의 다양한 어휘와 표현(이디엄)을 외워둔다. 글자만 외울 것이 아니라 소리 내어 읽으며 외워서 정확한 표현을 실제 대화 상황에서 써먹을 수 있을 정도로 외운다. 단어와 표현을 외울 때는 정확한 발음을 알아두도록 한다. 발음을 잘못 알고 있으면 의미를 아는 단어라도 제대로 알아 듣기가 힘들다.

2. 많이 듣고 따라 읽는다.

토플 리스닝 교재나 기타 듣기 자료 등을 활용하여 무조건 많이 듣는다. 일주일치 학습량을 하루에 몰아서 듣고 그 다음 주까지 아무 것도 듣지 않는 것보다 매일매일 조금씩 꾸준히 듣는 것이 훨씬 효과적이다. 내용의 이해가 최우선이지만 발음과 억양에도 신경을 집중하고 들으며 따라 읽는 연습을 한다.

3. 들으면서 note-taking을 한다.

듣기 연습을 할 때 note-taking을 하는 습관을 기르도록 한다. 키워드의 개념 정리를 시작으로 핵심 내용을 빠르고 체계적으로 적는다. Note-taking은 단순한 받아 적기가 아니라 듣는 사람이 자기만의 방식으로 내용을 간단하게 메모하는 것이다. 시험장에서 들려주는 내용을 놓치는 일 없이 note-taking을 제대로 활용하기 위해서는 많은 연습이 필요하다. Note-taking을 다 한 후에는 적어 놓은 내용이 스크립트의 흐름과 맥을 같이 하는지 확인해보고 본인이 적은 내용만 보고도 글의 내용을 이해할 수 있는지 확인해본다.

4. 글을 요약하는 연습을 한다.

들은 후 핵심 내용을 제대로 이해했는지 들은 내용을 요약해 보도록 한다. 요약 연습은 note-taking과 연계하여 해보는 것이 좋다. 메모에 스크립트의 중요 사항이 흐름대로 잘 적혀있다면, 이 메모가 요약의 틀을 짜는 바탕이 될 수 있기 때문이다. 요약할 때는 되도록 들려준 그대로의 어휘나 표현을 사용하지 말고 본인만의 표현으로 바꾸어 나타내본다.

5. 많이 읽는다.

토플 리스닝 강의에 등장하는 지문은 길이도 길뿐만 아니라 다양한 분야의 학구적인 내용을 다루기 때문에 내용 자체도 어려운 편이다. 낯선 분야의 강의 내용을 사전 지식 없이 바로 들으면 무슨 내용인지 이해하지 못할 때가 많다. 따라서 듣기와 더불어 평소에 많은 글을 접하여 읽어 본다.

6. 배경 지식을 늘린다.

토플 시험에 등장할만한 다양한 분야의 글을 읽고 들으며 배경지식을 쌓도록 한다. 특히 시험에 자주 등장하는 토픽은 내용을 간략히 정리해두는 것도 좋다. 대화 파트를 위해서는 영어 회화를 많이 해보고 대화 상황을 들으며 구어체 표현을 익히는 것이 효과적이다.

iBT Listening Note-taking

iBT Listening에서는 노트 테이킹이 허용된다. CBT에 비해 지문의 길이가 많이 길어졌지만, 내용이 많아지고 길어진 만큼 지문을 들으면서 내용을 적을 수 있기 때문에 노트 테이킹을 효과적으로 활용하면 더 높은 점수를 받을 수 있는 가능성도 높아졌다. 지문을 들으면서 노트 테이킹을 하면 내용의 전체적인 주제와 전반적인 흐름을 이해하고 세부 정보를 정리하여 기억해내는데 효과적이다. 노트 테이킹을 할 때는 먼저 도입부에 제시되는 글 전체의 주제를 파악하고 이 주제를 전개하기 위해 언급되는 중심 정보와 세부 정보를 간단 명료하게 적는 것이 중요하다. 노트 테이킹의 목적은 지문에 언급되는 모든 정보를 얼마나 잘 정리하느냐에 달린 것이 아니라 듣고 적은 내용이 문제를 풀며 내용을 기억해내고 정보간의 관계를 파악하는데 얼마나 도움을 주느냐에 있다. 따라서 내용 이해에 방해가 되지 않는 선에서 노트 테이킹을 해야 하며, 지문을 한 번 밖에 들을 수가 없고 들려주는 내용의 양이 상당히 많다는 Listening 섹션의 특성을 고려하여 내용을 효율적으로 받아 적을 요령이 필요하다.

Note-taking 핵심 요령

1. 주제 (main topic)를 먼저 명료하게 적는다.

도입부를 들으면서 핵심어(keyword)를 중심으로 앞으로 전개될 대화와 강의의 주제를 먼저 적는다.

2. 세부 정보를 하위 주제에 따라 구분하여 적는다.

도입부에 대화와 강의의 중심 정보가 나온 후, 그 뒤에는 이 중심 정보와 관련된 세부 정보가 언급된다. iBT Listening에서는 한 지문당 듣기 시간이 상당히 긴 편이므로, 이 세부 정보 역시 하위 주제별로 구분하여 정리해 두어야 한다. 특히 강의를 들을 때는 하위 주제가 전환될 때 이를 알려주는 전환어가 자주 등장하므로 이를 듣고 화제가 바뀌고 있음을 알 수 있다.

3. 가능한 간단히 적는다.

완전한 문장으로 적을 필요는 없다. 구(Phrase)를 사용하여 최대한 간단히 적는다.

4. 약어와 부호를 이용해 적는다.

자주 등장하는 어휘나 표현의 부호와 약어를 충분히 익혀두고 노트 테이킹을 할 때 적극 활용한다. 시간을 절약하는데 도움을 준다.

5. 잘 듣지 못한 부분은 넘어간다.

대화와 강의를 들으면서 알아듣지 못한 부분이나 놓친 부분은 넘어간다. 알아들었다고 해도 앞부분의 내용을 먼저 적다가 잊어버리는 수도 있다. 특히 이런 경우에는 지나간 내용에 집착하게 되는데, 잊어버린 내용을 기억해내려고 하는 동안에도 화자의 말은 계속 되고 있음을 잊지 말아야 한다. 한 번 지나간 부분은 다시 들을 수 없다. 따라서 놓친 부분에 연연해하지 말고 앞으로 들어야 할 내용에 더 신경을 쓴다.

Note-taking 부호

다음의 표에 자주 쓰이는 표현의 의미를 대신하는 부호들이 정리되어 있다.

부호	의미	예
=	equals, to be	family = core of society
↔	opposite	Democratic party ↔ Republican party
〉	more than, larger than	disadvantages of home schooling > advantages
〈	less than, smaller than	rate of left-handed < right-handed
↑	increase; more	↑ air pollution → smog
↓	decrease; less	↓ investment in industry ← economic panic
←	come from	sales increase ← advertising
→	become, result in, lead to	regular eating habits → good health
X	not, no	X possibility of developing a new medicine
+, &	and, plus	political, economic + cultural factors
/	or	issue – construction of new factories / environmental protection
$	money	$ for research ← subsidy
#	number	# of students
∴	therefore, so	signs of the prevalence of epidemics ∴ should have a preventive injection
∵	because	low crime rate ∵ maintenance of public order
~	approximately, about	~ 2,000 endangered species
∞	infinite	∞ natural resources
%	percent	80% of the schools
@	at	@ the bookstore

다음의 표에 자주 쓰이는 표현을 간단히 표기할 수 있는 약어들이 정리되어 있다. 약어는 어휘의 뒷부분 철자를 생략하여 표기하거나, 모음을 생략하고 표기하거나, 중간 철자를 생략하고 처음과 뒷부분만을 써서 표기할 수 있다.

약어	원형	약어	원형
e.g.	for example	lang.	language
ppl.	people	int'l	international
prof.	professor	fem.	female
univ.	university	ea.	each
etc.	and so on, et cetera	com(p).	computer
ltd	limited	max.	maximum
bldg	building	min.	minimum
dept	department	diff.	different
w/	with	avg.	average
w/o	without	s/o	someone
c.f.	compare	s/t	something
b.f. (b4)	before	tech.	technology
vs.	versus	pics	pictures
info.	information	reg.	regular
edu.	education	i.e.	that is
env't	environment	intro.	introduction
comfrt	comfortable	concl.	conclusion
convt	convenient	rsn	reason
imprt	important	tho'	though
excl.	excluding	thro'	through
incl.	including	prob.	probably
c.	century	probs.	problems

Script

Today, let's take a brief look at <u>how the reindeer can survive in freezing</u>
강의 토픽: 삼림순록이 추운 날씨에서 어떻게 살 수 있는가
<u>weather</u>. The reindeer are a species of deer indigenous to the Arctic and near-
Arctic regions. Reindeer range from Russia and Mongolia across Scandinavia
and Scotland into Greenland, Canada, and Alaska. They are fascinating
animals, with <u>numerous adaptations to the cold climates</u>.
삼림순록의 다양한 추위 적응 방식

<u>First, the hooves of the reindeer change depending on the time of year</u>. During
추위 적응 방식 1: 발굽이 계절에 따라 변함
<u>summers</u>, when the tundra environment is wet and muddy, the reindeer's
여름
<u>footpads become spongy and coarse</u>. During <u>winter</u>, the <u>footpads shrink and</u>
각부(다리 부분)가 폭신폭신해지고 결이 거칠어짐   겨울   각부가 오그라들고 더 단단해짐
<u>become more solid</u>. This exposes the edge of the hoof, which is sharp enough
to dig into ice and packed snow.

For additional protection from cold, <u>the fur and the body fat deposits of</u>
추위 적응 방식 2: 털과 체지방량의 독특한 발달
<u>reindeer have evolved in novel ways</u>. There is <u>a thick woolly layer of fur</u>
두꺼운 털
closest to the reindeer's body, and <u>the outer layer of fur consists of hollow</u>
바깥쪽 층은 공기로 가득 차 있는 속이 텅 빈 털로 되어 있음
<u>hairs that are filled with air</u>. In addition, the reindeer <u>maintain a balance of</u>
체지방의 균형을 유지
<u>body fat</u> just enough to <u>insulate themselves and to store energy for the winter</u>.
스스로를 단열하고 겨울을 날 에너지를 저장할 수 있을 정도로

Surprisingly, reindeer have remarkably <u>adapted to a barren habitat where food</u>
추위 적응 방식 3: 먹이 부족 해결을 위해 초식을 함
<u>is scarce</u> much of the year. They are a <u>plant eater</u>, and their diet mostly
초식 동물
comprises vegetable matter. They <u>eat reindeer moss</u>, grasses that grow on
이끼를 먹음
the tundra, and <u>the leaves of certain trees</u>. During the <u>winter months</u>, the
특정 나무의 잎을 먹음   겨울
reindeer have difficulty finding enough to eat. They <u>dig holes in the snow to</u>
눈 속에 구멍을 팜
<u>get to the lichens and moss</u> underneath. They also <u>feed on the twigs of any</u>
땅 속에 있는 이끼를 구하기 위해   관목의 나뭇가지를 먹는다
<u>shrubs</u> they can find under or above the snow.

Topic: The reindeer

    - adaptations to cold climates   토픽: 삼림순록의 추위 적응 방식

1. Hooves change over seasons   추위 적응 방식 1
   - summer: spongy, coarse
   - winter: footpads shrink/more solid

2. Fur/body fat   추위 적응 방식 2
   - thick woolly layer of fur
   - outer layer: hollow hair
   - body fat balance: insulate & store energy

3. Food shortage → eat plant   추위 적응 방식 3
   - moss, leaves, lichen, twig

iBT Listening 화면

1. 헤드셋 착용 화면

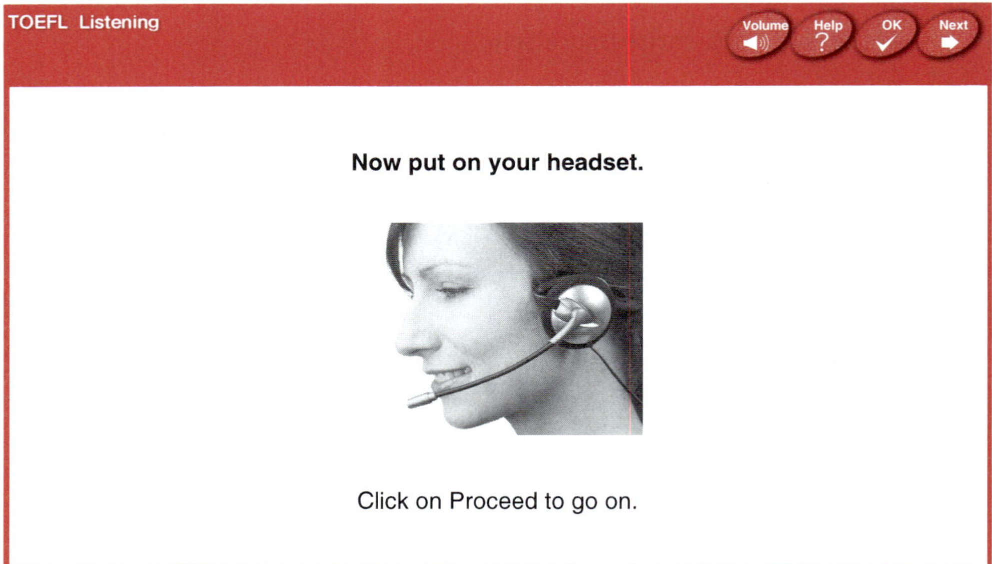

2. 볼륨 조절 화면

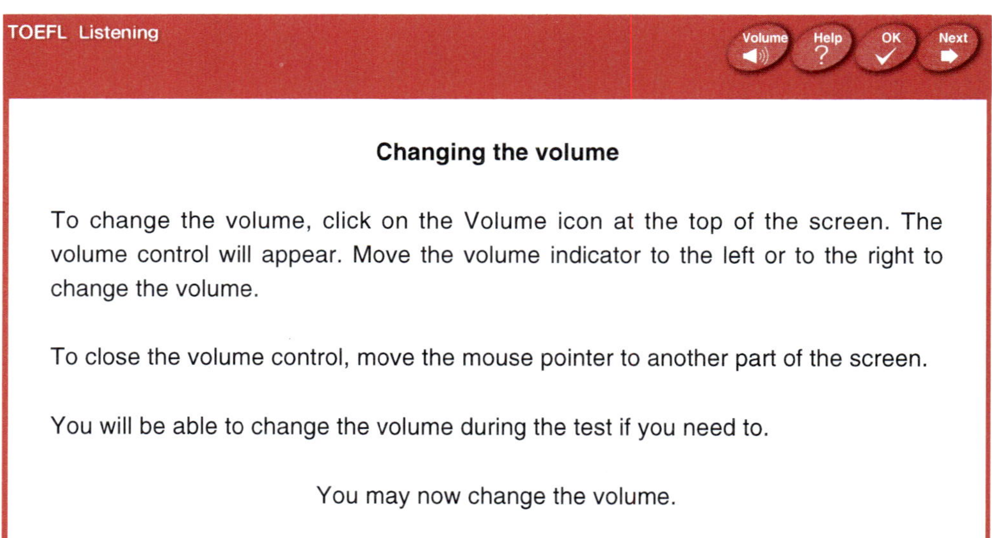

Listening Section Directions

This section measures your ability to understand conversations and lectures in English. The listening section is divided into 2 separately timed parts. In each part you will listen to 1 conversation and 2 lectures. You will hear each conversation or lecture only one time.

After each conversation or lecture, you will answer some questions about it. The questions typically ask about the main idea and supporting details. Some questions ask about a speaker's purpose and attitude. Answer the questions based on what is stated or implied by the speakers.

You may take notes while you listen. You may use your notes to help you answer the questions. Your notes will not be scored.

If you need to change the volume while you listen, click on the Volume icon at the top of the screen.

In some questions, you will see this icon: This means that you will hear, but not see part of the question. Some of the questions have special directions. These directions appear in a gray box on the screen.

Most questions are worth one point. If a question is worth more than one point, it will have special directions that indicate how many points you can receive.

You must answer each question. After you answer, click on Next. Then click on OK to confirm your answer and go on to the next question. After you click on OK, you cannot return to previous questions.

4. Part Directions 화면

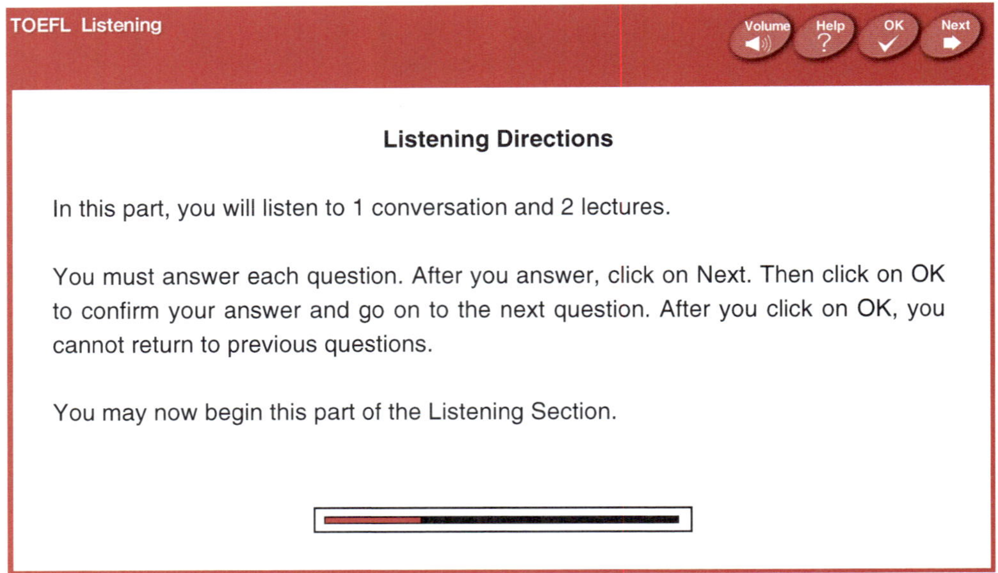

5. 강의 과목명 화면

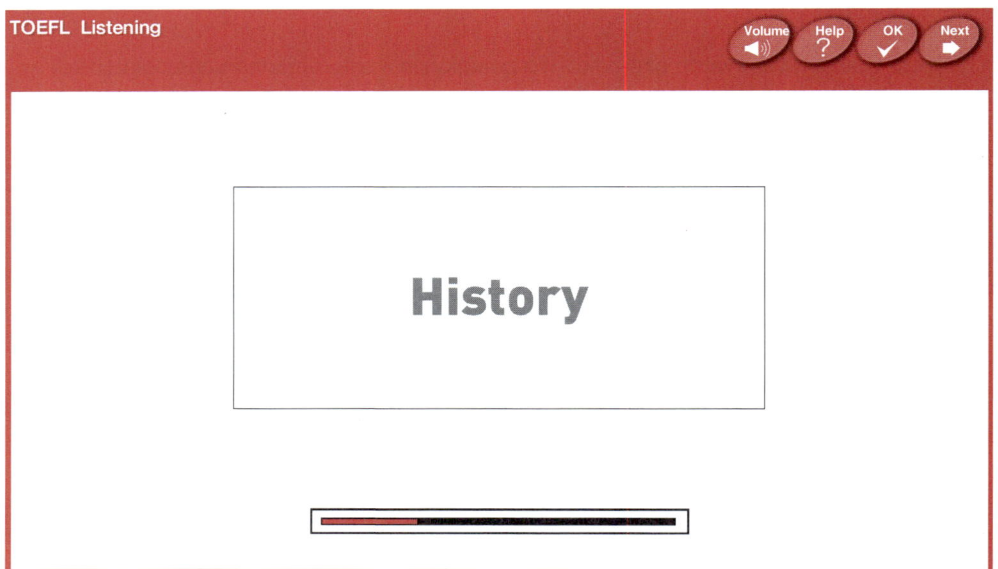

6. 지문을 듣는 동안 등장하는 사진 화면

7. 문제가 제시되는 화면

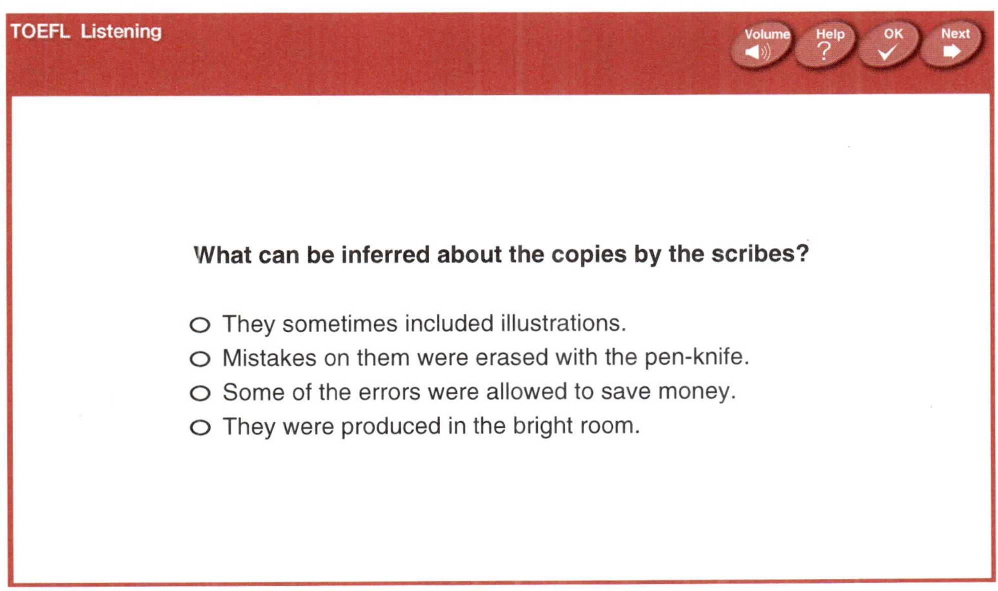

8. 강의 중 언급되는 중요 용어 화면

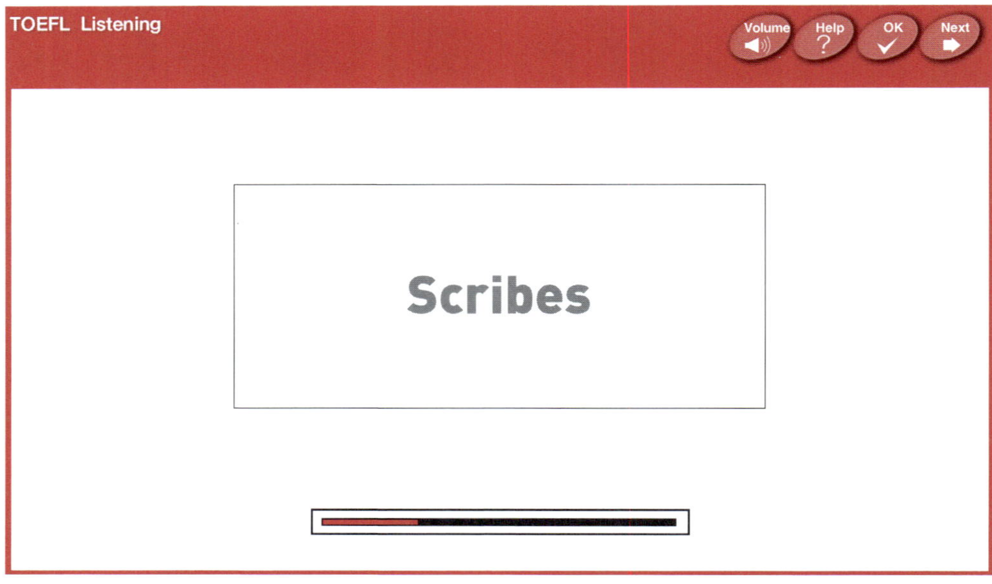

9. 지문의 일부를 다시 들려주는 문제 Direction 화면

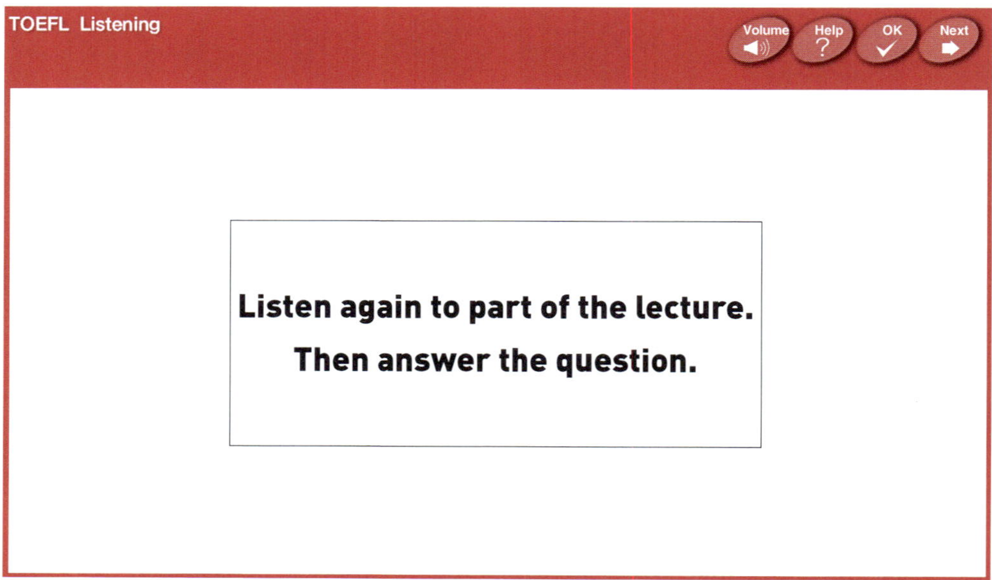

iBT TOEFL 특징

토플은 비영어권 국가의 수험생들의 영어 능력 측정을 목표로 한다. 특히 영어권 국가의 대학 생활과 같은 학술적 환경에서의 영어 사용 능력을 측정하는 데 초점을 맞추고 있다. 학문적 지식이나 컴퓨터 활용 능력을 평가하려는 것이 아니므로 모든 문제는 시험에 제시되는 내용만을 근거로 정답을 골라야 한다. iBT (Internet-based test) 토플은 인터넷을 통해 시험이 치러지며 언어의 네 가지 영역인 읽기(Reading), 듣기 (Listening), 말하기(Speaking), 쓰기(Writing) 능력을 종합적으로 평가한다.

1. Speaking(말하기) 영역이 평가된다.

영어를 읽고 듣고 쓰는 능력에 비해 말하기 실력이 부족한 사람들이 많다는 것을 감안해 iBT 토플에서는 Speaking 영역이 평가된다. 글을 듣거나 읽으면서 이해하는 것으로만 그치지 않고 이해한 내용을 체계적으로 말할 수 있어야 한다.

2. 언어의 통합적(Integrated) 사용 능력이 중요하다.

Speaking과 Writing에서는 말하고 쓰는 독립적 능력 외에, 언어의 통합적 사용 능력이 함께 평가된다. Speaking 영역에서는 강의나 대화를 듣고 말하거나 지문을 읽고 강의나 대화를 들은 후 말하는 통합형 문제가 출제된다. Writing 영역에서는 지문을 읽고 강의를 들은 후 내용을 요약해야 하는 통합형 문제가 출제된다.

3. 문법 실력만을 측정하는 별도의 영역은 없다.

CBT에서는 문법(Grammar) 영역이 별도로 있었으나 iBT에서는 문법 실력만을 별도로 측정하는 영역은 없다. 이는 문법이 언어 구사에 있어 기본적인 요소인 만큼 읽고 듣고 말하고 쓰는 실용적 상황에서의 기본적인 문법 활용을 측정하기 위함이다.

4. Note-taking이 허용된다.

시험 내내 Note-taking을 할 수 있는 별도의 용지가 제공된다. 따라서 평소에 공부할 때도 기억력보다는 이해력과 논리력에 중점을 두고, 시험 중에 Note-taking을 위해 이를 최대한 활용할 수 있도록 충분히 연습해 두어야 한다.

5. Writing 영역의 답안 작성시에는 타이핑만 가능하다.

종이에 답안을 작성할 수 없으므로 능숙한 영자 타이핑 실력이 필요하다. 시험 도중 서투른 타이핑으로 시간을 낭비하는 일이 없도록 시험 전에 많은 연습을 해두도록 한다.

6. 인터넷으로 성적을 확인할 수 있다.

인터넷 기반 시험인 만큼 시험일로부터 15일 후에 인터넷으로 성적 확인이 가능하다.

iBT TOEFL 구성

영역	시간	문항 수	점수	특징
Reading	60~100분	지문 수 : 3~5개 문제 수 : 각 12~14개	0~30점	• 지문은 약 700자로 구성되어 있다. • 일부 지문에는 그림이 등장한다. • 지문의 종합적인 이해를 요구하는 표 채워넣기 문제(Summary, Category chart)가 출제된다.
Listening	60~90분	대화 지문 수 : 2~3개 대화 문제 수 : 각 5개 강의 지문 수 : 4~6개 강의 문제 수 : 각 6개	0~30점	• 대화는 약 400~500자로 구성되어 있고, 강의는 약 500~800자로 이루어져 있다. • 대화는 3분간 들려주고 강의는 3~5분간 들려준다. • 화자의 억양과 발음이 다양화되어 미국식, 영국식, 호주식 발음을 들려준다.
Break (휴식)	10분			
Speaking	20분	독립형 문제 수 : 2개 통합형 문제 수 : 4개	각 문제 : 0~4점 총점 : 0~30점	• 독립형은 개인적 경험을 말하는 문제 1개와 두 가지 선택사항 중 하나를 선택하여 말하는 문제 1개로 구성되어 있다. • 통합형은 지문을 읽고 강의나 대화를 들은 후 말하는 문제 2개와 강의나 대화를 듣고 말하는 문제 2개로 이루어져 있다. • 헤드셋과 연결되어 있는 마이크에 대고 답을 녹음하며, 이는 디지털화되어 채점 기관으로 전송된다.
Writing	55분	통합형 문제 수 : 1개 독립형 문제 수 : 1개	각 문제 : 0~5점 총점 : 0~30점	• 통합형 문제는 먼저 독해 지문을 읽고 강의를 들은 후 강의 내용을 독해 지문과 연계하여 요약해야 한다. • 독립형 문제는 주어진 주제에 대해 개인적 경험이나 생각에 기초하여 글을 작성해야 한다. • 답안은 타이핑으로 작성해야 한다.

iBT TOEFL 시험 등록

1. www.ets.org/toefl 웹사이트를 방문하여 인터넷 접수를 한다. 상시 등록이 가능하며 응시일로부터 최소 7일 전까지 등록을 해야 한다. 응시료는 신용카드로 결제한다.

2. 한미교육위원단으로 전화를 하여 시험을 접수한다. 응시일로부터 최소 7일 전까지 등록을 해야 하며 응시료는 신용카드로 결제한다. 전화번호는 02-3211-1233.

3. 한미교육위원단으로 우편접수를 한다. 등록 신청서(registration form)를 작성하고 수표나 우편환을 동봉하여 보낸다. 응시일로부터 최소 4주 전까지 등록을 해야 한다. 주소는 서울특별시 마포구 염리동 168-15 한미교육위원단(121-874).

4. 응시료는 US S140, 시험일자 변경 비용은 US $40, 취소한 성적 복원 신청 비용은 US $20, 성적 추가 리포팅 비용은 US $17이다.

5. 등록한 시험을 취소하기 위해서는 직접 등록 센터를 방문하거나 웹사이트에 접속하여 절차를 밟아야 한다. 우편으로는 등록 취소가 불가능하다. 응시일로부터 최소 4일 전까지 등록 취소가 가능하며 US $85를 환불 받을 수 있다.

6. 시험 당일에는 반드시 신분증(주민등록증, 운전면허증, 여권 중 택일)을 지참해야 하며 등록 번호(registration number)를 알고 있어야 한다.

7. 시험은 약 4시간 동안 진행되고 두 영역이 끝난 후 10분간의 휴식시간이 주어진다.

8. 성적은 응시일로부터 15일 후 인터넷으로 확인 할 수 있다. 시험 당일에 원하는 4개 기관으로 성적 리포팅이 가능하다

9. 성적표에는 영역별 점수와 함께 총점이 기재되며 각 영역별로 수험자의 실력을 진단해주는 feedback이 들어있다. 성적표의 유효 기간은 2년이다.

10. 시험 당일 날 시험을 마치면서 성적을 취소할 수 있으며 취소한 성적을 복원하기 위해서는 응시일로부터 10일 이내에 시험주최측에 연락을 해야 한다. 앞서 언급한 대로 성적 복원 신청 비용은 US $20이다.

학습 계획표

	Day 1	Day 2	Day 3	Day 4	Day 5	Day 6	Day 7
Week 1	Ch. 1 Overview, Preview	Ch. 1 OH	Ch. 1 SE	Ch. 1 Lectures	Ch. 1 Practice	Ch. 2 Overview, Preview	Ch. 2 OH
Check							
Week 2	Ch. 2 SE	Ch. 2 Lectures	Ch. 2 Practice	복습	Ch. 3 Overview, Preview	Ch. 3 OH	Ch. 3 SE
Check							
Week 3	Ch. 3 Lectures	Ch. 3 Practice	Ch. 4 Overview, Preview	Ch. 4 OH	Ch. 4 SE	Ch. 4 Lectures	Ch. 4 Practice Preview
Check							
Week 4	복습	Ch. 5 Overview, Preview	Ch. 5 OH	Ch. 5 SE	Ch. 5 Lectures	Ch. 5 Practice	복습
Check							

* OH: Office Hours   SE: Service Encounters

주제
Main Idea

Main Idea

주제

Overview

- Main Idea(주제) 유형은 들려주는 대화와 강의의 중심 내용인 주제를 고르는 문제
- 모든 대화와 강의 스크립트의 첫 번째 문제로 항상 한 문제씩 출제됨
- 반복해서 들리는 keyword가 주제와 밀접한 관련이 있음
- 대개 첫머리에 무엇에 관해 이야기가 진행될 것인지 방향이 제시되는 편이므로 도입부를 놓치지 않고 잘 들으면 비교적 쉽게 주제를 고를 수 있음
- 강의의 경우에는 주제와 관련하여 지난 시간에 배운 내용이나 다음 시간에 배울 내용 등이 언급되는 경우가 많은데, 이를 이용한 보기가 오답으로 자주 제시됨
- 화자들이 언급한 내용들 가운데 세부적인 정보에 해당하는 보기는 주제 찾기 문제의 답이 될 수 없음

Sample Questions

- What are the speakers mainly talking about?
- Why does the man talk to the woman?
- Why does the man go see his professor?
- What is the man's problem?
- What problem does the woman have?
- What is the professor mainly discussing?
- What is the main topic of the lecture?
- What is the lecture mainly about?

Preview

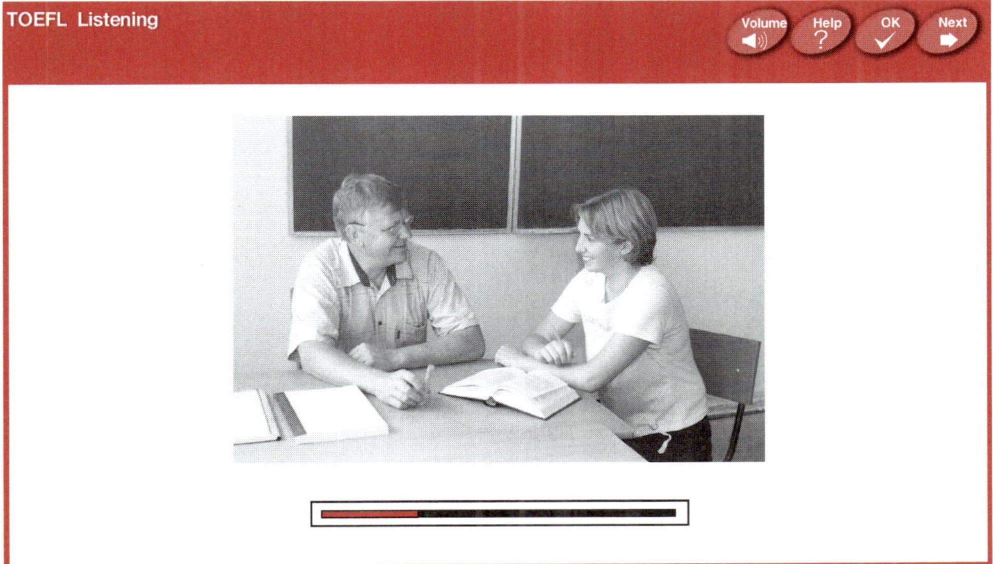

Why does the professor want to speak to the student?

Ⓐ The student has been in poor health.
Ⓑ The student seems to less participate in class.
Ⓒ The professor is interested in a photography exhibition.
Ⓓ The professor asks the student not to do a part-time job.

🎧 Listen to part of a conversation between a student and a professor.

M : Jennifer, last semester you were a leader in class, and this semester... <u>you can hardly stay awake during the class</u>. Can you tell me what's going on?
대화 토픽 : 학생이 수업 시간에 제대로 집중을 하지 않음

W : I guess <u>I'm doing too many things</u>. I'm in <u>the photography club</u>, and we're
너무 많은 활동을 하고 있음   사진 클럽
having an exhibition soon. I'm also <u>taking extra classes</u>, and I've got <u>a
수업을 추가로 더 듣고 있음
part-time job</u>, too. I'm really tired these days.
아르바이트도 함

M : <u>Then you need to cut back</u>. You can't do everything.
교수의 조언: 하는 일을 줄여야 함

W : But I manage my time very well!

M : If that's true, why are you yawning? <u>Your grade in my class is lower</u> than it
학생의 성적이 낮음
should be. Plus, <u>exhaustion is bad for your health</u>. You should <u>either drop
피곤하면 건강에도 안 좋음
the class or spend less time on your other activities</u>.
교수의 제안: 수강을 취소하던가 다른 활동 시간을 줄여야 함

W : All right. I guess you're right.

남 : Jennifer, 지난 학기에는 수업 시간에 돋보이더니, 이번 학기에는 눈을 뜨고 수업에 집중하는 모습조차도 거의 볼 수가 없구나. 무슨 일인지 얘기해보겠니?

여 : 아무래도 너무 많은 일을 하고 있는 것 같아요. 제가 사진 클럽 활동을 하고 있는데, 곧 전시회가 있어요. 강의도 더 듣는 것이 있고, 아르바이트도 해요. 요즘 정말 피곤해요.

남 : 그럼 하는 일을 좀 줄여야지. 모든 걸 다할 수는 없단다.

여 : 하지만 시간 관리를 잘 하고 있는 걸요!

남 : 네 말대로라면, 왜 하품을 하니? 내 수업에서 네 성적은 예상했던 것보다 더 낮단다. 그리고, 피로하면 건강에도 나쁘지. 수강을 취소하던가 다른 활동을 하는 데 쓰는 시간을 줄여야겠구나.

여 : 알겠습니다. 교수님 말씀이 맞는 것 같아요.

해설 대화의 첫머리에 교수가 학생에게 왜 요즘 수업 시간에 제대로 집중을 하지 않는지 이유를 묻고 있다. 학생은 수업 외에도 하는 일이 많아서 그렇다고 대답하고 있다. 주제 찾기 문제의 답은 거의 대부분 들려주는 대화와 강의의 초반부에 등장하므로 이 부분을 놓치지 말고 들어야 한다.

M : Jennifer, last semester you were a leader in class, and this semester... <u>you can hardly stay awake during the class</u>. Can you tell me <u>what's going on</u>?
W : I guess <u>I'm doing too many things</u>.

교수의 첫 번째 말을 다른 말로 바꾸어 표현한 것이 보기 ⑧이다. 교수가 한 말 중 'you can hardly stay awake during the class'가 보기 ⑧에서 'less participate in class'로 paraphrase(바꾸어 쓰기) 되어 있다.

해석 교수는 왜 학생과 이야기하기를 원하는가?
ⓐ 학생의 건강이 안 좋다.
ⓑ 학생의 수업 참여도가 적은 것 같다.
ⓒ 교수는 사진전에 관심이 있다.
ⓓ 교수는 학생에게 아르바이트를 하지 말라고 한다.

어휘 hardly 거의 ~ 않다 | photography 사진 | exhibition 전시회 | yawn 하품하다 | exhaustion 피로

정답 ⑧

Office Hours

01 What are the speakers mainly talking about?

    Ⓐ The woman's paper for her class
    Ⓑ The final exam for Professor Murakami's class
    Ⓒ The writing for the campus newspaper
    Ⓓ Another professor's farewell party

> *Topic:*
>
> *Details:*

02 Why does the student go see her professor?

    Ⓐ She needs more information about editing techniques.
    Ⓑ She wants to make a 20-minute film instead of a 12-minute one.
    Ⓒ She is confused about the length of her film project.
    Ⓓ She is seeking advice on the subject of her film project.

> *Topic:*
>
> *Details:*

03 Why does the woman go see her professor?

Ⓐ She wants to know about well-known philosophers during the class.
Ⓑ She has a C in the class and wants to improve her grade.
Ⓒ She is considering dropping the philosophy class.
Ⓓ She is thinking of majoring in philosophy.

Topic:

Details:

04 What is the reason for the student's discussion with her professor?

Ⓐ Her grade in the chemistry lab course is not good.
Ⓑ Her lab partner doesn't show up for class too many times.
Ⓒ She wants the professor to give her one more chance.
Ⓓ She needs a couple of extra days to finish her first assignment.

Topic:

Details:

Dictation : Office Hours

01

W : Professor Blair, here's my paper — sorry I had to be late. Thanks again
　　① ______________________________ . Oh, before I go, is there going to be
　　② ______________________________ for Professor Murakami?

M : Yes, ③ ______________________________ , there is. It'll be held just before
　　final exams. Would you like to come?

W : Actually, I was hoping to help organize it. He is one of my favorite
　　professors, and I'd like to help out.

M : Oh, that won't be necessary. The department is ④ ______________________________
　　______________ .

W : But I'd really like to do something, you know?

M : Um, Shirley, you write for the student newspaper, right?

W : Yes, why? Do you have an idea?

M : Why don't you write about Dr. Murakami's career in the newspaper? He
　　has written ⑤ ______________________________ , and I bet he'd appreciate
　　it more.

W : That's a great idea!

W : I've got a couple of questions about the semester film project.

M : Sure. What do you need to know?

W : It's, uh, the instruction sheet said ① _________________________ 12 minutes long, but in class you said 20. I don't understand.

M : Oh, I see. This is an editing assignment. You're supposed to make ② _________________________ that's 20 minutes long, and then you have to ③ _________________________ 12 minutes.

W : So that's like the midterm project and the final project?

M : Right. Think of the 20-minute film as your midterm exam. Use the techniques we learn about filmmaking, and ④ _________________________ ______. In the second half of the semester, we'll learn more about editing. You have to cut the film down to 12 minutes, but it still has to ⑤ _________________________ .

W : Oh, I get it now! Thanks!

W : Do you have a few minutes? I'd like to talk about your *Intro to Philosophy* class.

M : Sure, how can I help?

W : Well, I'm really ① ________________________ keeping up with it. The readings are too hard to understand. I may have to ② ________________ ________________ .

M : I see. In fact, the initial readings are the hardest. Um, you've still got a C average, so I think you should ③ ________________________ . We'll be doing more group discussions and individual activities for the rest of the semester. Students usually do better ④ ________________________ of the course.

W : Really?

M : Of course. Once we cover the introductory concepts, I let the students explore topics and philosophers that interest them.

W : That's encouraging.

M : Good. Think it over, because I'm sure you'll be able to ⑤ ________________ ________________ .

W : I will!

W : Can you help me ① _________________________ ? It's about your chemistry lab course, and I'm afraid it's going to ② _________________________ .

M : Sure. I guess it's about your lab partner, isn't it?

W : How did you know that?

M : I forgot her name... uh, what is it?

W : Justine. She's ③ _________________________ ! I barely remember what the girl looks like!

M : Yes, I know what you mean. Let me check her attendance... hmm, that's what I thought. She has only come to lab 4 times.

W : So you can see why I wanted to talk to you.

M : I see. Do you have ④ _________________________ in mind? Do you want to give her one more chance, or is it time to ⑤ _________________________ ?

W : No more second chances. Our first assignment is ⑥ _________________________ , and she won't be able to contribute. I want to do it ⑦ _________________________ .

M : All right. You can have a couple of extra days, if you need. After all, this isn't your fault.

W : I think there are a couple of new students in the class. Next time, would you ⑧ _________________________ ?

M : Sure. We can also have groups of three.

W : Great. That ought to ⑨ _________________________ . Thanks!

Service Encounters

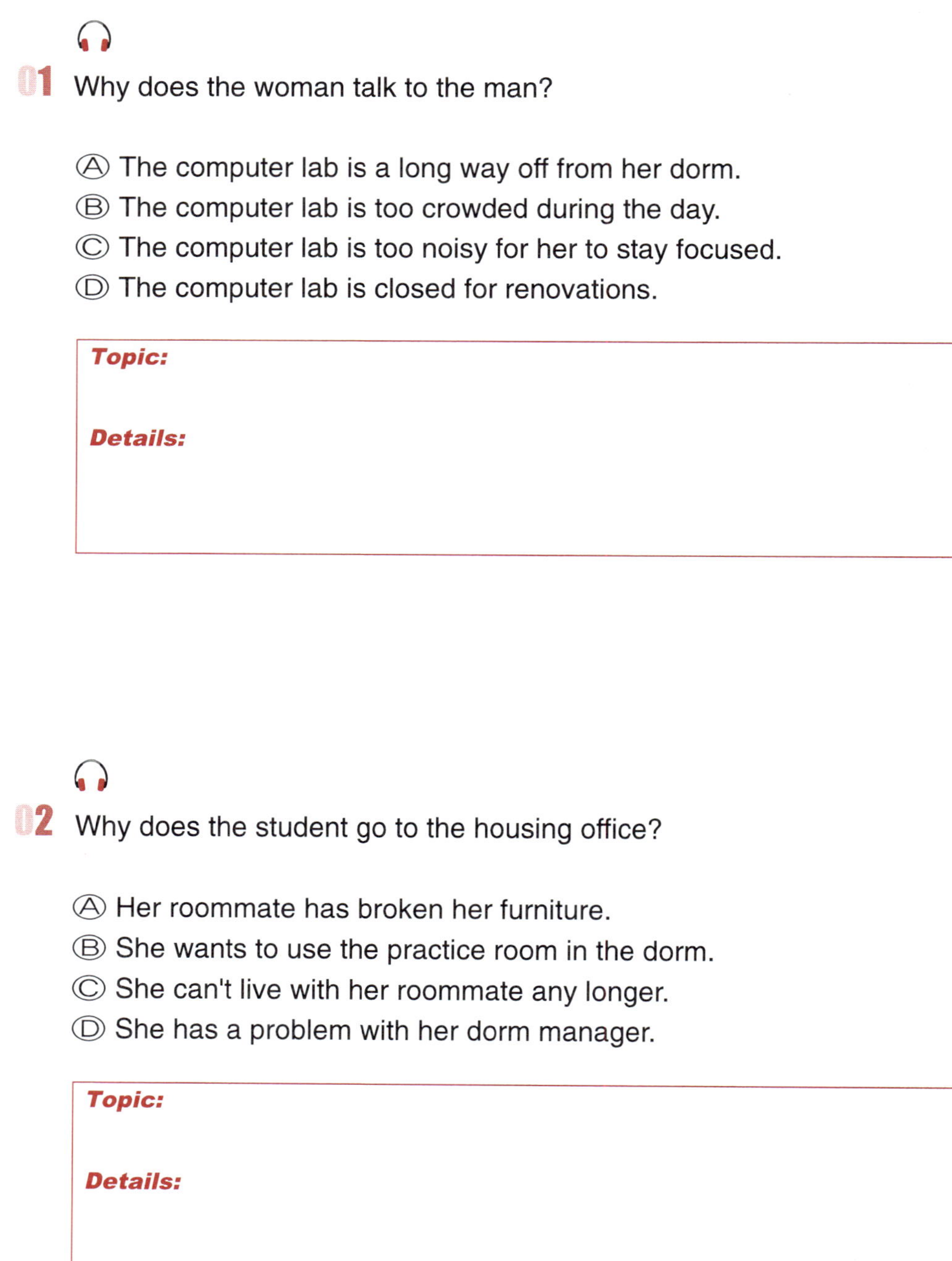

01 Why does the woman talk to the man?

    Ⓐ The computer lab is a long way off from her dorm.
    Ⓑ The computer lab is too crowded during the day.
    Ⓒ The computer lab is too noisy for her to stay focused.
    Ⓓ The computer lab is closed for renovations.

Topic:

Details:

02 Why does the student go to the housing office?

    Ⓐ Her roommate has broken her furniture.
    Ⓑ She wants to use the practice room in the dorm.
    Ⓒ She can't live with her roommate any longer.
    Ⓓ She has a problem with her dorm manager.

Topic:

Details:

03 Why does the student go see the woman?

Ⓐ To complain about the charges for printing documents
Ⓑ To complain about the lack of printers in the lab
Ⓒ To complain about the type of paper used in the printers
Ⓓ To complain about the price of the printers in the lab

Topic:

Details:

04 What are the speakers mainly discussing?

Ⓐ The student wants to live in a dorm that is not being renovated.
Ⓑ The student wants to use a kitchen to cook for her friends.
Ⓒ The student wants to open her own snack bars on campus.
Ⓓ The student wants to study in the nutrition department.

Topic:

Details:

Dictation : Service Encounters

W : Could you help me with something? I'm ① _________________________
   in the computer lab.

M : What's going on? Are you okay?

W : It's ② _________________________ in the lab. It's really loud in there, and I
   can't focus on my research. I've got a paper due on Wednesday, and I
   really need to concentrate.

M : Oh, I understand. That building is ③ _________________________ :
   new floors, fresh paint, and so on. I bet it's pretty loud right now.

W : It is, and I don't know what to do. The other computer labs are ④ _________
   _________________________ my dorm, and they're usually full.

M : You'd better go late at night or early in the morning. The workers are only
   there during the day.

W : Oh, I didn't know ⑤ _________________________ . I'll go then.
   Thanks for your help!

W : Hi. I'd like to ask about changing my dorm room?

M : What's the matter?

W : Well, I'm having some trouble with my roommate. She's making a lot of noise, and I ① ____________________ .

M : What kind of noise? Have you talked to her about it?

W : Yes, we've talked about it. The ② ____________________ has also talked to her, too, but she keeps doing it. She's in a band, so she ③ ____________________ . She listens to a lot of music in the room, too.

M : I see. Normally we cannot change rooms ④ ____________________ , but we should call your dorm manager now. We need to have a meeting with your roommate here, in my office. She will be in a lot of trouble if she ⑤ ____________________ .

W : That's a relief.

M : Excuse me, are you ① _____________________________ the computer labs?

W : Yes, I'm the general manager for all of them. Can I help you with something?

M : Well, yes. Uh, it's about the new fee system for printouts. It's a lot more expensive ② _____________________________ , and it's becoming kind of a problem.

W : I'm sorry it's a problem. The reasons for it are pretty simple, though. The cost of paper ③ _____________________________ , and we have to pay for it somehow.

M : I understand that, but still — it's so expensive!

W : But it's not something that ④ _____________________________ , I guess. The other issue is to ⑤ _____________________________ . We've discovered that a lot of students print things out that they don't actually need, or they're not careful. They waste a lot of paper.

M : I get it. I guess it's better for the environment that way, too.

W : Hi, I'd like to ask about using the kitchen in one of the other dorms? The one in mine ① ________________________ for renovations.

M : All right, is there ② ________________________ ?

W : Yes, I've got friends staying with me this weekend, and there's no place to cook in my dorm. Cooking is my favorite thing, and we don't want to eat ③ ________________________ .

M : I see. Ah, you can reserve a kitchen in either of the dorms next to yours. You can also reserve one of the teaching kitchens in the nutrition department.

W : Oh, students can use those?

M : Yes, on weekends, if no one else is using them. But you have to clean up, and you can't open a cafe ④ ________________________ the dining halls on campus.

W : No selling food. Don' worry, and ⑤ ________________________ !

Lectures

01 🎧 In a marketing class

1. What is the topic of the lecture?

Ⓐ For-profit businesses and not-for-profit organizations
Ⓑ The elements of a business plan
Ⓒ The steps to start up a business
Ⓓ Development of a new product

2. What are the two types of business plans?

Ⓐ Forms and paperwork
Ⓑ Financial projections and market research
Ⓒ Investing and hiring
Ⓓ Internal and external

Topic:

Details:

 🎧 **In an architecture class**

1. What is the professor mainly talking about?

Ⓐ Current trend in climate change
Ⓑ The importance of reducing energy consumption
Ⓒ Advantages of eco-friendly buildings
Ⓓ Innovative construction technologies

2. What is the main benefit of green building techniques?

Ⓐ Cost savings
Ⓑ Improvement in indoor air
Ⓒ Decrease in the construction time
Ⓓ Better interior design

3. Why is architectural salvage an important part of the green building philosophy?

Ⓐ Bamboo can be used in many parts of the new buildings.
Ⓑ The components of the old buildings may be recycled.
Ⓒ The new buildings look more attractive than the old ones.
Ⓓ Architectural salvage makes the urban temperature go down.

> *Topic:*
>
> *Details:*

Dictation : Lectures

P(M) : You all have a seat, so let's get started, shall we? Um, can somebody
tell me what a business plan is?

S(W) : Isn't it, like, when you're going to ① _________________________ ?
You have to fill out a lot of forms and paperwork?

P : Yes, something like that. A business plan is one of the important first steps
in setting up a business, whether it's a for-profit business or
② _________________________ . It's a statement of your goals for the
business, or if you're trying to start up a non-profit organization, then it would
be ③ _________________________ you want to offer. What else do
you think you'd need to include in a good business plan?

S : How about financial data? Or something about ④ _________________________
you'd need to hire?

P : Right. Often a business plan will include background data about your
team, either the people already involved or the ones you'll need to hire. For
that, ⑤ _________________________ is required. Realistic ⑥ _________
_________ are also important, plus detailed market and competitor
research. A business plan can either be externally directed, meaning you
focus on goals that are important to people outside of the organization.
This usually means financial stakeholders or ⑦ _________________________ .
Internal business plans are typically about ⑧ _________________________
the business might have. Would anyone like to give me an example?

S : Maybe you're developing or launching a new product?

P : Yes, exactly. Or your business is trying to rebrand itself, or
⑨ _________________________ in the market. Maybe you'd use the
business plan to chart your path, to identify all the objectives that need to
be met as you work ⑩ _________________________ , and so on. Next,
I want to talk more specifically about it, but first, are there any questions?

P(M) : In this day of global climate change, we need to consider how we can
① ________________________________ . New and more environmentally-
friendly construction techniques are an important part of this process. You
might have heard the term *green building.* What does that mean? Green
building techniques attempt to make buildings healthier for
② ________________________________ . Green building doesn't just mean making
buildings more energy-efficient. Care is taken with the materials chosen for
construction, the location, the way the building faces the sun, heating and
cooling technologies, and so on. However, by choosing paint, insulation,
and flooring materials that do not ③ ________________________________ , air
quality may be significantly better in a green building than in one
constructed from traditional methods and materials. Better air quality leads
to better health and ④ ________________________________ from work.
A number of innovations go into green buildings. Traditional insulation may
be made of fiberglass, for example. However, a newer form of insulation is
made from recycled denim, from clothes. Paint may be made from milk or
other safe organic substances. Bamboo, which grows quickly and can be
harvested six years after it is planted, is an excellent substitute for wood
from slower-growing trees. Architectural salvage is also encouraged in
green building design: when ⑤ ________________________________ , a great deal
of useful wood, glass, and metal is left behind. Rooftop gardens may cool
the building during summer and insulate the roof during winter. This
contributes to a reduction ⑥ ________________________________ in the
surrounding city.

Practice

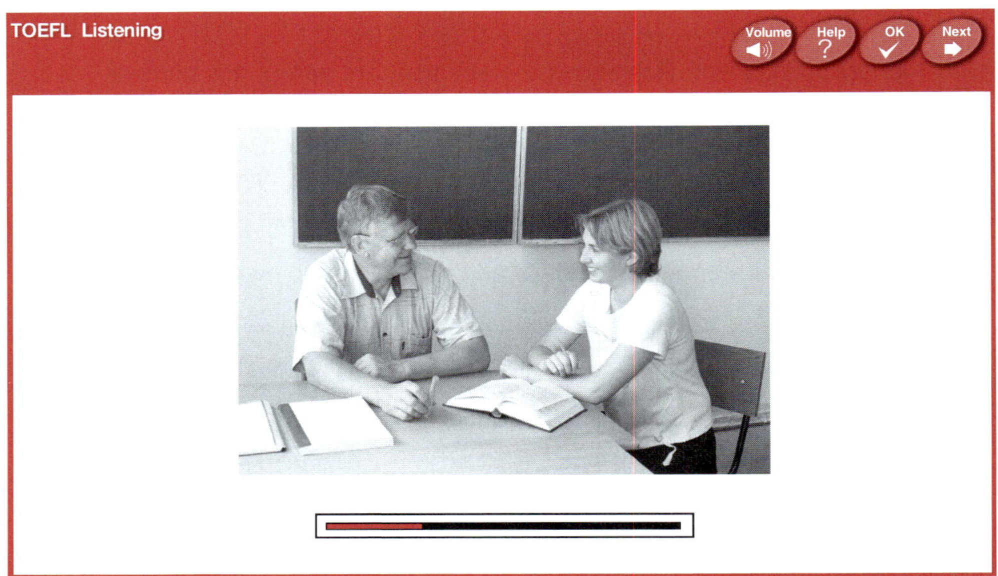

Note-taking

Topic: _________________ for class

1. Student: want to take SLA
   - already _________________
2. Prof.'s suggestions
   - _________________ → risky
   - similar course: Bilingualism
   - take next semester when it is decided _________________

01 Why is the student talking to her professor?

    &Ⓐ She wants to conduct a linguistics research project.
    Ⓑ She wants to take one of the professor's courses.
    Ⓒ She wants to discuss her plan after graduation.
    Ⓓ She wants to be hired as a new professor.

02 What course does the professor recommend as an alternative to Second Language Acquisition?

    Ⓐ Languages of Asia
    Ⓑ Comparative Linguistics
    Ⓒ Intro to Applied Linguistics
    Ⓓ Bilingualism

Listen again to part of the conversation. Then answer the question.

03 What does the professor imply when he says this:

    Ⓐ The student had better look into the undergraduate courses.
    Ⓑ The student is not qualified for taking the master courses.
    Ⓒ The student is pursuing a master's degree in linguistics.
    Ⓓ The student will be a leading expert in the field of linguistics.

04 What does the student imply about Languages of Asia class?

 Ⓐ She is interested in taking the class next semester.
 Ⓑ It is not an advanced course.
 Ⓒ She has already taken the course.
 Ⓓ It is intended for Asian students.

05 In the conversation, the professor offers several possible solutions to the student. Indicate in the table below whether each of the following is mentioned as one of the solutions.

Click in the correct box for each phrase.

	Mentioned	Not Mentioned
Ⓐ Take the course online from another university		
Ⓑ Put her name on the wait-list		
Ⓒ Write a letter to the department head		
Ⓓ Register for the course later, when it is definite who will be teaching it		
Ⓔ Take another course as a substitute		

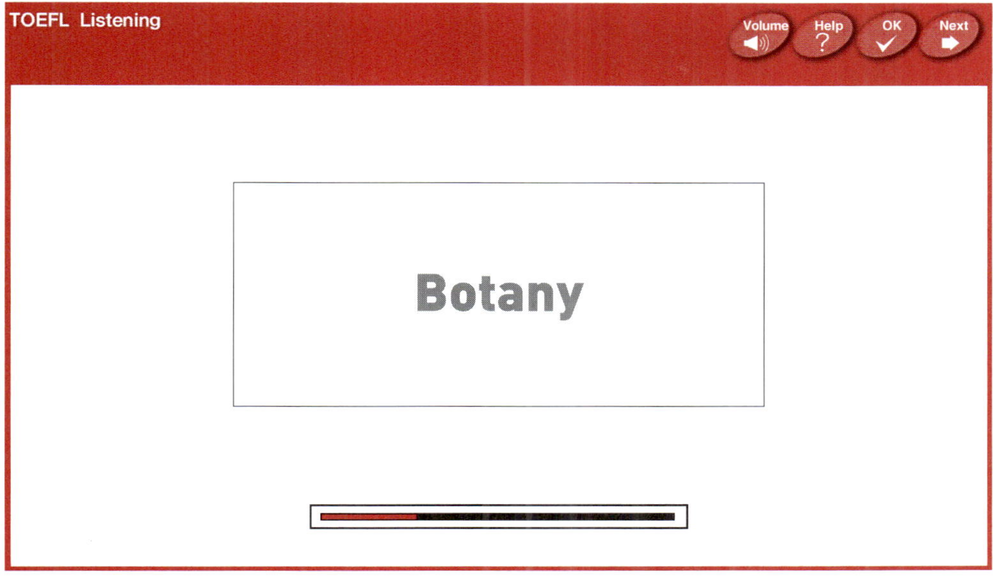
TOEFL Listening
Volume
Help
?
OK
Next
Botany

TOEFL Listening
Volume
Help
?
OK
Next

Topic: Tea

1. Def.

   - different from ___________________ : antiseptic, *Melaleuca* tree

   - C.S. tree leaves

   - ___________________ in hot water

2. Many types

   - ___________________ : black, oolong, green, white, yellow, dark green

   - others: ___________________

3. Tea culture in ___________________

   - Chinese legend: emperor found by accident

   - used as ___________________

4. ___________________

   - begin 17th C.

   - ___________________

06 What is the topic of this lecture?

    Ⓐ Types of herbal tea
    Ⓑ The British East India Company
    Ⓒ Properties of tea tree oil
    Ⓓ Tea and its history

07 Which of the following is true of tea tree oil?

    Ⓐ It is used for medicinal purposes.
    Ⓑ It is derived from *Camellia sinensis*.
    Ⓒ It is mainly made in China.
    Ⓓ It is difficult to come by.

Listen again to part of the lecture. Then answer the question.

08 What does the professor imply when she says this: 🎧

 Ⓐ The list of tea is provided at the supermarket.
 Ⓑ Tea is not an everyday item.
 Ⓒ There are many types of tea.
 Ⓓ The name of tea is difficult to read.

09 In the lecture, the professor mentions the basic types of tea and some of herbal tea. Indicate in the chart below to which each of the following is related. Click in the correct box for each phrase.

	Basic Types	Herbal Tea
Ⓐ Rooibos tea		
Ⓑ Oolong tea		
Ⓒ White tea		
Ⓓ Chamomile tea		
Ⓔ Black tea		

10 What is likely one of the reasons that the Chinese became fond of tea?

 Ⓐ It was an emperor's favorite drink.
 Ⓑ It is easy to prepare tea.
 Ⓒ It has many different colors.
 Ⓓ It proves effective as a stimulant.

11 What does the professor imply about the British's tea consumption?

 Ⓐ They used sugar to purchase tea.
 Ⓑ They depended on the imports.
 Ⓒ They liked to sweeten their tea with sugar.
 Ⓓ They cultivated sugar and tea in the same places.

ALL ABOUT
JUNIOR
TOEFL
Listening

세부사항
Detail

Chapter 2

- Overview
- Preview
- Office Hours
- Service Encounters
- Lectures
- Practice

Overview

- Detail(세부사항) 유형은 화자들이 언급한 내용 중 세부적인 정보에 관한 질문의 답을 고르는 문제
- 대화에서는 1~2문항, 강의에서는 2문항 이상이 출제됨
- 대화에서는 육하원칙(who, when, where, what, how, why)과 관련된 문제와 함께 대화의 내용과 일치하는 것 또는 일치하지 않는 것을 고르는 문제가 주로 출제됨
- 강의에서는 강의 주제에 관한 설명 중 맞는 것과 맞지 않는 것을 고르는 문제가 자주 출제되고, 구체적인 내용과 관련된 질문의 답을 올바로 고를 수 있는지를 묻는 문제 역시 자주 출제됨
- 정답은 대부분 스크립트에서 질문과 관련된 내용(clue)과 비슷한 의미를 가진 다른 표현으로 paraphrase(바꾸어 쓰기)되어 있으므로, 평소 이 부분을 중점적으로 학습하는 것이 Detail 문제 공략의 핵심임
- 스크립트에서 언급되었던 단어나 표현이 똑같이 제시되어 있는 보기는 오답일 확률이 높기 때문에, 보기 내용을 꼼꼼히 확인해야 함
- 답을 2개 골라야 하는 2 click 문제도 출제됨
- 세부 정보에 관한 질문이기는 하지만 너무 세세한 내용에 대해서 묻는 일은 거의 없으므로, 대화와 강의를 들으면서 note-taking을 할 때 들리는 내용 전부를 받아 적으려고 하지는 말아야 함

Sample Questions

- What is ~?
- Why is ~?
- Where will ~?
- Who will ~?
- When will ~?
- How will ~?
- Which of the following is true of ~?
- Which of the following is NOT true of ~?
- What does the professor suggest the student do? Click on 2 answers.
- What are two reasons for ~? Click on 2 answers.

Preview

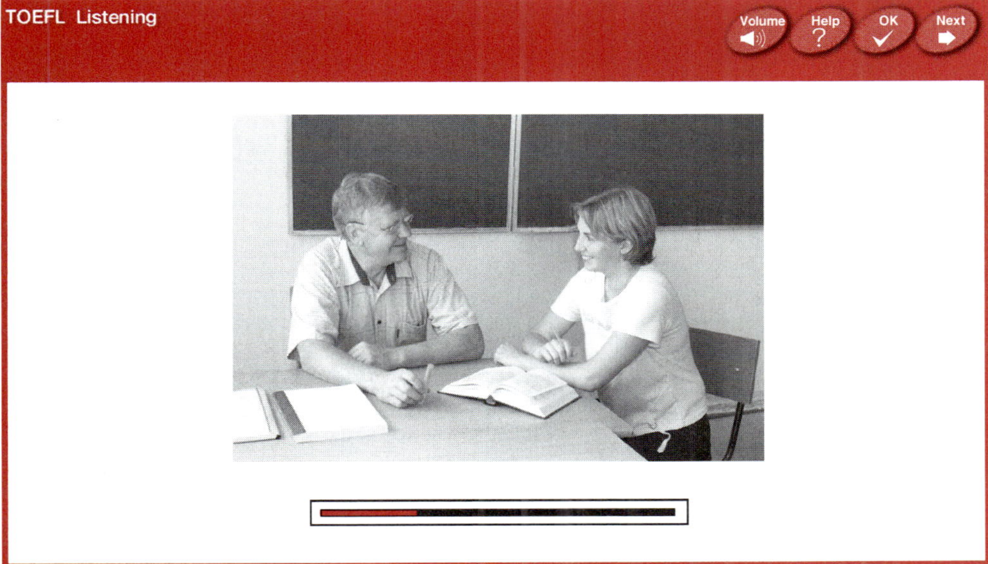

What does the professor suggest the student do?

Ⓐ Take a few extra classes
Ⓑ Hold a photo exhibition
Ⓒ Take good care of her health
Ⓓ Reduce the time spent on the club activity

🎧 Listen to part of a conversation between a student and a professor.

M : Jennifer, last semester you were a leader in class, and this semester...
<u>you can hardly stay awake during the class</u>. Can you tell me what's going
대화 토픽: 학생이 수업 시간에 제대로 집중을 하지 않음
on?

W : I guess <u>I'm doing too many things</u>. I'm in <u>the photography club</u>, and we're
너무 많은 활동을 하고 있음   사진 클럽
having an exhibition soon. I'm also <u>taking extra classes</u>, and I've got <u>a
수업을 추가로 더 듣고 있음
part-time job</u>, too. I'm really tired these days.
아르바이트도 함

M : <u>Then you need to cut back</u>. You can't do everything.
교수의 조언: 하는 일을 줄여야 함

W : But I manage my time very well!

M : If that's true, why are you yawning? <u>Your grade in my class is lower</u> than it
학생의 성적이 낮음
should be. Plus, <u>exhaustion is bad for your health</u>. You should <u>either drop
피곤하면 건강에도 안 좋음
the class or spend less time on your other activities</u>.
교수의 제안: 수강을 취소하던가 다른 활동 시간을 줄여야 함

W : All right. I guess you're right.

남 : Jennifer, 지난 학기에는 수업 시간에 돋보이더니, 이번 학기에는 눈을 뜨고 수업에 집중하는
모습조차도 거의 볼 수가 없구나. 무슨 일인지 얘기해보겠니?

여 : 아무래도 너무 많은 일을 하고 있는 것 같아요. 제가 사진 클럽 활동을 하고 있는데, 곧 전시회
가 있어요. 강의도 더 듣는 것이 있고, 아르바이트도 해요. 요즘 정말 피곤해요.

남 : 그럼 하는 일을 좀 줄여야지. 모든 걸 다할 수는 없단다.

여 : 하지만 시간 관리를 잘 하고 있는 걸요!

남 : 네 말대로라면, 왜 하품을 하니? 내 수업에서 네 성적은 예상했던 것보다 더 낮단다. 그리고,
피로하면 건강에도 나쁘지. 수강을 취소하던가 다른 활동을 하는 데 쓰는 시간을 줄여야겠구
나.

여 : 알겠습니다. 교수님 말씀이 맞는 것 같아요.

해설 학생은 사진 클럽 활동과 아르바이트, 추가 강의 수강 때문에 피곤하여 수업 시간에 집중을 잘 못하고 있다. 그 때문에 성적도 낮게 나오고 있다. 교수는 학생이 모든 것을 한꺼번에 할 수는 없기 때문에 수강을 취소하던가 다른 활동 시간을 줄이라고 조언하고 있다. 대화의 마지막 부분에 문제 해결의 단서가 있다.

> M : <u>Then you need to cut back</u>. You can't do everything.
> W : But I manage my time very well!
> M : If that's true, why are you yawning? Your grade in my class is lower than it should be. Plus, exhaustion is bad for your health. You should <u>either drop the class or spend less time on your other activities</u>.

문제에서 교수가 학생에게 제안하는 것이 무엇인지를 묻고 있으므로, 교수의 말을 주의 깊게 들어야 한다. 수강 취소나 클럽 활동 시간 줄이기와 관련된 보기를 답으로 고르면 된다. 스크립트에 그대로 언급되었던 표현이 쓰인 보기는 오답일 확률이 높다.

교수의 말 : spend less time on your other activities

↓

보기 ⓓ : Reduce the time spent on the club activity

해석 교수가 학생에게 제안하는 것은 무엇인가?
Ⓐ 강의를 추가로 더 듣기
Ⓑ 사진전 열기
Ⓒ 건강을 돌보기
Ⓓ 클럽 활동 시간을 줄이기

어휘 hardly 거의 ~ 않다 | photography 사진 | exhibition 전시회 | yawn 하품하다 | exhaustion 피로

정답 ⓓ

Office Hours

01 What is the student supposed to do at the faculty screening committee?

Ⓐ She will evaluate the professors' research performance.
Ⓑ She will carry out a survey of public opinion.
Ⓒ She will participate in the professor hiring process.
Ⓓ She will review the students' reports.

Topic:

Details:

02 What does the professor suggest the student do?

Click on 2 answers.

Ⓐ Take an extracurricular lesson
Ⓑ Borrow books from the library
Ⓒ Join a study group
Ⓓ Enter a graduate school

Topic:

Details:

03 What does the student need to submit to the competition along with his essay?

Ⓐ A photograph
Ⓑ A reference letter
Ⓒ Writing about himself
Ⓓ A transcript

> **Topic:**
>
> **Details:**

04 Which data should the student see to classify the cities?

Ⓐ The average wages of the cities
Ⓑ The population of the cities
Ⓒ The growth rate of the cities
Ⓓ The real estate cost of the cities

> **Topic:**
>
> **Details:**

Dictation : Office Hours

01

M : Hey, congratulations, I heard you were elected to the faculty screening committee!

W : Yes, thanks... actually, I was chosen to be the head of the student representatives ① ________________________ , too.

M : Wow, double congratulations, then!

W : Thanks. I'm ② ________________________ , though. It's a pretty big job, choosing professors for the university. You don't want to choose the wrong person, after all.

M : I know ③ ________________________ . But I also think you'll do a good job, and it's definitely a good opportunity for you. It'll ④ ________________________ on your resume. Oh, maybe you could probably use the experience in my class, too. Like conducting an opinion poll on campus, ⑤ ________________________ , and using it in a report.

M: Well, since you put it like that, I think I feel better already!

M : May I ① _________________________ about your calculus class,
professor?

W : Sure, what's the matter?

M : Well, I'm having a hard time studying for the class. During class, I
understand ② _________________________ , but after I leave, I start
to forget.

W : Have you tried the calculus study group? It meets on Tuesday evenings in
the library.

M : Yes, a few times, but we always ③ _________________________ ,
and we didn't ④ _________________________ .

W : Well, that's not good. What about the tutoring center on campus? Have
you been there?

M : No, I'm not sure whether that's ⑤ _________________________ . I
can't afford to pay much for a tutor.

W : You're right, it's not free, but it's also not expensive. You should check it
out. You can get some help from graduates. I think it would help you a lot.

M : Great, I will!

W : I have some great news for you, Carlos!

M : What is it?

W : Do you remember the ① _______________________? The English Department's essay committee selected yours. It will be entered in the national competition.

M : That's great! I can't believe it!

W : It's true. We all thought your essay was fantastic. It's very well-written. You have a lot of talent. Of course, I ② _______________________ whether it will win or not, but you should be very proud.

M : That's amazing! What do I need to do now?

W : Well, you need to write ③ _______________________. It should let the reader know who you are. Talk about your family, your ④ _______________________, and your interests... whatever you consider the most important.

M : Sure! How soon should I do that?

W : Can you give it to me by this Friday?

M : Of course! Is there anything else?

W : Actually, there is. A letter of recommendation is required, but you don't have to worry about that. I've asked Professor Frederick to write one.

M : I really appreciate that! Um, won't it be necessary to ⑤ _______________________ _______________________ or something?

W : No, it won't.

M : How're things going with your proposal?

W : Actually, uh, could I get some advice, please? ① ________________ , it's not that going well.

M : Sure, ② ________________________________ ?

W : Well, what I want to do is to look at wages in America's smaller cities, and I want to compare them to the cost of real estate.

M : That's an interesting proposal, considering what's been happening to the real estate market this year.

W : That's ③ ________________________________ . But I'm having trouble deciding ④ ________________________________ .

M : Well, my advice would be to do it two ways: both by population and by growth rate. They might give you very different results, but you should be able to see ⑤ ________________________________ . Also, you should get statistics for the whole metropolitan area.

W : I'll remember that. I think that will ⑥ ________________________________ .

Service Encounters

01 What is the requirement for working at the computer center?

    Ⓐ Being a full-time student at the university
    Ⓑ Taking a basic computing course
    Ⓒ Majoring in a computer-related subject
    Ⓓ Talking to the director of the center

Topic:

Details:

02 Which of the following is NOT the information that the student needs to provide?

    Ⓐ A period of posting
    Ⓑ A host organization
    Ⓒ An e-mail address
    Ⓓ A phone number

Topic:

Details:

03 What will the student do to use the books he needs?

Click on 2 answers.

    Ⓐ Check them out for research
    Ⓑ Read them in the library
    Ⓒ Print out the books of sagas
    Ⓓ Make a duplicate of some pages

> *Topic:*
>
> *Details:*

04 Why are the student's parents calling on him at his school?

    Ⓐ He misses his parents.
    Ⓑ He recently had knee surgery.
    Ⓒ He will be playing in a concert.
    Ⓓ He will be out of hospital.

> *Topic:*
>
> *Details:*

Dictation : Service Encounters

01

M : Hi, I wanted to ① ____________________ this application.

W : You're applying for a job in the computer center?

M : Yes. The university website said that you're hiring?

W : That's right, and what's your major?

M : I'm an English major.

W : English major... have you taken ② ____________________ ?

M : No, I haven't, but I know a lot about computers. Is it a problem?

W : Well, I'm afraid the center just changed ③ ____________________ .
Our student assistants have to have taken – and passed – the first introductory-level course before working here.

M : I didn't know that. But what about someone who already knows a lot about a computer? Isn't there any way to get the job?

W : It's ④ ____________________ . It's a new policy, so I don't think the center head will want to ⑤ ____________________ yet. I'll take your application anyway, though.

M : Thanks for your help, anyway.

W : I don't know if I came to the right place, but I need to ① ___________

___________ to put up posters around the campus.

M : OK, what's the occasion?

W : We're ② ___________________________ .

M : Sure, there's a form you need to fill out, with your name, the organization's

name, the type and number of posters, and how long they'll be up.

W : That should be no problem.

M : Uh, have you already printed the posters?

W : We're about to do that. We wanted to make sure there ③ ___________

___________ , though. It wouldn't make sense to print a hundred

posters if we're only allowed to post fifty.

M : Good thinking. And you're right, there is a limit on that. There are only 27

④ ___________________________ around campus, so you probably

shouldn't print a hundred posters!

W : Thanks for letting me know that. And... here's the form. What happens

next?

M : We'll e-mail you to ⑤ ___________________________ .

W : Thanks!

M : Excuse me, I have a question about the Icelandic dictionary and the books of sagas. They're ① ___________________________ , but I'm writing a paper, and I really need them for my research.

W : I understand completely, but they're reference books, and we can't ② ___________________________ .

M : But I really need them! What can I do?

W : You should do what everyone else does. Use them here in the library, and ③ ___________________________ you need if you ④ ___________________________ .

M : But the library's about to close!

W : Then you should come back tomorrow, earlier in the day. I'm sorry, but those books aren't easy to replace. Actually, the book of sagas is ⑤ ___________________________ . We really can't let them leave the library.

M : All right. I'll come back tomorrow, then.

04

M : Hi, I need to ① ________________________ a parking permit for my
parents.

W : Are they coming to visit you on campus?

M : Yes. I'm actually in the orchestra, and they're ② ________________________
________ this weekend.

W : They can use the regular visitor lots, can't they? Those ③ ________________
________________ the performance hall.

M : Well, my father had ④ ________________________ last week, and
he still can't walk too far yet.

W : Oh, why didn't you say so? They can park in a handicapped space if
they've already got an official permit. Tell your parents to display it on the
dashboard when they park. They won't get a ticket or ⑤ ________________
________________ .

M : I thought I had to get a special permit for that, myself.

W : Well, if you were a disabled student and you needed to use those parking
spaces, yes. But your parents are just coming down for this performance...

M : Well, for the weekend, actually.

W : For the weekend, then. All they need is the official permit, which they
⑥ ________________________ from the hospital or the Department
of Motor Vehicles. It's very simple.

M : Oh, that is simple!

Lectures

01 🎧 In an ichthyology class

1. Which of the following is true of an electric organ of electric fish?

 Ⓐ It makes the fish lose its consciousness.
 Ⓑ It is not useful for attacking a prey.
 Ⓒ It is located near the end of the body.
 Ⓓ It reduces the function of the brain.

2. How much of the electric eel's body is used in the generation of electricity?

 Ⓐ 4/5
 Ⓑ 20%
 Ⓒ Half
 Ⓓ 18%

Topic:

Details:

---

1. Why is fast mapping of interest to developmental psychologists?

    Ⓐ Because it explains children's rapid vocabulary growth
    Ⓑ Because it takes place during elementary school
    Ⓒ Because it shows how good children's memory is
    Ⓓ Because it is also an important area in linguistics

2. Where do small children pick up most of their vocabularies?

    Ⓐ From school
    Ⓑ From maps
    Ⓒ From the environment
    Ⓓ From their lexicon

3. What happens when infants hear a new word?

    Ⓐ They instantly figure out what it exactly means.
    Ⓑ They associate it with what they already know.
    Ⓒ They confuse it with the words from their lexicon.
    Ⓓ They refuse to memorize it at first.

Topic:

Details:

Dictation : Lectures

01

P(M) : I guess the electric eel is one of those species we're all somewhat familiar with. If you've visited an aquarium or if you've studied biology at all, you've probably seen one: either a picture, or perhaps even the real thing. Electric eels are the best-known electric fish, but they're ①________________________. First of all, I should point out that they are not eels. They're a type of knifefish, ②________________________. Electric fish species are ③________________________. What they all have in common is the ability to generate electricity. And the way ④________________________ is with an electric organ, which uses specialized muscle and nerve cells to emit the electric discharge. Usually the electric organ is found in the tail of the fish. This makes sense from ⑤________________________, because if it were in the head, it could ⑥________________________ of the brain. Electric shocks don't save you from predators if you knock yourself unconscious every time, do they?

There are relatively few electric fish species that produce a strong-enough discharge to ⑦________________________. The electric eels can do it, and so can the electric catfishes and the electric rays. The electric eel is particularly interesting because so much of its body, 80% of it, is devoted to electricity production. In the same way that a battery produces electricity via a series of plates, the electric eel has a series of structures called electroplaques. Their electric discharge is strong enough to ⑧________________________, and as a matter of fact, some countries like Australia have outlawed them. They are simply too dangerous.

P(W) : In developmental psychology, one subject we find very interesting is the process of language acquisition. The way ① _______________ has been studied extensively for many decades, and we have learned some fascinating things. Linguists and psychologists are particularly interested in fast mapping, which is one way children ② _______________ .

As you know, infants learn most words from the environment. Later, in elementary school, they learn words with the rest of their lessons. However, small children do ③ _______________ . How do they pick up so many words ④ _______________ , then? Fast mapping explains this process.

When a child hears a novel word for the first time – meaning a word that is different from anything else in his or her lexicon – then ⑤ _______________ . The child forms a hypothesis about what the word might mean. In other words, he or she can make a relationship with some other objects, and can ⑥ _______________ after hearing the word once. Only one time – that's all that is necessary in fast mapping. Later, when the child hears the word again, ⑦ _______________ the word will help to clarify its meaning. The child can figure out the basic idea right away, and in time, can come to understand the word perfectly.

Practice

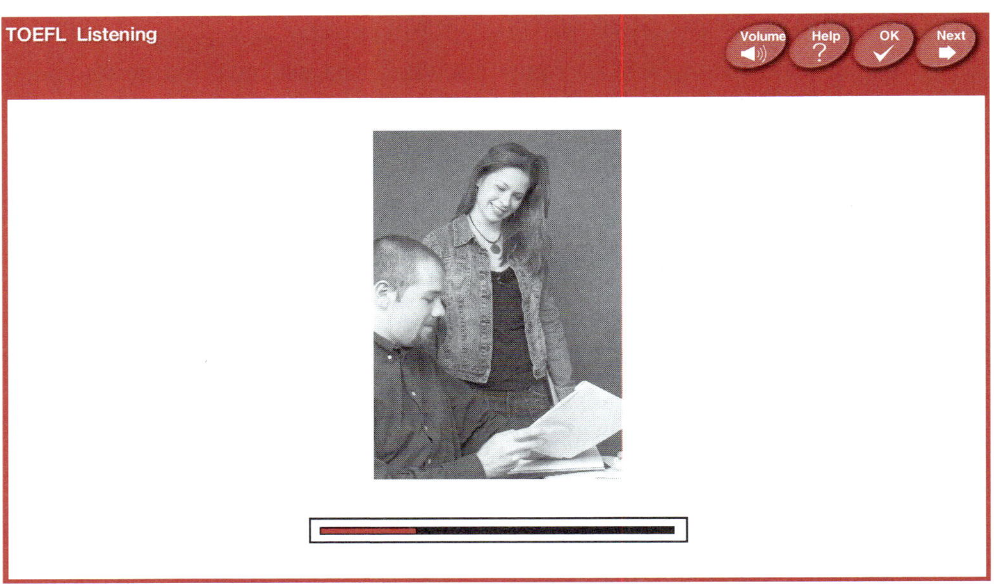

Note-taking

Topic: Switch day off

1. Student: want to take ____________________

   - ____________________ in sociology

   - visit com. org

2. Manager: X allowed

   - Mon is ____________________

   - short-staffed

3. Suggestion

   - student: post ____________________ for switching shift

   - manager: ____________________ project trip

01 Why is the student having this conversation with the cafeteria manager?

    Ⓐ She will get a job at a community organization.
    Ⓑ She wants to cover for one of her colleagues.
    Ⓒ She wants the manager to hire new workers.
    Ⓓ She needs a day off to work on a school project.

02 Why can't the manager allow the student to take Monday off?

    Ⓐ The student already had days off.
    Ⓑ The manager has no authority to decide it.
    Ⓒ The cafeteria is heavily crowded on Monday.
    Ⓓ The schedule is not subject to change.

Listen again to part of the conversation. Then answer the question.

03 What does the man imply when he says this: 🎧

    Ⓐ The student's idea is perfect.
    Ⓑ He is willing to hire someone.
    Ⓒ It is not possible to employ someone now.
    Ⓓ The world is a perfect place.

04 Why is it implied that the manager will have trouble finding new workers?

    Ⓐ Students are busy with projects and exams at the end of the semester.
    Ⓑ Cafeteria jobs are not popular with students.
    Ⓒ Students need money for activities during break, but the cafeteria does not pay well.
    Ⓓ The cafeteria has poor working conditions.

05 In the conversation, the speakers discuss several possible solutions, some better than others, to the schedule problem. Indicate in the table below whether each of the following is mentioned as one of the solutions.

Click in the correct box for each phrase.

	Mentioned	Not Mentioned
Ⓐ Asking the professor for an extension on the trip		
Ⓑ Rearranging the group project trip		
Ⓒ Having the student's friend cover for her one day		
Ⓓ Putting up a note for switching shifts		

TOEFL Listening
Volume
Help
OK
Next
Law

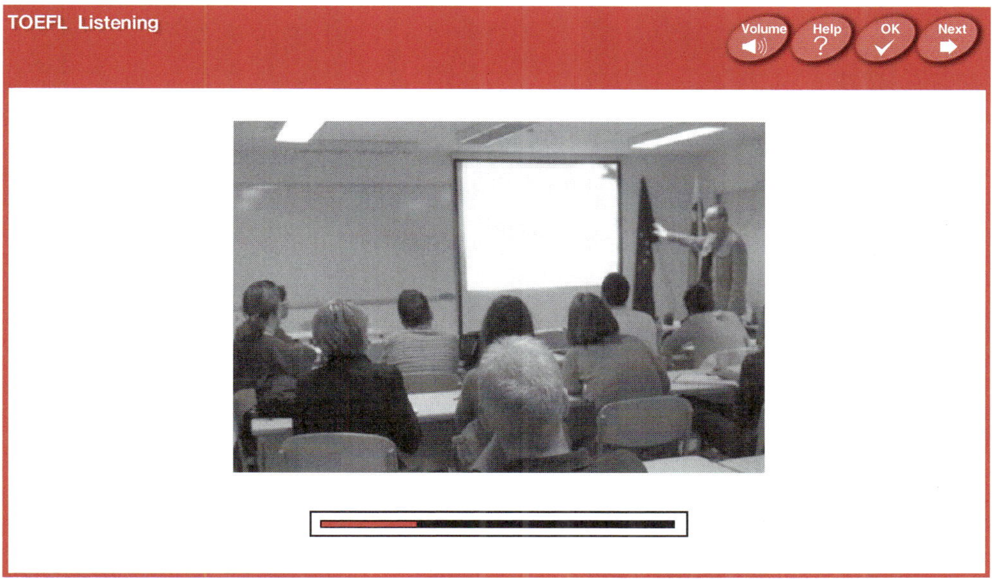

TOEFL Listening
Volume
Help
OK
Next

Topic: IP

1. _________________
   - illegal download
   - book, music, movie, software, etc.
   - legal restriction on _________________
2. Patent
   - _________________
   - e.g. Edison
3. Cons
   - _________________
   - X competition ← unique
4. Others
   - trademark: _________________
   - indus. design
   - _________________

06 What is the professor lecturing about today?

Ⓐ Copyrights and patents
Ⓑ Illegal downloading
Ⓒ A limited monopoly
Ⓓ Intellectual property rights

07 When a book is published, who does NOT earn a portion of the money?

Ⓐ The distributor
Ⓑ The writer
Ⓒ The reader
Ⓓ The publishing company

Listen again to part of the lecture. Then answer the question.

08 Why does the professor mention Thomas Edison: 🎧

    Ⓐ To emphasize Thomas Edison was a great inventor
    Ⓑ To give an example of wonderful inventions in history
    Ⓒ To suggest his inventions made people's lives more convenient
    Ⓓ To help the students understand the concept of a patent easily

09 According to the lecture, what is the apparent contradiction in IP laws?

    Ⓐ They completely control the competitors.
    Ⓑ They cause a form of monopoly to exist.
    Ⓒ They prevent a monopoly from being created.
    Ⓓ They disintegrate a regular monopoly.

10 How is a *limited monopoly* different from a regular monopoly?

    Ⓐ It defends capitalism.
    Ⓑ No rivalry is found.
    Ⓒ It is regulated by the government.
    Ⓓ It is universally respected.

11 In the lecture, the professor mentions several important IP rights.
Match them to which they relate.

Click in the correct box for each phrase.

IP rights	Features
Copyright	
Trademark	
Patent	
Trade secret	

Ⓐ A piece of writing or music
Ⓑ New inventions
Ⓒ A distinguishing symbol
Ⓓ Confidential information of a company

ALL ABOUT
JUNIOR
TOEFL
Listening

추론
Inference

Overview

- Inference(추론) 유형은 대화와 강의 내용을 통해 미루어 짐작 또는 추론할 수 있는 것을 고르는 문제
- 대화와 강의 모두 1문항 정도가 출제됨
- 화자의 다음 행동을 예측하는 단순한 추론 문제에서부터 강의 내용 전체를 바탕으로 새롭게 도출해낼 수 있는 결론을 묻는 까다로운 문제까지 다양한 형태의 추론 문제가 출제됨
- 언급된 사실에 대한 정확한 이해를 바탕으로 한 논리적 접근이 문제 해결의 핵심
- 반드시 스크립트에 언급되었던 내용들만을 근거로 하여 답을 골라야 함
- 스크립트에 언급되었던 단어나 표현이 그대로 등장하는 보기는 오답일 가능성이 높으므로 보기 내용을 꼼꼼히 확인해야 함

Sample Questions

- What can be inferred about ~?
- What does the man imply about ~?
- What will the woman probably do next?
- What can be concluded about ~?
- What would be a similar example of ~?
- Which of the following is probably true about ~?

Preview

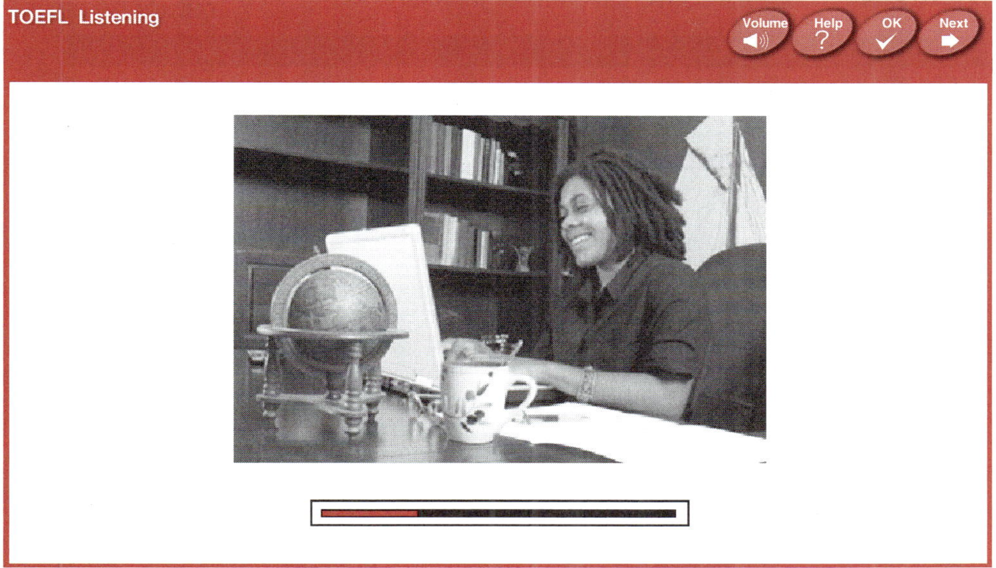

What can be concluded from the conversation?

Ⓐ The student got injured while playing basketball.
Ⓑ The student will miss some classes.
Ⓒ The student is not able to give a lecture.
Ⓓ The student will do the cooking.

🎧 Listen to part of a conversation at an infirmary.

M : Thanks for <u>taking care of my ankle</u>. I'm glad it's not worse!
　　　　　　　대화 토픽: 발목 치료

W : Well, <u>sprains are pretty bad</u>. A sprain can be more painful than a fracture.
　　　　　　발목을 삐었음
　　<u>You need to be careful with it</u>. <u>The less you can move around, the better</u>.
　　　　　조심해야 함　　　　　　　　　되도록이면 움직이는 것을 자제해야 함

M : But... I have <u>an intervarsity basketball match next week</u>!
　　　　　　　　　　다음 주에 대학 농구 대항전이 있음

W : <u>Are you out of your mind</u>? You should take this seriously. You don't want
　　　시합에 나가면 안 됨
　　it going from bad to worse, do you?

M : If you say so...

W : I want you to <u>go straight back to your room and stay there at least</u> <u>for a</u>
　　　　　　　　　　집으로 돌아가서 최소 이틀은 쉬어야 함
　　<u>couple of days</u>. You can <u>go to the bathroom and you can take a shower</u>. If
　　　　　　　　　　　　　　　　화장실에 가거나 샤워는 해도 됨
　　you can <u>get food delivered, do that</u>.
　　　　　음식을 배달시켜 먹기

M : Just the basics, in other words?

W : That's right. You've got a sprained ankle. <u>I don't care if you're *teaching* the</u>
　　　　　　　　　　　　　　　　　　　며칠간은 쉬어야 한다는 사실을 강조하여 말함
　　<u>class</u>. You need to rest!

M : All right. Will you give me a note?

W : Coming right up!

남 : 발목을 치료해주셔서 감사합니다. 심하지 않아서 다행이에요.

여 : 발목을 삔 것도 상당히 심한 상태가 될 수 있어요. 골절상보다 더 고통이 심하기도 하니까요. 조심하도록 하세요. 적게 움직일 수록, 더 빨리 낫죠.

남 : 하지만… 다음 주에 대학 농구 대항 경기가 있어요!

여 : 지금 제정신이에요? 지금 상태를 진지하게 받아들여야 해요. 상태가 악화되기를 바라지는 않겠죠?

남 : 그렇게 말씀하신다면…

여 : 기숙사로 곧장 가서 며칠 정도는 쉬도록 해요. 화장실에 가거나 샤워는 할 수 있어요. 음식을 배달시킬 수 있으면, 그렇게 하는 것이 좋고요.

남 : 아주 기본적인 것만 하라는 말씀이시죠?

여 : 맞아요. 발목을 삐었잖아요. 학생이 직접 강의를 한다 해도 상관없어요. 꼭 쉬어야 해요.

남 : 알겠습니다. 진단서 좀 적어주시겠어요?

여 : 바로 해줄게요.

해설 학생은 발목을 삐어서 학교 양호실에서 치료를 받고 있다. 여자는 학생에게 다친 부위의 상태가 안 좋아질 수도 있으니, 되도록 몸을 움직이지 말라고 충고하고 있다. 각 보기와 지문의 해당 부분을 비교하며 이 대화를 통해 결론 너릴 수 있는 것이 무엇인지 확인해보자.

보기 Ⓐ : 여자가 몸을 되도록 움직이지 말라고 말하자 학생이 다음 주에 농구 경기가 있다고 하였는데, 이 말을 통해 학생이 농구를 하다가 발목을 다쳤는지는 알 수 없다. 다친 이유에 대해서는 언급이 되지 않았다. 따라서 보기 Ⓐ의 내용은 오답이다.

보기 Ⓑ : 여자는 학생에게 며칠간은 쉬어야 한다고 강조하여 말했다. 학생이 강의를 해야 하는 입장이라도 상관없다고 하자, 학생이 여자의 말대로 하겠다고 했다. 이를 통해 학생이 며칠간 수업을 빼먹게 될 것임을 짐작할 수 있다. 따라서 보기 Ⓑ가 정답이다.

보기 Ⓒ : 여자가 학생이 직접 강의를 한다 해도 상관 없다고 한 것은 학생이 실제로 강의를 하고 있다는 것이 다니라 무슨 일이 있어도 며칠간은 쉬어야 한다는 사실을 강조하여 말하는 것이다. 따라서 보기 Ⓒ의 내용은 오답이다.

보기 Ⓓ : 여자가 학생에게 음식을 배달시켜 먹을 수 있으면 그렇게 하라고 했기 때문에 보기 Ⓓ의 내용은 오답이다.

해석 대화를 통해 결론 내릴 수 있는 것은 무엇인가?
Ⓐ 학생은 농구를 하다가 다쳤다.
Ⓑ 학생은 일부 수업에 결석할 것이다.
Ⓒ 학생은 강의를 할 수 없다.
Ⓓ 학생은 요리를 할 것이다.

어휘 ankle 발목 | sprain 발목을 삠 | fracture 골절상 | in other words 즉, 다른 말로 | intervarsity match 대학 대항 경기

정답 Ⓑ

Office Hours

01 Which of the following is probably true about the photography club?

    Ⓐ There are many talented photographers in the club.
    Ⓑ It needs funds granted by the university.
    Ⓒ It will publish the magazine as planned.
    Ⓓ Few of the members have experience with publication.

Topic:

Details:

02 What does the professor imply about writing the letter of recommendation?

    Ⓐ He believes the student needs at least 2 letters.
    Ⓑ He does not know the student well.
    Ⓒ He thinks the academic advisor is the best person to write it.
    Ⓓ He does not know what to say in the letter.

Topic:

Details:

03 What does the professor imply about the student?

Ⓐ The student is one of the best in the class.
Ⓑ The student has not been fully prepared for the presentation.
Ⓒ The student was busy with presentations for other classes.
Ⓓ The student doesn't know much about computer software programs.

Topic:

Details:

04 What will the student probably do next?

Ⓐ He will try to do the entire thing at a different time.
Ⓑ He will finish as much as possible in the remaining 20 minutes.
Ⓒ He will give up and leave the exam unfinished.
Ⓓ He will bring the professor a doctor's note.

Topic:

Details:

Dictation : Office Hours

**1**

W : Would you mind giving me some suggestions about the magazine the photography club is ① _______________________ ?

M : Sure, is there any problem?

W : Well, the problem is that there aren't enough really good photos. We thought we'd have more, but fewer students submitted work ② _______________________ ...

M : I see. How often were you planning to publish it?

W : Monthly?

M : In that case, I think you have two choices. One, you could include photographs that are just good, ③ _______________________ that are really good. Two, you could publish ④ _______________________ , or even once per semester. Lots of university publications operate that way.

W : Maybe monthly is too ambitious... I'll talk about it with others, and I'll see what they think. Thanks for the suggestions!

M : No worries. Let me know if I can help again.

W : Hi, I'm wondering if you could ① _______________________? I'm

applying for an internship at B&G, and the deadline is coming up soon.

M : Sure, I can do that. In fact, I know a couple of former students from our

program who work there now.

W : Thanks!

M : But you should know, those jobs are very competitive. Many people apply

for them, including people with a lot of experience. I can't

② _______________________.

W : I understand.

M : By the way, isn't Dr. Douglas your academic advisor? Have you asked

him?

W : Yes, he is, but he's ③ _______________________ at a conference

in Kyoto.

M : Oh, that's right. And we've got ④ _______________________, so

he's staying in Japan. Lucky man. Well, I know you from my own classes,

so it won't be a problem. How soon do you need it?

W : How about Friday?

W : You wanted to see me after class?

M : Yes, I did. Did you ① _______________________ for this presentation? I passed it out in class on the 23rd, and I also posted the instructions on my website for this class.

W : Um... yes, I got a copy. Was there a problem?

M : Well, the instructions ② _______________________. In addition to your talk, you needed to prepare a PowerPoint presentation, and you needed to have a handout for the class. Apparently, you didn't have ③ _______________________.

W : Oh. Um...

M : I also noticed you were ④ _______________________ too often during your talk. If you want to pass this class, you will need to do a better job with the remaining two presentations. Do you understand?

W : I'm sorry.

M : That's all. Have a good afternoon.

M : I'm sorry I'm just ① _______________________! I'm sorry I'm late!

Is it too late to take the exam?

W : Not if you can do it in 20 minutes. That's ② _______________________

_________ in the period.

M : Oh, no. I'm sorry. I... I overslept. Um... can I make an appointment to take

it later?

W : I can't do that. The department head is very clear on that point — unless

there's a doctor's note, she ③ _______________________. And if

you don't agree with the decision, then you have to ④ _______________________

_____________ of academic affairs.

M : I haven't been late all semester! Please... can't I just make an

appointment?

W : You're ⑤ _______________________. I suggest you do as much as

you can now, and we'll talk about it afterward, OK?

M : Oh... I've ruined everything.

Service Encounters

01 What will probably happen next?

Ⓐ Most students will stay in their rooms because they need to study.
Ⓑ Many students will get bad grades on their midterm exams.
Ⓒ Some of the students in the noisy area will move to the new dorm.
Ⓓ The university will halt renovation work on the dorm.

> *Topic:*
>
> *Details:*

02 What do you think the Spanish phrase *de nada* means?

Ⓐ You're welcome.
Ⓑ I understand.
Ⓒ That's too bad.
Ⓓ See you later.

> *Topic:*
>
> *Details:*

03 What does the man imply about the students at the student lounge?

Ⓐ They are very fond of watching TV.
Ⓑ They don't like to study in the library.
Ⓒ They are studying hard now.
Ⓓ They don't usually use the student lounge.

Topic:

Details:

04 What can be inferred about the student?

Ⓐ He will search his room for the book.
Ⓑ He will have to pay for the book.
Ⓒ He will not be allowed to check out other books.
Ⓓ He will talk to the author of the book.

Topic:

Details:

Dictation : Service Encounters

01

M : I can't ① _________________________ any longer!

W : What's the problem?

M : Well, I live next to the dorm that's ② _________________________ .
You know...

W : Oh, yeah, I bet the construction noise is pretty bad right now.

M : Tell me about it, and even worse, I'm on that side of the building. Plus, midterm exams start next week, and it's hard to study. What can I do?

W : I understand. We've decided to let students affected by the construction noise ③ _________________________ . Our original plan was to wait until next semester to open it, but these renovations have been louder than anyone expected.

M : Will there be ④ _________________________ for that?

W : No, of course not. It's not your fault that the construction is loud. We're going to provide movers ⑤ _________________________ , also, because we understand this will affect a lot of students during midterms.

M : That's fantastic! I'll text my roommate now.

W : Glad I could help.

M : Hi, I've been selected for ① ____________________ , and I'm going to Mexico for a semester.

W : Oh, you look excited. Did you just get the news?

M : Yes! But I just looked at the Mexican university's website, and some of the courses I want to take don't seem to ② ____________________ here.

W : Um, which courses are those?

M : Advanced Spanish, and a couple of the advanced literature classes as well. I think they're new. Is that going to be a problem for me?

W : No, it shouldn't be. If they're new courses, we only need ③ ____________________ from the university, and we can give you credit.

M : Do I need to contact the university?

W : No, we do, because it means we need to ④ ____________________ of eligible courses. Thanks for letting us know about this!

M : *De nada.*

M : There's a little bit of a problem in the student lounge.

W : Is something wrong? Has anyone been hurt?

M : No, it's not that. It's not an emergency. It's just that the volume on the TV is too loud, and ① _________________________ without the remote control. We're trying to study.

W : Oh... um, can't you ② _________________________ ?

M : The library's full. Finals start next week, and everyone's there. The lounges ③ _________________________ , too. This was the only place we could find.

W : But, you know, there are also other students ④ _________________________ there.

M : I'm sure nobody's watching it tonight.

W : All right, let me get the remote control, and I'll go and ⑤ _________________________ _________________ . Should I turn it down, or should I just turn the TV off?

M : I guess you can ⑥ _________________________ .

W : All right.

M : Thanks!

M : Excuse me, um, I've lost a book, and I'm not sure what I need to do now.

W : I see. Will you ① ______________________ of the book, and the author's name if you remember it? Here's some paper and a pen.

M : Oh, thanks. But actually I don't remember the names. There were three, I think. Anyway, you can ② ______________________ , right?

W : Yes, as long as I have some basic information, it'll be easy to find. I'll need your student ID, too.

M : Uh, will I have to pay a fine, or buy a new book, or what? I don't know ③ ______________________ .

W : You're absolutely sure you've lost the book?

M : Yes. I've looked all over my room for it, and I've retraced all my steps. I can't find it anywhere.

W : All right... well, you're ④ ______________________ .

M : Oh? Losing a book doesn't feel lucky to me.

W : Well, fortunately the book isn't ⑤ ______________________ . We, actually, you can replace it easily, and it's not a very expensive book. That's why I said you were lucky.

M : Oh, OK. That's a relief. How much will it cost me?

W : $24.95.

Lectures

1. Which of the following is NOT true of the Pony Express?

    Ⓐ It didn't get to every city in the western.
    Ⓑ It usually took 10 days for mail to be delivered.
    Ⓒ It made up for the weak points in a telegraph.
    Ⓓ It was in service for 18 months.

2. What is probably true if Pony Express stations were set up at intervals of ten miles?

    Ⓐ Stations ten miles apart would be the cheapest option for the Pony Express company.
    Ⓑ Ten miles is the longest distance a horse could run before getting too tired to continue.
    Ⓒ Real estate was not available for the stations to be closer together.
    Ⓓ Riders could not endure more than ten miles on a galloping horse.

Topic:

Details:

1. What is the main topic of this lecture?

    Ⓐ Decrease in responsiveness to unchanging conditions
    Ⓑ Various concepts in psychology
    Ⓒ Observation of habituation in humans
    Ⓓ Advantages of habituation

2. What can be concluded about an experiment on a stuffed owl and a bird?

    Ⓐ The bird recognizes that the stuffed owl is not real from the beginning.
    Ⓑ The bird never gets used to the stuffed owl.
    Ⓒ The bird eventually attacks the stuffed owl.
    Ⓓ The bird considers the stuffed owl no threat over time.

3. What would be another example of habituation?

    Ⓐ Talking to someone in a secret place
    Ⓑ Listening to the radio while driving a car
    Ⓒ Participating in a discussion
    Ⓓ Reading a book in a quiet room

Topic:

Details:

Dictation : Lectures

P(W) : If you're familiar with the United States and its history, you've probably heard of the Pony Express. The name has become a legend, even though it was ① _______________________ for about a year and a half, from April 1860 to October 1861. Pretty short, right? It was set up to be ② _______________________ across the Western states and territories, and the company's real goal was to win government mail contracts. Uh, the eastern terminus and company headquarters were in St. Joseph, Missouri, and ③ _______________________ was Sacramento, California. Well, in Sacramento, mail ④ _______________________ to the west like San Francisco and Oakland would be carried the rest of the way on a steam ship.

Look, the Pony Express was a pioneering outfit in many ways, which is why we remember it today. Prior to this, people hadn't thought it was possible to ⑤ _______________________. Mail either had to go by ship down below the South American continent, or it had to be sent across Panama, or it had to take a southern route across the regions like Arizona and New Mexico. None of these routes offered fast delivery. For example, using a ship would take upward of six months! But Pony Express stations were staged about every ten miles, so a rider could ⑥ _______________________ _______________________. In this way, the riders made their deliveries within ten or eleven days, almost unheard-of back then. Moreover, they proved it could be done even during the winter. Unfortunately, ⑦ _______________________ _______________________, and two days after telegraph cables were extended to Salt Lake City, the Pony Express announced it was closing... and in a way, it was ⑧ _______________________ in American history.

P(W) : Uh, habituation is an important concept in psychology, and it's one that you're experiencing right now. Well, can you feel your clothes? If you think about it a little, you'll probably answer with something like 'Sort of.' When you get dressed, you are ① _________________________ of your clothes against your skin. After a while, you ② _________________________ . Only if something you're wearing is uncomfortable – maybe you've gained a little weight, and your pants are too tight – will you continue to notice.

Habituation is a natural phenomenon. It has been observed in all animals, even protozoa. When a particular stimulus is presented long enough, we stop noticing. The only time we begin paying attention again is ③ _________________________ . For example, um, if a stuffed owl is put in a cage with birds for which it is a predator, they will panic. But as time passes, they will stop reacting to it completely. That doesn't mean they have ④ _________________________ between a real owl and a false one, though: if you take out the stuffed owl and ⑤ _________________________ , the birds will react again.

From that, we know that habituation is about changes in stimuli. It acts as a filter, in other words, and it allows us to tune out background stimuli. The brain simply can't ⑥ _________________________ , so we have developed habituation in order to cut out stimuli that we've already experienced. This is helpful in many ways. For instance, it's the reason we stop noticing, uh, odors after a while. When you walk into a classroom, you may smell dust or cleaning products, but if you kept smelling them, you might not ⑦ _________________________ . So you should be thankful to have this ability!

Practice

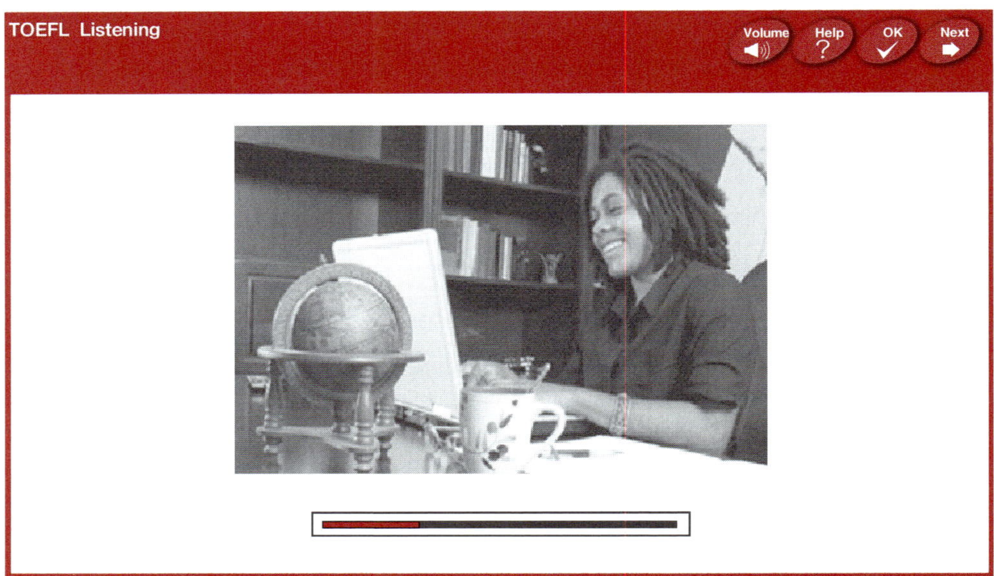

Note-taking

Topic: _________________ options

1. Want a _________________

   - closer to _________________

   - _________________ room

   - private bathroom

2. Deposit

   - in 2 weeks

   - scholarship fund coming _________________

   - W's suggestion: _________________

01 What are the speakers mainly talking about in the conversation?

Ⓐ Moving into an off-campus apartment
Ⓑ Reserving a room in a residence hall
Ⓒ Switching the dorm room
Ⓓ Finding a new roommate

02 Why does the student want no roommate?

Ⓐ He wants to use a spacious room alone.
Ⓑ He does not get along well with other people.
Ⓒ He does not like a lazy and untidy person.
Ⓓ He wants to study without interruption from a roommate.

03 What does the woman imply about Buchanan Hall?

Ⓐ It is very large.
Ⓑ It has a small student body.
Ⓒ It is on main campus.
Ⓓ It doesn't have a single room.

 In the conversation, the student lists several criteria for his accommodations. Indicate on the table below whether each of the following is mentioned as one of them.

Click in the correct box for each phrase.

	Mentioned	Not Mentioned
Ⓐ A dorm near the bus stop		
Ⓑ A personal bathroom		
Ⓒ A room with no roommate		
Ⓓ A study room of his own		
Ⓔ A dorm not far from main campus		

Listen again to part of the conversation. Then answer the question.

05 What does the student imply when he says this: 🎧

Ⓐ He is concerned he will not pay the deposit soon enough.
Ⓑ He wants to make sure he has enough money in his checking account.
Ⓒ He thinks he might change his mind after he pays the deposit.
Ⓓ He is going to ask his professor to lend him the deposit.

TOEFL Listening
Volume
Help
?
OK
Next
Modern Art

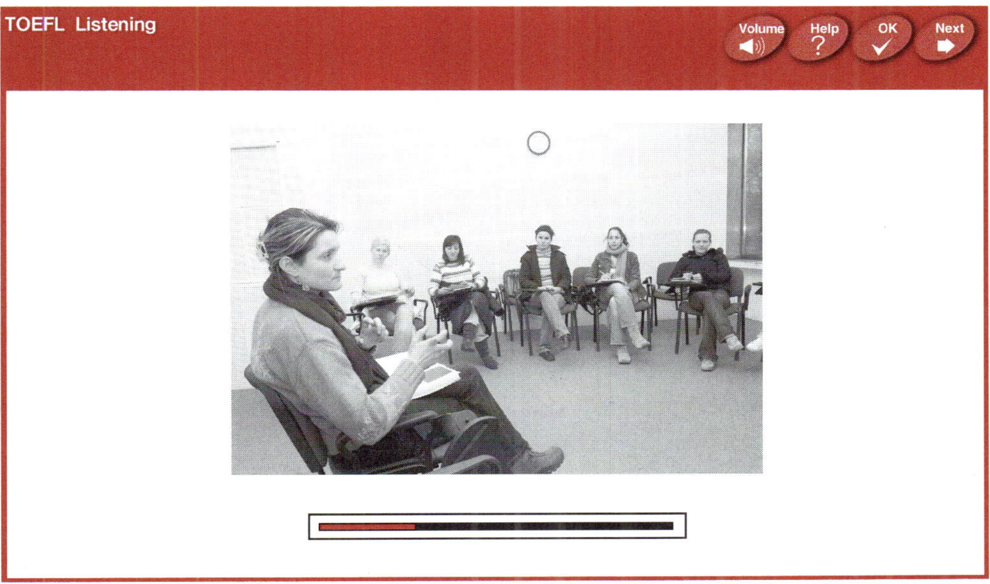

TOEFL Listening
Volume
Help
?
OK
Next

Topic: Georgia O'Keeffe

1. Represent changes in society regarding ________________
   - feminist artist
2. Work from New Mexico
   - painted ________________
3. 1st exhibit by Stieglitz
   - ________________ drawing
   - she ________________
   - married him
4. 1920s,30s, 40s, ________________
   - mainly painted ________________
   - calla lilies sold for $25,000
   - success & popularity → ________________ exhibit
5. Stieglitz's death → ________________
   - got ________________
   - landscape paintings
   - The Georgia O'Keeffe Museum

06 What is the discussion mainly about?

    Ⓐ Famous female artists
    Ⓑ Georgia O'Keeffe and her work
    Ⓒ Georgia O'Keeffe and Alfred Stieglitz
    Ⓓ The Georgia O'Keeffe Museum

07 Why is Georgia O'Keeffe considered an important figure in American art history?

    Ⓐ Her paintings were exhibited at the Museum of Modern Art in New York.
    Ⓑ She represented the change in the social recognition of women.
    Ⓒ Her work had the strength and elegance.
    Ⓓ She married the world famous photographer.

08 What influence did O'Keeffe's Southwest period have on her life?

    Ⓐ She got an opportunity to hold several exhibitions.
    Ⓑ She spent the rest of her life with her husband there.
    Ⓒ She found a site to build The Georgia O'Keeffe Museum.
    Ⓓ She drew inspiration for much of her work from images there.

Listen again to part of the lecture. Then answer the question.

09 Why does the professor mention this: 🎧

    Ⓐ To indicate O'Keeffe started painting quite early in her life
    Ⓑ To emphasize O'Keeffe was the most prominent female artist
    Ⓒ To make the students think of how society would be different from today
    Ⓓ To compare O'Keeffe with other artists working these days

10 What does the lecture imply about the first exhibition of O'Keeffe's paintings by Alfred Stieglitz?

    Ⓐ O'Keeffe took advantage of his fame and reputation.
    Ⓑ O'Keeffe managed to attract public attention on her own.
    Ⓒ O'Keeffe consented to let him display the paintings in the end.
    Ⓓ O'Keeffe made a great deal of money out of the exhibition.

11 In the lecture, the professor mentions O'Keeffe's subject matter in her paintings. Indicate on the table below whether each of the following is mentioned. **Click in the correct box for each phrase.**

	Yes	No
Ⓐ Animal skeletons		
Ⓑ Charcoal		
Ⓒ New York streets		
Ⓓ Flowers		
Ⓔ The scenery of New Mexico		

ALL ABOUT
JUNIOR
TOEFL
Listening

Overview

Preview

Office Hours

Service Encounters

Lectures

Practice

Chapter 4

Connecting Information 정보 연결

Overview

- Connecting information (정보 연결) 유형은 대화와 강의를 들으면서 주제와 관련된 세부 정보들 사이의 관계를 파악하여 질문에서 요구하는 대로 표에 분류 또는 재구성하는 문제
- 대화와 강의 모두 1문항 정도가 출제됨
- 대화에서는 학생이 가진 문제에 대해 교수나 학교 직원의 제안으로 맞는 것과 아닌 것을 구분하기, 전공 선택과 관련하여 각 전공 분야의 장점을 분류하기, 학교 시설 이용 절차 등의 문제가 출제됨
- 강의에서는 주제에 대한 특징으로 맞는 것과 아닌 것을 구분하기, 비교/대조되어 있는 두 대상의 특징을 해당 종류에 맞게 분류하기, 제작 과정 순서 맞추기 등의 문제가 출제됨
- 특히 강의를 들을 때는 주제 전개 방식을 파악하고 그 구성 방식에 맞추어 note-taking을 해두면 문제를 풀 때 메모 내용과 보기 내용을 각각 비교해 볼 수 있어서 도움이 됨

주제 전개 방식과 note-taking

학생이 공연장을 예약하기 위해 담당 직원을 찾아가는 대화 내용

이런 내용의 대화에서는 직원이 학생에게 공연장 예약에 따른 절차나 여러 가지 조건을 제시하는 경우가 대부분이므로, 조건에 해당하는 것(Required)과 해당하지 않는 것(Not Required)을 구분하는 문제를 예상할 수 있다. 절차를 순서대로 적거나 새로운 조건이 언급될 때마다 차례대로 내용을 간단히 적는다.

Note-taking

Topic: Reserve auditorium

Requirement
1. present student ID
2. put down $50 deposit: refundable
3. sign paper

:: 교수가 두 종류의 화산에 관해 설명하는 강의 내용

◎ 각 보기가 어떤 화산의 특징인지를 분류하는 문제를 예상할 수 있다. 두 범주의 특징을 비교(공통점, 차이점) 및 대조(차이점)하여 설명하는 강의에서는 각 범주별 특징을 분류하는 문제가 빠지지 않고 출제되는 편이다. 강의를 들으면서 각각의 특징을 구분해서 적는다.

> ## Note-taking
>
> Topic: 2types of volcano
>
> Hawaiian
> 1. plates move over hot spot
> 2. frequently erupt
>
> Stromboli
> 1. high viscosity
> 2. booming sound, but small eruptions
> 3. once 25~30 years

:: 교수가 파리 지옥이 먹이를 잡는 과정을 설명하는 강의 내용

◎ 먹이 잡는 과정을 올바르게 배열하라는 문제를 예상할 수 있다. 역사적 사건이 일어난 순서, 사물의 제작 순서 등을 중심으로 강의가 전개되면 대개 보기를 순서에 맞게 배열하는 문제가 출제된다. 강의를 들으면서 선후 관계를 구분하여 차례대로 내용을 적는다.

> ## Note-taking
>
> Topic: The Venus Flytrap capturing preys
>
> Step
> 1. produce nectar
> 2. short hairs on the leaves are touched
> 3. cells in the leaves inflate

Sample Questions

- In the conversation, the student wants to reserve a concert hall. Indicate on the chart below whether the student is required to do each of the following.

  Click in the correct box for each phrase.

  대화에서, 학생은 공연장을 예약하기를 원한다. 공연장 예약을 위해 학생이 다음 각 보기의 내용을 해야 하는지 아래 표에 표시하시오. 각 보기에 맞는 칸에 클릭하시오.

	Required	Not Required
Ⓐ Provide identification	∨	
Ⓑ Write a pledge to keep the date		∨
Ⓒ Leave a sum of refundable money	∨	

- In the lecture, the professor discusses two types of volcanoes. Indicate on the chart below to which group each of the following is attributed.

  Click in the correct box for each phrase.

  강의에서, 교수는 두 종류의 화산을 설명하고 있다. 아래의 각 보기가 어떤 화산의 특징인지 아래 표에 표시하시오. 각 보기에 맞는 칸에 클릭하시오.

	Hawaiian	Stromboli
Ⓐ Makes a loud noise when erupting		∨
Ⓑ Forms when the plates move over the hot spot	∨	
Ⓒ Spills out small amount of lava that's highly sticky		∨

- The professor describes how the Venus Flytrap captures its prey. Put the steps in correct order. Drag each sentence to the space where it belongs.

  교수는 파리지옥이 먹이를 잡는 과정을 설명하고 있다. 각 단계를 순서대로 배열하시오. 보기를 해당되는 표의 빈 칸으로 드래그하시오.

	How the Venus Flytrap captures its prey
Step 1	
Step 2	
Step 3	

Ⓐ Small hairs are stimulated.

Ⓑ Nectar is produced.

Ⓒ Leaf cells expand.

   ALL ABOUT JUNIOR TOEFL

Preview

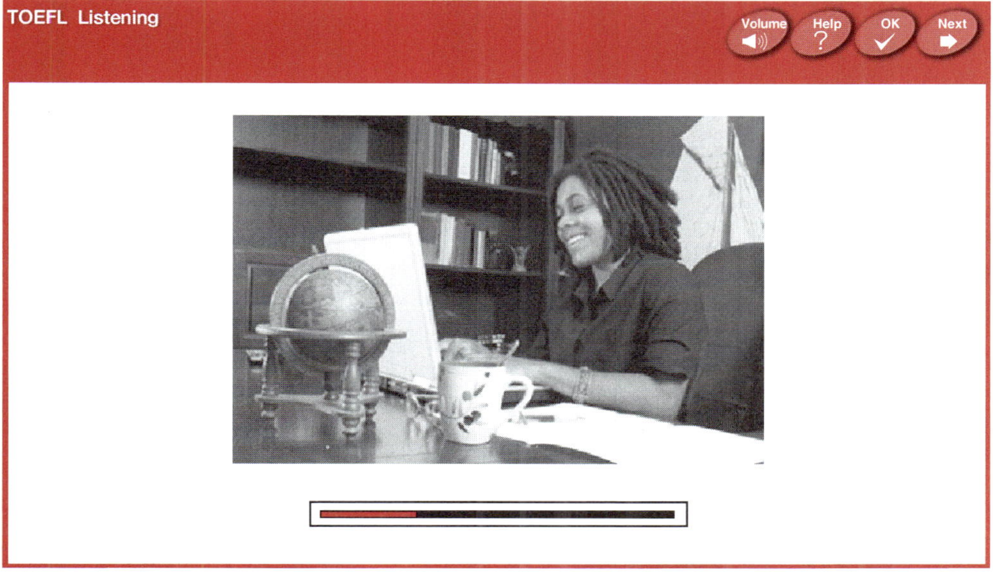

In the conversation, the woman mentions several things to do and not to do for the man. Indicate on the chart below to which each of the following is attributed. **Click in the correct box for each phrase.**

	To Do	Not To Do
Ⓐ Have a short bath		
Ⓑ Take part in a basketball game		
Ⓒ Prepare a dish by himself		
Ⓓ Take a rest in bed		

🎧 Listen to part of a conversation at an infirmary.

M : Thanks for <u>taking care of my ankle</u>. I'm glad it's not worse!
대화 토픽: 발목 치료

W : Well, <u>sprains are pretty bad</u>. A sprain can be more painful than a fracture.
발목을 삐었음
<u>You need to be careful with it</u>. <u>The less you can move around, the better</u>.
조심해야 함   되도록이면 움직이는 것을 자제해야 함

M : But... I have <u>an intervarsity basketball match next week</u>!
다음 주에 대학 농구 대항전이 있음

W : <u>Are you out of your mind</u>? You should take this seriously. You don't want
시합에 나가면 안 됨
it going from bad to worse, do you?

M : If you say so...

W : I want you to <u>go straight back to your room and stay there at least for a</u>
집으로 돌아가서 최소 이틀은 쉬어야 함
<u>couple of days</u>. You can <u>go to the bathroom and you can take a shower</u>. If
화장실에 가거나 샤워는 해도 됨
you can <u>get food delivered, do that</u>.
음식을 배달시켜 먹기

M : Just the basics, in other words?

W : That's right. You've got a sprained ankle. <u>I don't care if you're teaching the</u>
며칠간은 쉬어야 한다는 사실을 강조하여 말함
<u>class</u>. You need to rest!

M : All right. Will you give me a note?

W : Coming right up!

남 : 발목을 치료해주셔서 감사합니다. 심하지 않아서 다행이에요.

여 : 발목을 삔 것도 상당히 심한 상태가 될 수 있어요. 골절상보다 더 고통이 심하기도 하니까요.
조심하도록 하세요. 적게 움직일 수록, 더 빨리 낫죠.

남 : 하지만… 다음 주에 대학 농구 대항 경기가 있어요!

여 : 지금 제정신이에요? 지금 상태를 진지하게 받아들여야 해요. 상태가 악화되기를 바라지는 않
겠죠?

남 : 그렇게 말씀하신다면…

여 : 기숙사로 곧장 가서 며칠 정도는 쉬도록 해요. 화장실에 가거나 샤워는 할 수 있어요. 음식을
배달시킬 수 있으면, 그렇게 하는 것이 좋고요.

남 : 아주 기본적인 것만 하라는 말씀이시죠?

여 : 맞아요. 발목을 삐었잖아요. 학생이 직접 강의를 한다 해도 상관없어요. 꼭 쉬어야 해요.

남 : 알겠습니다. 진단서 좀 적어주시겠어요?

여 : 바로 해줄게요.

해설 | 여자는 학생어 게 최대한 몸을 움직이지 말고 적어도 이틀간은 푹 쉬라고 말했다. 보기 내용을 스크립트의 내용과 구체적으로 비교하여 보자.

> 보기 Ⓐ : 대화에서 여자가 샤워는 해도 된다고 말했다. 스크립트의 take a shower라는 표현이 보기 Ⓐ에서 have a short bath로 바뀌었다.
>
> 보기 Ⓑ : 여자가 되도록이면 몸을 움직이는 것을 자제하라고 하자 학생이 다음 주에 농구 시합이 있다고 하였는데, 이에 대해 여자가 제정신이냐고 되물었다. 이를 통해 농구 시합에 참여해서는 안 된다는 것을 알 수 있다.
>
> 보기 Ⓒ : 가능하다면 음식은 배달시켜 먹으라고 말한 것으로 보아 요리를 직접 하지 않는 것이 좋다는 것을 알 수 있다.
>
> 보기 Ⓓ : 바로 집으로 돌아가서 최소한 이틀은 쉬라고 하였다.

해석 | 대화에서, 여자는 남자에게 해야 할 일과 하지 말아야 할 일을 알려주고 있다. 다음 보기가 어떤 쪽에 속하는지 표시하시 오. 각 보기에 맞는 칸에 클릭하시오.

	To Do	Not To Do
Ⓐ 간단히 목욕하기		
Ⓑ 농구 시합에 참가하기		
Ⓒ 직접 요리하기		
Ⓓ 침대에 누워 쉬기		

어휘 | ankle 발목 | sprain 발목을 삠 | fracture 골절상 | in other words 즉, 다른 말로 | intervarsity match 대학 대항 경기

정답 | To Do − Ⓐ, Ⓓ Not To Do − Ⓑ, Ⓒ

Office Hours

01 In the conversation, the professor mentions the job duties in the language lab. Indicate on the table below whether each of the following is mentioned as one of the duties.

Click in the correct box for each phrase.

	Mentioned	Not Mentioned
Ⓐ Teaching classes		
Ⓑ Helping students learn languages		
Ⓒ Tidying up the lab		
Ⓓ Visiting students' homes		
Ⓔ Writing reports		

Topic:

Details:

🎧

02 In the conversation, the professor suggests ways to help the student with creative writing. Indicate on the table below whether each of the following is suggested by the professor.

Click in the correct box for each phrase.

	Suggested	Not Suggested
Ⓐ Read widely		
Ⓑ Spend less time using a computer		
Ⓒ Get regular writing practice		
Ⓓ Reflect one's own experience		
Ⓔ Imitate other writers' novels		

Topic:

Details:

03 In the conversation, the professor mentions a number of reasons to establish a French club. Indicate on the chart below whether each of the following is mentioned by the professor.

Click in the correct box for each phrase.

	Mentioned	Not Mentioned
Ⓐ French is the most popular foreign language at this university.		
Ⓑ A lot of students would enjoy participating in the club.		
Ⓒ The Swiss club was a huge success last year.		
Ⓓ The potential leader is from a city in France.		
Ⓔ The university now has money to support the club.		

Topic:

Details:

04 In the conversation, the speakers talk about the professor's two presentations at the upccming music symposium. Indicate on the table below to which each of the following is related.

Click in the correct box for each phrase.

	2:00~2:45	3:00~3:45
Ⓐ Being held in the music building's media lab		
Ⓑ Providing refreshments		
Ⓒ Discussing social networking sites and their effect on music		
Ⓓ Speaking about work to encourage students in music composition		
Ⓔ Introducing an innovative local band		

Topic:

Details:

Dictation : Office Hours

M : Thanks for staying after class to speak with me. Do you already have a
job ① ____________________?

W : Well, no, as a matter of fact, I don't.

M : Good, I mean for me. I was hoping you'd be interested in working in the
language lab.

W : I'd love to! What would the job duties be?

M : It's pretty simple. You'd be a tutor for students in the summer classes.
This would include helping with homework. You'd also be responsible for
helping to keep the place ② ____________________.

W : Sure. Would there be ③ ____________________?

M : Yes, there would be very ④ ____________________ to show
how many students had used the center, how long they stayed, and so on.

W : That sounds great! It'll really help me later when I start looking for a job.
Thanks for the offer!

M : I'm wondering if I could get some ① _________________.
I've never tried it before, and the course is a lot harder than I thought it would be.

W : Well, sure. Well, there's a process to follow if you want to write effectively, but before you learn to use those techniques, do you write much? That's probably the most important thing you can do as a writer, after actually sitting down with your computer. Just write.

M : So doing the writing, that's the most important part? Then reading?

W : Yes. Read ② _________________. Not just your assignments, but everything: novels, newspapers, magazines... read it all. Also, write what you know.

M : You mean, write ③ _________________?

W : That's right. It's important to have some life experience to ④ _________________ _________________. That's why so many first novels are very autobiographical.

M : That's great advice. Thank you!

M : Carla, do you have a few minutes? I'd like to talk to you about setting up a French club on campus.

W : Of course.

M : I've been thinking you'd be a good person ① ______________________. Well, you're from Nimes.

W : Oh, you know that. Sure, what's your idea?

M : Well, as you probably know, there was the campus French club, but ② ______________________ when the university ③ ______________________. This year, all the funding has been restored.

W : Um, would the students be interested?

M : Absolutely. I'm sure you've seen that we have a strong French program here. I guess many students will be happy to join the club, you know, if there's one. And I'll be happy to serve as the faculty advisor. We've got the funds and we've got the students. I also know that the French Department is ④ ______________________ France and Switzerland next semester, and if the club's doing well, we could join them.

W : I like the idea very much — let's do it! Wow, I guess ⑤ ______________________ from now on.

04

M : I understand you're giving two different presentations ① _______________ _______________ next Tuesday. Is that right?

W : Yes, it's going to be a rather busy day for me.

M : What will you be talking about, and where will you be? I'd enjoy attending your talks.

W : That's good to hear. Well, ② _______________ I'll be talking about the work I'm doing on adapting the Writers Workshop model to music education. The purpose is to foster students music composition. There's not enough attention ③ _______________ these days, and it's a real loss for the music world.

M : Where will that be?

W : The main presentation's in the music building, room 1172. My portion runs from 2:00 to 2:45 p.m. There's food, by the way.

M : That sounds more interesting! And what's next?

W : Then, I'm going to give a presentation on ④ _______________ _______________ in music education. As you know, sites like Facebook, MySpace, and blogs are really changing the music industry. That'll be from 3:00 until 3:45, in the music building's media lab. Ah, there's a special guest. I'm going to introduce the local band. They've just gotten their first ⑤ _______________. They're doing interesting things with technology, including distributing music via USB drive ⑥ _______________.

M : Oh, I'm really looking forward to it.

Service Encounters

01 The woman describes the process of registering a bicycle on campus.
Put the steps in correct order.

Drag each sentence to the space where it belongs.

	Registering a bicycle on campus
1	
2	
3	
4	
5	

Ⓐ Take a picture of the bike's unique details
Ⓑ Bring a bike to school
Ⓒ Stick a special decal on the bike
Ⓓ Pay $25 fee
Ⓔ Fill out an application form

Topic:

Details:

02 In the conversation, the librarian explains the criteria for long-term lending. Indicate on the table below whether each of the following is mentioned.

Click in the correct box for each phrase.

	Mentioned	Not Mentioned
Ⓐ Sign up for the long-term lending service		
Ⓑ Make sure all contact information is accurate		
Ⓒ Make a list of the borrowed books		
Ⓓ Leave a deposit of $25		
Ⓔ Make photocopy of the student's ID		

Topic:

Details:

🎧

03 In the conversation, the financial aid employee tells the student to do several things to solve her problem. Indicate on the table below whether each of the following is mentioned by the man.

Click in the correct box for each phrase.

	Mentioned	Not Mentioned
Ⓐ Fill out a form to show the virus delay of the loan company		
Ⓑ Call the loan company and explain her situations		
Ⓒ Obtain extension on deadline for tuition		
Ⓓ Apply for emergency loan to cover textbooks and other expenses		
Ⓔ Talk to her professors about the problem		

Topic:

Details:

 ALL ABOUT JUNIOR TOEFL

04 In the conversation, the campus bookstore clerk gives the steps for taking a return on several items. Put the steps below in correct order.

Drag each answer choices to the space where it belongs.

	Taking a return on items
Step 1	
Step 2	
Step 3	
Step 4	

Ⓐ Submit the receipts that accompanied the purchases
Ⓑ List the authors and titles of the textbooks
Ⓒ Inspect the lantern to make sure it is real
Ⓓ Provide a copy of the student's ID

Topic:

Details:

Dictation : Service Encounters

M : Ah, would you mind telling me what I need to do if I want to
①______________________________ on campus?

W : Sure, it's pretty simple. Um, first of all you need to bring your bike.

M : I brought mine from home today. It's chained up outside.

W : Good. All right, in that case, you need to ②______________________________
next. Here's a form to fill out, and we'll take a digital photo of
③______________________________ . That's in case it's stolen.

M : Does that happen often?

W : No, but we ④______________________________ very seriously. Once I do
those things, I'll give you a decal, which you should put on the bike.

M : Fine. Um, is there a fee?

W : Yes, it's $25 a month. Pay me that last, and you'll be all done!

M : All right, thanks!

M : Good afternoon. What can I do for you?

W : Yes, I hope so. I am a senior, and I'll need these books for a bit longer than the usual 10-day period. I can keep them ① ____, right?

M : That's right, because you're a senior. There are ② ________________________, though.

W : Uh oh, everything's so complicated. OK, what are they?

M : You have to register for extended lending before you can keep the books that long. We also have to verify your cell phone number, e-mail address, and ③ ________________________________, because we're very serious about getting our books back.

W : Sure, um, didn't I read that there was a deposit for extended senior lending, also?

M : Yes, it's $25, which isn't expensive, but it's not an amount ④ ________________________________, either.

W : All right, that's fine. I'm interested!

M : Hi, can I help you?

W : Well, my student loan company's computer network ① _________________________ _________________________, and it has delayed everything by a couple of weeks. But I need to pay my tuition, buy books, and so on...

M : Oh, don't worry: we've already seen a few other students with the same problem.

W : Really? So, is there something I can do about it?

M : Well, first, you need to fill out this form to show you were ② _________________________ _________________________.

W : OK, and what next?

M : You'll need an emergency loan for your textbooks and basic expenses. Plus, you need to apply for ③ _________________________. Here are the forms.

W : I'm glad you already knew about it. How long will this take?

M : 24 hours on the emergency loan, and ④ _________________________. The only other thing you need to do is be patient until the virus problem is solved!

W : Thanks, you've saved my life!

W : Hi, I'd like to bring these things back. I think I'm still ① _______________

_______________ , right?

M : When did you buy those?

W : 4 days ago.

M : Then, you are within the refund period, but because you've got several things to return, it'll be a little complicated.

W : Oh... is there a problem?

M : No, it's just ② _______________________________ . First, I need a copy of your student ID. Next, I'll need ③ _______________________________ for all these things.

W : OK, no problem. I have all that with me.

M : Good. I'll process the books now. I just need you to ④ _______________

_______________ on this form, along with the classes you bought them for.

W : All right...

M : And last, for the lantern, I just need to verify that it is in that box, and you'll need to fill out a different form for the refund.

W : OK, that's easy. Thanks for helping me with this!

Lectures

01 🎧 In a European history class

1. What is the main idea of this passage?

      Ⓐ Coeducation systems of ancient Athens
      Ⓑ Importance of Military training in ancient Spartan society
      Ⓒ Comparison between ancient Athenian and Spartan educational systems
      Ⓓ History of schools in ancient Athens

2. The professor discusses two forms of education system. Indicate on the chart below to which form each of the following is attributed.

Click in the correct box for each phrase.

	Athens	Sparta
Ⓐ Teachers chose among various subjects for students.		
Ⓑ Military training was emphasized.		
Ⓒ Girls were taught at home.		
Ⓓ The only academic subjects were basic reading and writing.		
Ⓔ Memorization was an important part of study.		

Topic:

Details:

1. Where were the first Dead Sea Scrolls found?

    Ⓐ In an ancient temple
    Ⓑ At the bottom of the Dead Sea
    Ⓒ In Jerusalem
    Ⓓ In a cave

2. The professor mentions several types of information included in the Dead Sea Scrolls. Indicate on the chart below whether each of the following is mentioned.

Click in the correct box for each phrase.

	Yes	No
Ⓐ Religious texts		
Ⓑ Social aspects of the time		
Ⓒ Pottery-making process		
Ⓓ Extinct animals		
Ⓔ Location of valuable objects		

Topic:

Details:

Dictation : Lectures

01

P(W) : This afternoon, we'll be discussing education in ancient Sparta and
Athens. Athenian schools trained citizens in the arts and prepared them
① _________________________ , as well as peace. Girls did not
attend school, but many were ② _________________________ at
home. Boys were taught in the home until age 6 or 7, either by their mother
or ③ _________________________ . From 6 through 14, boys would
attend a school near their home, or they would be sent to a private school.
Books were ④ _________________________ , so teachers would read
them aloud, and lessons had to be memorized. The teacher, always male,
could choose ⑤ _________________________ he wanted to teach. The
poetry of Homer was required. The teacher might also choose to teach
drama, public speaking, civics, art, reading, math, or other subjects. After
primary school, boys attended a higher-level school for four more years,
then two years of ⑥ _________________________ .

In contrast, Sparta's education system was intended to
⑦ _________________________ . Spartan society demanded strict
discipline, self-denial, simplicity, and ⑧ _________________________ .
Therefore, boys entered military school at an early age: they were taught
⑨ _________________________ and other skills needed for military life. These
studies were very difficult and painful. Students were taught to read and
write, but those skills were considered less important to the ancient
Spartans than warfare. The result was a terrifying army.

P(M) : Today, in our discussion of important holy documents from around the world, we'll touch on the Dead Sea Scrolls. You might be surprised to learn that there are approximately 900 of them. The scrolls were discovered between 1947 and 1956 ① ___________________________ near the Dead Sea, in the West Bank. At first, access to the scrolls was ② ___________________________. The reason they're so important is that they're the only copies of documents from Biblical times, from before 100 A.D. Carbon dating has shown that the oldest ones ③ ___________________________ the 2nd century B.C., and they were created over a period of about 200 years. They are written ④ ___________________________ of Hebrew, as well as Aramaic and an ancient dialect of Greek.

Uh, the important thing you should remember here is that they tell us a great deal about the beliefs of Judaism as it was practiced then. And actually, they're a very ⑤ ___________________________: some seem to be the record of ancient Jewish religion, some explain more about how those societies functioned at that time, and one even appears to be a treasure map that shows stashes of gold, weapons, more scrolls, and other valuables. As many important finds often are, the first scrolls were ⑥ ___________________________. According to legend, a boy ⑦ ___________________________ to the opening of a cave. He threw a rock inside, to drive the animal — and the story doesn't specify what kind of animal it was — out. The sound of ⑧ ___________________________ told him there might be something worthwhile inside. That's when he discovered the scrolls, wrapped in linen. They're now housed in a museum in Jerusalem, but their route to the museum was very ⑨ ___________________________. Today, because there are so few other documents to compare them to, it's hard to understand them perfectly. Even so, there's no denying how important they are.

Practice

🎧 **Questions 1-5**

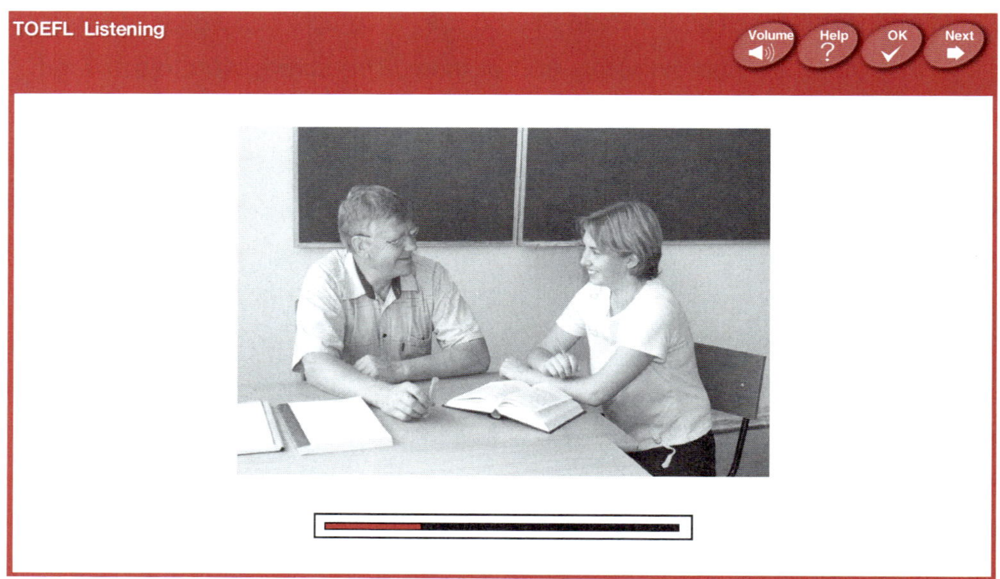

Note-taking

Topic: ________________

1. English lit major
   - concerned about ________________
2. Interested in ________________
   - Adult education
   - going to grad school
3. Prof.'s suggestion
   - ________________ major
   - switch to education in ________________

01 What is the reason for this conversation between the professor and the student?

    Ⓐ The student is considering majoring in economics.
    Ⓑ The student is thinking of changing her major.
    Ⓒ The student hasn't decided her major yet.
    Ⓓ The student is thinking of going to graduate school.

02 Why does the student have a second thought about her current major?

    Ⓐ She doesn't have a talent for writing.
    Ⓑ She is interested in teaching children.
    Ⓒ She wants to have number-related jobs.
    Ⓓ Her major might not be useful in the job market.

Listen again to part of the conversation. Then answer the question.

03 What does the professor imply when he says this:

    Ⓐ Many students are changing their major to the humanities.
    Ⓑ Those majoring in the humanities have no doubts about their choice.
    Ⓒ Economics and accounting are more interesting than the humanities.
    Ⓓ The number of students majoring in the humanities is decreasing.

04 According to the conversation, what is the student's minor?

    Ⓐ Applied linguistics
    Ⓑ Economics
    Ⓒ Spanish
    Ⓓ Adult education

05 In the conversation, the professor suggests several ideas that the student should consider. Indicate on the table below whether each of the following is suggested.

Click in the correct box for each phrase.

	Suggested	Not Suggested
Ⓐ Work in a Spanish-speaking country		
Ⓑ Transfer to another university		
Ⓒ Get a master's degree in adult education		
Ⓓ Keep her current major		

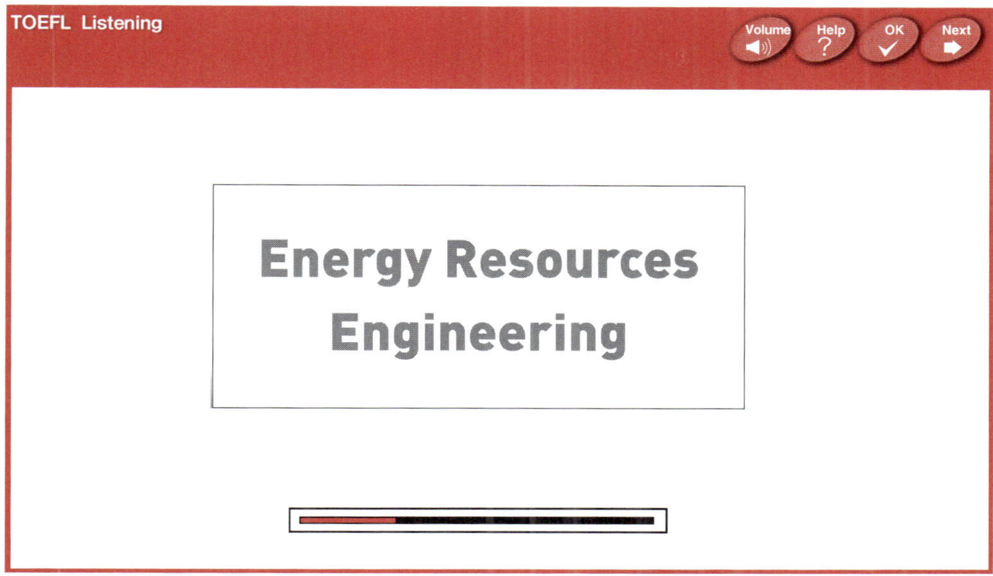

TOEFL Listening
Volume
Help
?
OK
Next

Energy Resources
Engineering

TOEFL Listening
Volume
Help
?
OK
Next

Topic: Natural gas

1. 1/3 of the _________________
2. _________________ has the most
   - Iran: 2nd
   - huge reserves in ocean trench, but _________________
3. Fossil fuel
   - _________________: 1st ingredient
4. Benefits compared w/ oil
   - burn more _________________: less carbon dioxide
   - no ash left
   - purifying: _________________, less labor
   - produce _________________
5. CNG vehicles
   - the same _________________ as oil

06 What are the speakers discussing in the lecture?

    Ⓐ Advantages of natural gas
    Ⓑ Different types of fossil fuels
    Ⓒ Energy production
    Ⓓ CNG vehicles

Listen again to part of the lecture. Then answer the question.

07 What does the student mean when he says this: 🎧

    Ⓐ He wants the professor to give him the answer.
    Ⓑ He is not sure of his answer.
    Ⓒ He doesn't have any idea what the professor is talking about.
    Ⓓ He knows the precise rate.

08 What country has the largest reserves of natural gas?

    Ⓐ Iran
    Ⓑ The U.S.A
    Ⓒ Saudi Arabia
    Ⓓ Qatar

09 What is needed to exploit large natural gas reserves in the ocean depths?

    Ⓐ Exploration expenses
    Ⓑ Technological development
    Ⓒ Human resources
    Ⓓ Government support

10 What does natural gas primarily consist of?

    Ⓐ Nitrogen
    Ⓑ Hydrogen
    Ⓒ Carbon
    Ⓓ Methane

11 In the lecture, the professor mentions several benefits of natural gas compared with oil. Indicate on the table below whether each of the following is mentioned as one of them.

Click in the correct box for each phrase.

	Mentioned	Not Mentioned
Ⓐ It is extracted with high technology.		
Ⓑ It generates much less carbon dioxide.		
Ⓒ It is cheaper to produce.		
Ⓓ It is easily stored and delivered.		

**ALL ABOUT
JUNIOR
TOEFL
Listening**

태도/발화 목적
Stance/Function

Overview

- Stance/Function(태도/발화 목적) 유형은 화자가 특정한 말을 왜 했는지, 어떤 목적과 의도를 가지고 그 말을 했는지, 그 말을 했을 때의 화자의 입장과 태도는 어떤지, 그 말이 암시하는 바는 무엇인지를 이해하여 답을 고르는 문제
- 대화와 강의 모두 1문항 정도가 출제됨
- 대개 대화와 강의의 일부를 다시 들려주는(Replay) 형태로 문제가 출제됨
- 문제 출제 부분만을 듣고서는 답을 명확하게 고르기가 쉽지 않으며, 앞뒤 내용의 흐름 속에서 그 말이 가지는 의미나 기능을 파악하는 것이 중요함
- Stance(태도) 문제는 화자의 말투, 어조, 뉘앙스 등을 주의 깊게 들으면 비교적 쉽게 풀 수 있는 문제로, 놀람, 걱정, 의심, 재확인, 강조 등의 상황과 관련된 문제가 자주 출제되고 있음
- Function(발화 목적) 문제는 화자가 특정한 말을 했을 때의 의도와 목적을 파악해야 하는데, 확인 및 재확인, 확신 및 불확신, 제안, 요청 등의 상황과 관련된 문제가 자주 출제되고 있음
- 문제 형태는 다시 듣기 문제로 출제되지만 질문의 답은 추론 과정을 거쳐 찾아야 하는 문제도 있음

Sample Questions

- Listen again to part of the conversation. Then answer the question.
  What does the woman mean when she says this: 🎧
- Listen again to part of the lecture. Then answer the question.
  Why does the professor say this: 🎧
- Listen again to part of the lecture. Then answer the question.
  What does the professor imply when she says this: 🎧
- Why does the professor mention ~?
- What is the man's stance toward ~?
- How does the student seem to feel about ~?

Preview

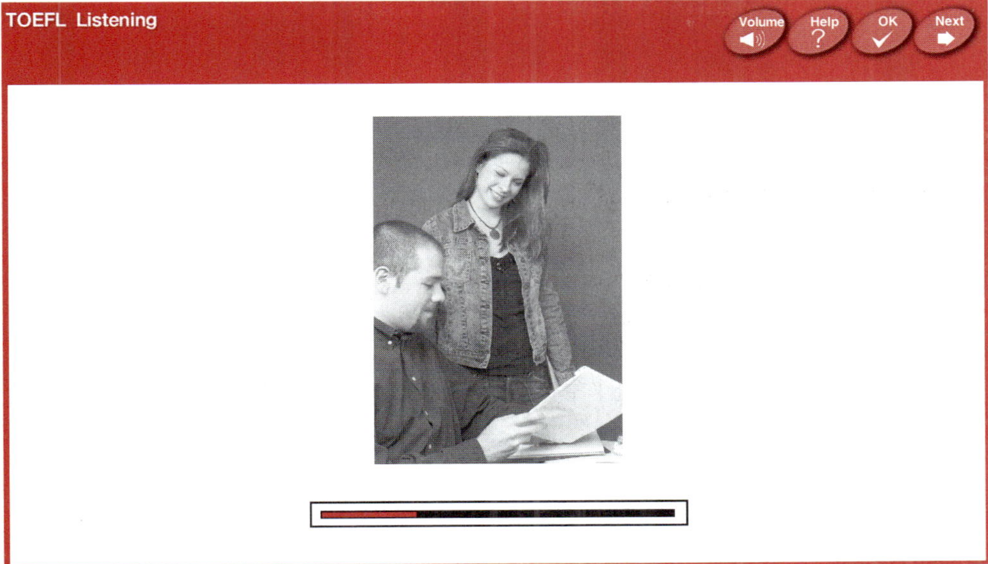

Listen again to part of the conversation. Then answer the question.

What does the man imply when he says this: 

Ⓐ The campus police often make mistakes with parking tickets.
Ⓑ The woman can sign up for classes at the campus police office.
Ⓒ The woman can register for classes only after the problems with the fine are settled.
Ⓓ The woman should show the man the receipts of the parking tickets.

Listen to part of a conversation at a registrar's office.

W : Excuse me, I've been trying to register for a couple of hours, <u>but the system won't let me</u>. Would you check and see what's going on?
수강 신청을 해야 하는데 시스템 접속이 안됨
M : Sure. What's your student ID number?

W : Here you go.

M : Just one second... oh, I see. <u>You have a couple of unpaid parking tickets</u>. That's the reason.
접속이 안되는 이유 : 학생이 주차 위반 벌금을 내지 않았음

W : Oh, no... I think there's a mistake. I've only gotten two parking tickets this semester, and <u>I've paid them both</u>!
학생의 주장 : 이미 벌금을 모두 냈음
M : *Then you need to <u>go to the campus police office, and show them your receipts</u>.*
직원의 입장 : 학생이 캠퍼스 경찰서에 가서 벌금 납부 영수증을 보여줘야 함

W : But what if the classes I want are already closed by then, and this is all a mistake?

M : If it's a mistake, then we'll help you. Don't worry about that. But you should take care of this as soon as possible!

W : All right, thanks. I'm on it!

여 : 제가 두 시간 동안 계속 수강 신청을 하려고 했는데요, 시스템에 접속이 안되고 있어요. 무슨 일인지 한 번 확인해 주시겠어요?
남 : 네. 학생증 번호가 뭐죠?
여 : 여기 있습니다.
남 : 잠깐만 기다려요… 아, 여기 있네요. 아직 주차 위반 벌금을 몇 차례 내지 않았네요. 그게 이유에요.
여 : 그럴리가요… 뭔가 착오가 있는 것 같아요. 이번 학기에 주차 위반을 두 번 밖에 안 했는데, 이미 다 벌금을 냈어요!
남 : 그럼, 캠퍼스 경찰서에 가서, 납부 영수증을 보여주도록 하세요.
여 : 만약 제가 듣고 싶어하던 수업이 그 때쯤이면 다 마감되면 어쩌죠? 게다가 이게 모두 착오로 생긴 일이라면요?
남 : 착오였다면, 도와주도록 할게요. 그 부분은 걱정 말아요. 하지만 이 일을 최대한 빨리 처리하도록 하세요!
여 : 알겠습니다, 감사합니다. 지금 바로 가서 처리할게요!

해설 학생이 수강 신청을 해야 하는데 시스템 접속이 안되어서 학적과로 찾아왔다. 직원은 확인 결과 학생이 주차 위반 벌금을 내지 않았기 때문이라고 말하는데, 학생은 이미 벌금을 납부했다고 대답한다. 그러자 직원이 학생에게 캠퍼스 경찰서에 가서 벌금 납부 영수증을 보여주고 오라고 하는데, 문제에서는 직원의 이 말이 암시하는 것이 무엇인지를 묻고 있다. 경찰서에 직접 가서 납부 영수증을 보여주고 제대로 처리되었는지 확인하고 오라는 것은 이 문제가 해결되어야만 수강 신청이 가능하다는 의미다. 따라서 보기 ⓒ가 정답이다.

해석 대화의 일부를 다시 들으시오. 그러고 나서 질문에 답하시오.

W : Oh, no... I think there's a mistake. I've only gotten two parking tickets this semester, and I've paid them both!

M : Then you need to go to the campus police office, and show them your receipts.

여 : 그럴리가요... 뭔가 착오가 있는 것 같아요. 이번 학기에 주차 위반을 두 번 밖에 안 했는데, 이미 다 벌금을 냈어요!

남 : 그럼, 캠퍼스 경찰서에 가서, 영수증을 보여주도록 하세요.

남자가 이것을 말할 때 암시하는 것은 무엇인가: 

M : Then you need to go to the campus police office, and show them your receipts.

M : 그럼, 캠퍼스 경찰서에 가서, 영수증을 보여주도록 하세요.

Ⓐ 교내 경찰은 주차 위반 스티커와 관련하여 실수하는 일이 자주 있다.
Ⓑ 여자는 교내 경찰서에서 수강 신청을 할 수 있다.
ⓒ 여자는 벌금 문제가 해결된 후에만 수업에 등록할 수 있다.
Ⓓ 여자는 남자에게 주차 위반 벌금 영수증을 보여주어야 한다.

어휘 unpaid 지불하지 않은 | parking ticket 주차 위반 스티커

정답 ⓒ

Office Hours

Listen again to part of the conversation. Then answer the question.

01 What does the professor mean when she says this: 🎧

    Ⓐ The student is going to fail the class.
    Ⓑ The student should completely get over his shyness.
    Ⓒ The student needs to put aside his homework and be more active.
    Ⓓ The low participation score will harm the student's overall grade.

Topic:

Details:

Listen again to part of the conversation. Then answer the question.

02 Why does the professor say this: 🎧

    Ⓐ The student appears he's really excited about the job.
    Ⓑ The student needs to be more prepared for the job.
    Ⓒ The student seems to have changed his mind about the job.
    Ⓓ The student will need to have a second job to earn more money.

Topic:

Details:

Listen again to part of the conversation. Then answer the question.

03 What does the professor mean when she says this:

    Ⓐ The student was an excellent intern.
    Ⓑ Loss of property has been caused by the student.
    Ⓒ The evaluation of the student is quite negative.
    Ⓓ The student has been careful with items at the museum.

Topic:

Details:

Listen again to part of the conversation. Then answer the question.

04 What does the student mean when he says this:

    Ⓐ He will make it to the lecture by any means.
    Ⓑ He doesn't care whether the lecture is given or not.
    Ⓒ His previous engagement is less important than extra credit.
    Ⓓ He should keep his promise to teach his student.

Topic:

Details:

Dictation : Office Hours

01

M : Professor, what did you want to see me about?

W : Well, I'm concerned about your participation this semester. Did you know that your participation score is 25% of your total grade?

M : Yes, I know. You talked about it ① __________________ .

W : But it doesn't seem to me that you're part of our class.

M : Well, the thing is... um, I'm really shy, and when talking ② __________________ __________________ , I really really get nervous.

W : Well, most people feel that way, ③ __________________ .

M : So, am I going to get a bad grade?

W : If you don't participate more, yes. I know you're very bright, and you do your homework. That part of your grade is fine. It's just your participation. [1] It'll pull you down.

M : There's still a month left in the semester. If I ④ __________________ __________________ , will that help me?

M : ∩ Professor Catherine, can we talk about the TA position, please? I'm supposed to start next week, and I still have some questions.

W : 2.Sure. Well, you look like ① ________________________. Are you still interested?

M : I think so. I've read the guidebook, but I still don't think I know enough about the subject to be a tutor.

W : Well, I have to ② ________________________, because you're doing very well in your classes. But don't worry: there's very little tutoring. Most of the time, you'll be doing ③ ________________________ like scoring exams.

M : It's just I'm just not sure I'm going to do a good job!

W : I'm sure you will. That's why I asked you to do it. Plus, this is your first time. People are always nervous ④ ________________________________

________________ .

M : OK, thanks. I feel a little bit better now.

M : So, how was my evaluation? I'm dying to know what they think of me...

W : 3·Well, ① ________________________ . You haven't burned the museum down or damaged anything in the collection...

M : Oh, I see.

W : Nate, this is the most important art museum in the city. If you want to get ② ________________________ , then a few things need to happen.

M : They don't like me?

W : You don't seem to be ③ ________________________ , and when the manager has spoken to you about this, you just ④ ________________________ .

M : Well...

W : I'm being very honest with you. I've read the manager's comments and talked to her a couple of times, and I've got my own opinions, as well. You need to ⑤ ________________________ . Arrive on time, dress nicely, and finish your tasks. I mean you should give your best shot at this.

M : I'm sorry I let you down.

W : All right. I hope you learn something from this.

M : Do you have a few minutes, Professor Danes?

W : Of course, Jake. What's on your mind?

M : I need to ask about the special lecture on Saturday. I'm afraid I won't be able to be there, and I need to find out ① ________________________ in any way.

W : You have ② ________________________ ?

M : Yes, I work as a private tutor, and my student has an exam next week. His parents have hired me to spend extra time with him, you know, ③ ________________________ . 4·I know this lecture is important, but I ④ ________________________ .

W : I see. Really, that's fine. We can't force students to attend these things outside of class hours, after all. I'm ⑤ ________________________ the people who show up, but there are plenty of chances to earn extra credit during the semester. I wouldn't worry about it.

M : OK, ⑥ ________________________ .

Service Encounters

Listen again to part of the conversation. Then answer the question.

01 What does the woman imply when she says this:

    Ⓐ Spanish DVDs are not available.
    Ⓑ The student can't check out the DVDs.
    Ⓒ The student should've used the media center.
    Ⓓ The student should watch Spanish DVDs more often.

Topic:

Details:

Listen again to part of the conversation. Then answer the question.

02 What does the professor imply when he says this:

    Ⓐ He thinks the student is doing great.
    Ⓑ He was expecting more from the student.
    Ⓒ He does not agree with the student.
    Ⓓ He already knows the student is failing.

Topic:

Details:

Listen again to part of the conversation. Then answer the question.

03 What does the woman mean when she says this:

A The rental fee is usually expensive.
B The fee is cheaper early in the year.
C It is free of charge during fall break.
D The fee is different at different times of the year.

> *Topic:*
>
> *Details:*

Listen again to part of the conversation. Then answer the question.

04 What does the man mean when he says this:

A The student can't change the meal plan.
B The student has to take morning classes.
C The student will receive a partial refund.
D The student shouldn't skip breakfast.

> *Topic:*
>
> *Details:*

Dictation : Service Encounters

01

M :  Hi, I'm taking Spanish and I'd like to ① _______________________.
How does that work?

W : [1.]You've never been here before, haven't you? They cost a fortune, and
we ② _______________________. So, you need to watch them
here, in one of the video booths. Actually, a group of your classmates is
watching the first Level 1 disc now, if you want to join them?

M : Thanks, but I'd ③ _______________________. When are the
booths available?

W : Same hours as the library. You can reserve the booths for 2 hours at a
time. That's usually more time than you need.

M : How do I reserve one?

W : You just sign up for the day and the time that you want it. You can usually
use one the same day, but ④ _______________________. I'd recommend
coming in the afternoon.

M : OK, thanks!

W : Professor Ducharme, do you have a few minutes to talk about the calculus final?

M : Sure, what's up?

W : 🎧 Well, um, I'm not doing so well in your class.

M : 2.Your grade could be a little better, yes.

W : Er, I'm pretty worried about the exam. There's still so much I don't understand. I mean, I think I have the basic concepts, but at some point, ① ________________________ , and the exam's only two weeks away...

M : Have you been working on it steadily?

W : Yes, maybe I just don't have an aptitude for it.

M : Well, ② ________________________! Here's what I suggest. I'm going to be here in my office more than usual in the next two weeks. Let's ③ ________________________ , and I'll help you. Also, you'd better go to the tutoring center to get some help ④ ________________________

________________ .

W : You have no idea how much I appreciate your help!

M : No problem. So here's my teaching schedule.

M : Are you in charge of facilities here on campus, if someone wants to

① _____________________________ ?

W : Yes, I am. Do you need space on campus for an event?

M : Yes, I do. I'm ② _____________________________ of the Sierra Club, and

we'd like to know if there's a place to hold a regional conference here.

W : When are you planning to do it?

M : Toward the end of the year. November or December.

W : Oh, there's plenty of time. You could use the campus conference center,

or if you want to do it during fall break, you could use one of the big

lecture halls ③ _____________________________ .

M : 🎧 Is there a charge for this?

W : [3.]It varies. Here's ④ _____________________________ . Why don't you

discuss it with your organization and let us know?

M : Yes, I will.

W : Hi, I'd like to ask about a refund I applied for? I sent e-mail about it, but I ①______________________.

M : What did you want to change?

W : I had purchased the plan that ②______________________. I changed my classes around, though, and I'm not taking morning classes this semester. I know I'll ③______________________, so there's no reason to pay for it. I wanted the 2-meal-a-day plan.

M : When did you e-mail us?

W : In late August. Here, I ④______________________ for you.

M : Oh. If that's the case, then it doesn't matter. You see, the contract includes ⑤______________________. You can't get a refund for changes made after August 15. You e-mailed us after the 15th, so there's nothing we can do.

W : Does that mean I'm paying for breakfasts I won't eat?

M : 4. I'm afraid so.

Lectures

01 🎧 In a psychology class

Listen again to part of the lecture. Then answer the question.

1. What does the professor mean when she says this: 🎧

    Ⓐ People should try to avoid aggressive behaviors.
    Ⓑ It is not hard to categorize different forms of aggression.
    Ⓒ It is common for people to experience aggression.
    Ⓓ Even imagining aggression may sometimes cause it to manifest itself.

Listen again to part of the lecture. Then answer the question.

2. What does the professor imply when she says this: 🎧

    Ⓐ Genetics is the most important cause of aggressive behavior.
    Ⓑ People sometimes blame genetics instead of taking personal responsibility for their actions.
    Ⓒ Aggressive parents often have even more aggressive children.
    Ⓓ Acts of self-defense are appropriate when one faces aggression, especially from one's parents.

Topic:
Details:

1. What are the speakers mainly discussing in the lecture?

    Ⓐ The number of regional languages
    Ⓑ Minority languages
    Ⓒ Language extinction
    Ⓓ An official language of each country

2. What regional language in Spain is not regarded as an endangered language now?

    Ⓐ Basque
    Ⓑ Catalan
    Ⓒ Leonese
    Ⓓ Aragonese

Listen again to part of the lecture. Then answer the question.

3. What does the professor imply when he says this, regarding the preservation of endangered languages in Indonesia: 🎧

    Ⓐ Young students are not interested in learning them.
    Ⓑ Adult speakers don't have the ability to teach their kids.
    Ⓒ Parents want their children to speak an official language.
    Ⓓ There is lack of public support and concern for the languages.

Topic:

Details:

Dictation : Lectures

01

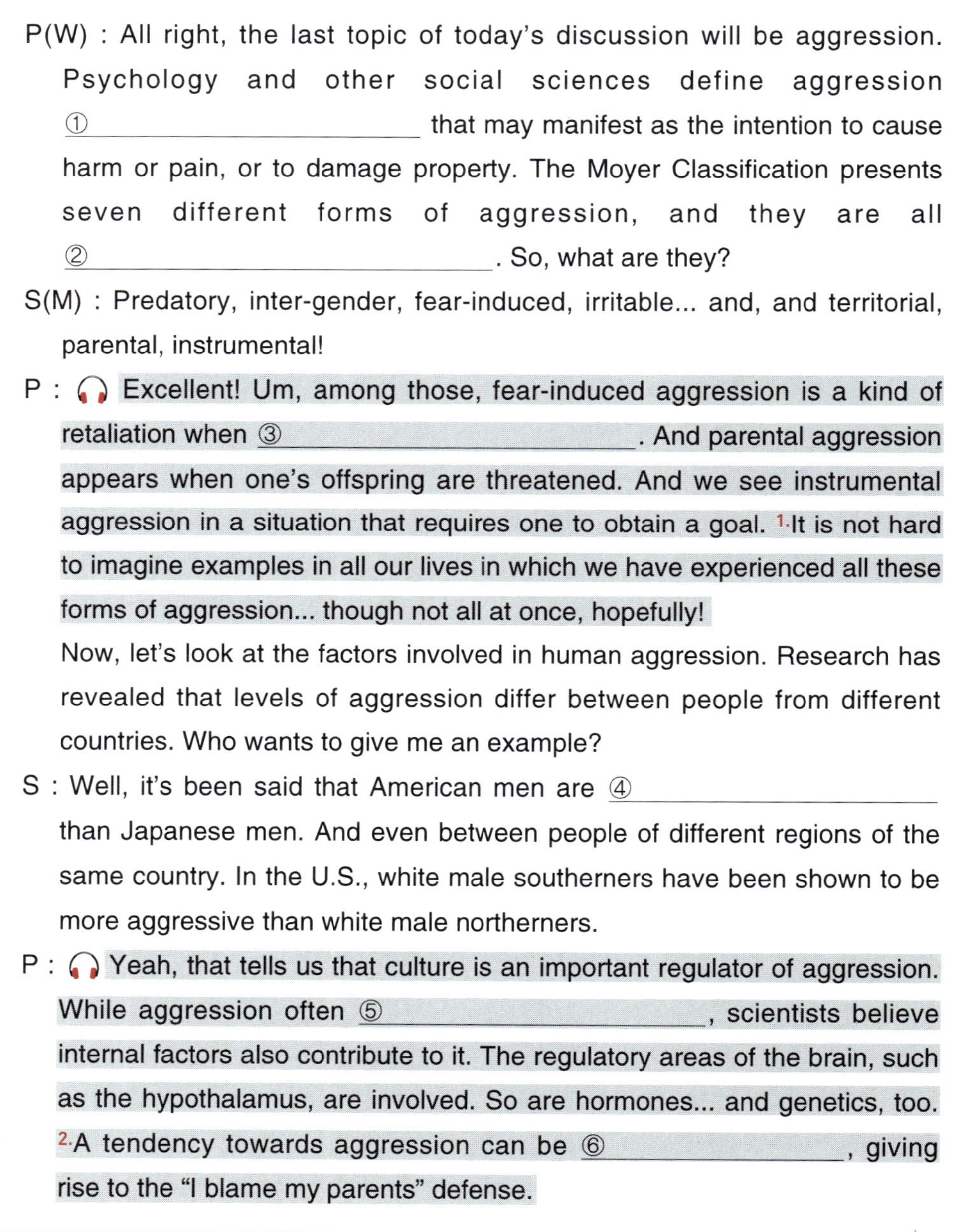

P(W) : All right, the last topic of today's discussion will be aggression. Psychology and other social sciences define aggression ① ________________________ that may manifest as the intention to cause harm or pain, or to damage property. The Moyer Classification presents seven different forms of aggression, and they are all ② ________________________. So, what are they?

S(M) : Predatory, inter-gender, fear-induced, irritable... and, and territorial, parental, instrumental!

P : Excellent! Um, among those, fear-induced aggression is a kind of retaliation when ③ ________________________. And parental aggression appears when one's offspring are threatened. And we see instrumental aggression in a situation that requires one to obtain a goal. [1] It is not hard to imagine examples in all our lives in which we have experienced all these forms of aggression... though not all at once, hopefully!

Now, let's look at the factors involved in human aggression. Research has revealed that levels of aggression differ between people from different countries. Who wants to give me an example?

S : Well, it's been said that American men are ④ ________________________ than Japanese men. And even between people of different regions of the same country. In the U.S., white male southerners have been shown to be more aggressive than white male northerners.

P : Yeah, that tells us that culture is an important regulator of aggression. While aggression often ⑤ ________________________, scientists believe internal factors also contribute to it. The regulatory areas of the brain, such as the hypothalamus, are involved. So are hormones... and genetics, too. [2] A tendency towards aggression can be ⑥ ________________________, giving rise to the "I blame my parents" defense.

P(M) : All right, now that you're back from break, let's look at our last topic for tonight, which is endangered languages. We would consider a language to be endangered if there is ① ________________________. In other words, if its speakers are likely to die out. When you think about the major world languages like English, Spanish, and Mandarin, it's hard to imagine a language with so few people speaking it that the last ones might die ② ________________________. This has happened many times, though, and it's still going on. Why do you think that is?

S(W) : Because some countries establish an official language, and children have to learn it in school, even if it's not the language spoken in the region where they live?

P : Yes, exactly. Can you think of a couple of examples?

S : France? I'm a French major, and I know France has strict laws about French ③ ________________________ of the republic.

P : Correct. So the minority languages of France — like Breton, Alsatian, and Occitan — are gradually dying out. There are ④ ________________________ than there used to be, and children aren't learning these languages in school. This has happened all over the world. Except for Catalan, all the regional languages of Spain are endangered: Leonese, Aragonese, and Basque are all declining. If you look into it, you'd be surprised ⑤ ________________________ all over the world. All over North and South America, as well as Africa and Australia, the same thing is happening. The native peoples' languages of Australia and the Americas ⑥ ________________________. In many African countries, tribal politics determine who's in government and therefore which languages are favored. The way we look at language endangerment is ⑦ ________________________ the number of fluent speakers, their average age, and the percentage of their children learning the language fluently. This means that some languages may have thousands of speakers, but if the fluent adult speakers of today aren't teaching their kids, ⑧ ________________________, those languages will be gone. 3·Indonesia is often cited as an example of this scenario.

Practice

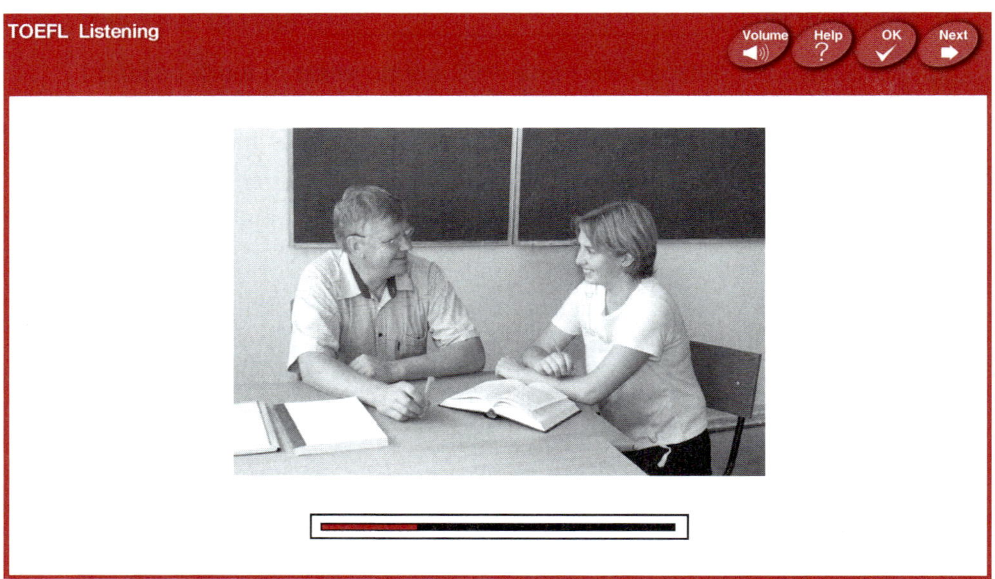

<table>
</table>

Note-taking

Topic: Turn in photos

1. Turned in _________________

   - busy ← language, paper, _________________

2. Photos

   - _________________ of day

   - long-exposure shots

   - good color contrast

3. Prof.'s advice

   - _________________

01 Why is the student having this conversation with her professor?

    Ⓐ She was late for class several times.
    Ⓑ She wants feedback on a photo project.
    Ⓒ She needed to submit an assignment late.
    Ⓓ She is interested in studying digital photography.

02 How did the student bring her photo assignments to the professor?

    Ⓐ Via e-mail
    Ⓑ In a laptop
    Ⓒ As a stack of pictures
    Ⓓ In a portable device

03 In the conversation, the student mentions several of the things she has been busy doing lately. Indicate on the chart below whether each of the following is mentioned as one of them.

Click in the correct box for each phrase.

	Mentioned	Not Mentioned
Ⓐ Practicing language with other students on campus		
Ⓑ Working at a part-time job		
Ⓒ Taking painting lessons		
Ⓓ Writing a paper for other classes		
Ⓔ Joining a photography club		

04 What can be inferred about the student in terms of her photo arrangement?

    Ⓐ She is a lazy person.
    Ⓑ She likes morning better than night.
    Ⓒ She is one of the professor's favorite students.
    Ⓓ She is very organized.

Listen again to part of the conversation. Then answer the question.

05 What does the professor imply when he says this: 🎧

    Ⓐ He will probably not be as flexible with the student again.
    Ⓑ The student is doing a good job managing all her responsibilities.
    Ⓒ The student should take care of her health.
    Ⓓ He suggests that the student reduce time spent on extracurricular activities.

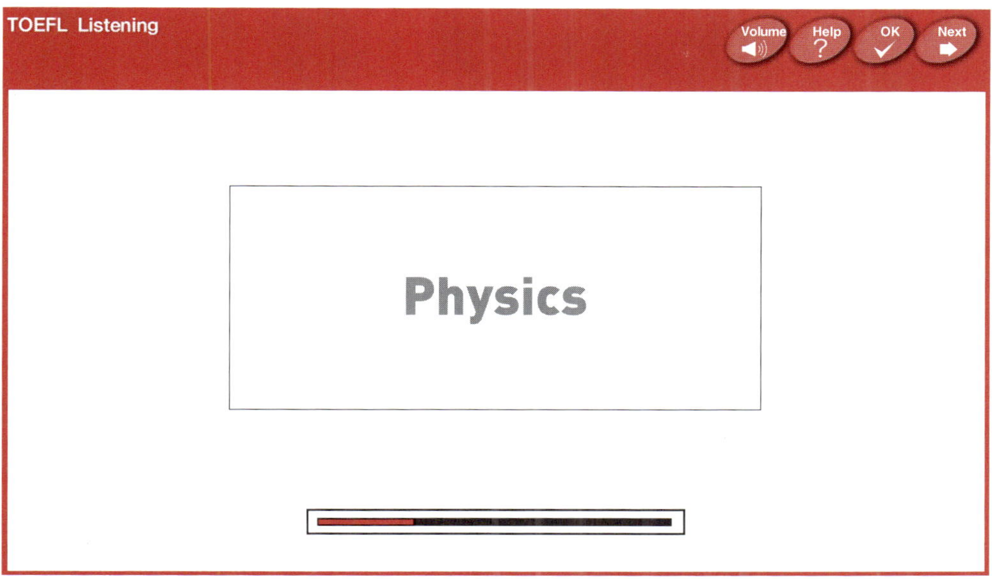

TOEFL Listening
Volume
Help
OK
Next
Physics

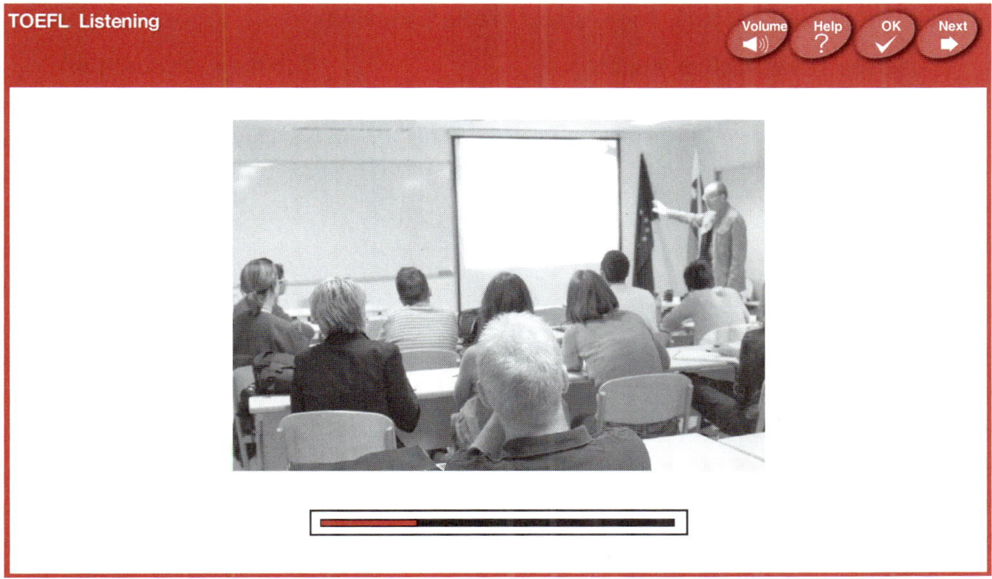

TOEFL Listening
Volume
Help
OK
Next

Topic: _________________

1. Low-level waste
   - medical supply
   - small amounts of radioactivity
   - _________________ in intensity
   - protective clothing,etc. become _________________ after exposure to neutron radiation

2. _________________ waste
   - used reactor fuel/waste after used fuel's reprocessed
   - hot and radioactive

3. Oil industry produces waste
   - oil shale: radium
   - coal: _________________

4. _________________
   - The amount of time to lose half its radioactivity
   - waste from nuclear reactor: _________________ for huge amounts of time

5. Long-term storage
   - deep underground
     :e.g. _________________
   - disposal at _________________ : legal issue/not likely

06 What is the main topic of this lecture?

Ⓐ Intensity of radioactivity
Ⓑ Types of radioactive waste and its storage
Ⓒ Nuclear waste disposal
Ⓓ Purpose of nuclear reactions

07 In the lecture, the professor explains both low-level waste and high-level waste. Indicate on the chart below to which each of the following is attributed.

Click in the correct box for each phrase.

	Low-level waste	High-level waste
Ⓐ Is produced when nuclear reactions occur		
Ⓑ Becomes radioactive through exposure to neutron radiation		
Ⓒ Remains very hot and radioactive		
Ⓓ Contaminates protective gear		
Ⓔ Releases small amounts of radioactivity		

08 Which of the following is considered sources of low-level waste?

Ⓐ Hospitals
Ⓑ Underground water
Ⓒ Uranium mines
Ⓓ Pure forms of oil

09 Which of the following is NOT a radioactive element in coal?

Ⓐ Thorium
Ⓑ Uranium
Ⓒ Radium
Ⓓ Barium

10 What is the half-life of a radioactive substance?

Ⓐ The time it takes for all the substance's radiation to diminish to a safe level
Ⓑ The time it takes for a living organism to be out of radiation's influence
Ⓒ The time it takes for half the radiation to decay
Ⓓ The time it takes for a living organism to be radioactivated

Listen again to part of the lecture. Then answer the question.

11 What does the professor imply when he says this:

Ⓐ Disposal in a subduction zone will probably not happen in the near future.
Ⓑ Disposal at sea is the safest possible method among other things.
Ⓒ Progress is being made for disposing of radioactive waste.
Ⓓ Using an abyssal plain would be better than using a subduction zone for disposal.

Actual Test

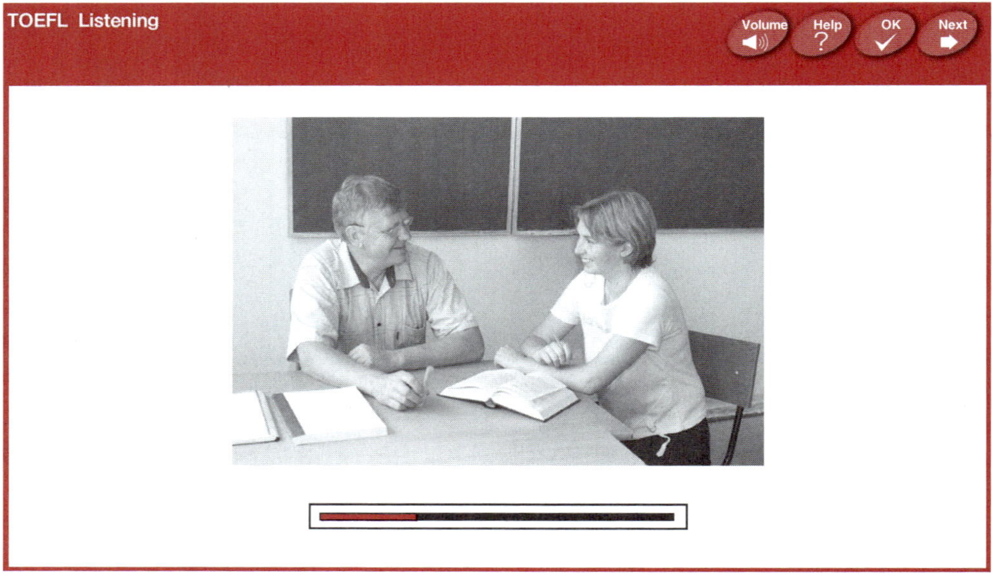

01 Why does the student go see her professor?

    Ⓐ To explain why she was not in class
    Ⓑ To reschedule the presentation that she missed
    Ⓒ To discuss changing her project topic
    Ⓓ To confirm the schedule of her presentation

02 Why was the woman unable to attend the seminars?

    Ⓐ She was visiting Chicago.
    Ⓑ She had to take an exam.
    Ⓒ She had a doctor's appointment.
    Ⓓ She had a terrible cold.

03 In the conversation, the professor explains several problems that have arisen during the student's absence from class. Indicate in the table below whether each of the following is one of the problems the professor mentioned.

Click in the correct box.

	Mentioned	Not Mentioned
Ⓐ She has missed a lot of information while away.		
Ⓑ Her classmates have already covered the material.		
Ⓒ Another student did the topic of her presentation.		
Ⓓ There is not enough time left in the course.		
Ⓔ The assistant flunked her for not attending class.		

Listen again to part of the conversation. Then answer the question.

04 What does the professor mean when he says this: 🎧

    Ⓐ The student will be docked for her absence.
    Ⓑ The student should take the course again.
    Ⓒ The student must change her topic.
    Ⓓ The student cannot give a presentation.

05 What must the student do before she can take the oral exam?

    Ⓐ Pick up medication from the clinic
    Ⓑ Obtain a signed letter documenting her illness
    Ⓒ Attend an appointment with her doctor
    Ⓓ Get permission from university administration

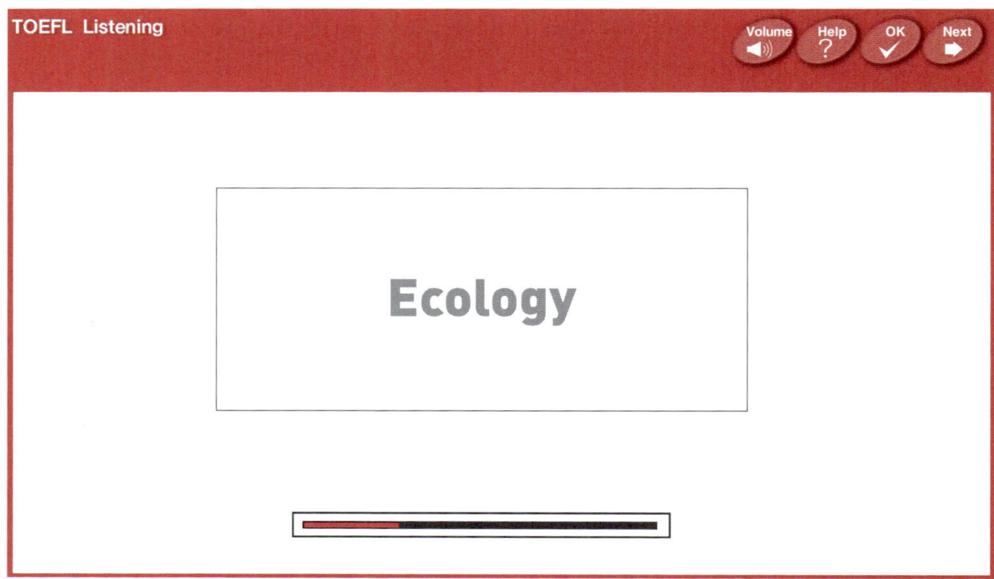

TOEFL Listening
Volume
Help
?
OK
Next
Ecology

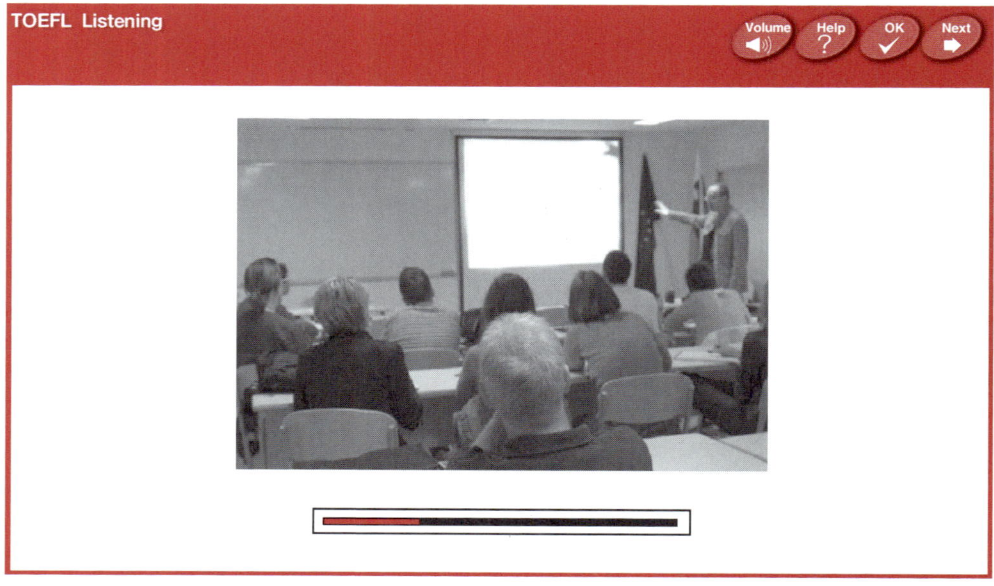

TOEFL Listening
Volume
Help
?
OK
Next

06 What is the lecture mainly about?

Ⓐ The creation of a dry ecosystem
Ⓑ A survey of plants that live in the desert
Ⓒ Survival strategies of desert species
Ⓓ Heat management in ungulates

07 Why was the professor surprised when the student asked a question?

Ⓐ The student should have already studied the material.
Ⓑ There are a few more weeks left till the assignment deadline.
Ⓒ The topic that the student is interested in is not related to the lecture.
Ⓓ The student has already started a paper that has not been assigned.

08 In the lecture, the professor discusses the camel's ability to survive in the desert. Indicate whether each of the following adaptations is mentioned by the professor.

Click in the correct box for each phrase.

	Mentioned	Not Mentioned
Ⓐ Rough hair on the body		
Ⓑ Varied natural body temperature		
Ⓒ Fat storage in its hump		
Ⓓ Rapid water intake		
Ⓔ Diet consisting of succulent plants		

09 What are two common features of the cactus and the camel?

   Ⓐ They can take in incredible amounts of liquid.
   Ⓑ They can survive off stored fat supplies.
   Ⓒ They can only remain active at night.
   Ⓓ They can tolerate periods of extreme heat.

10 Which of the following can be inferred about photosynthesis?

   Ⓐ It cannot function without carbon dioxide.
   Ⓑ It is only performed during sunny days.
   Ⓒ It is the plant's only way to obtain nutrients.
   Ⓓ It can provide excess energy supplies.

Listen again to part of the lecture. Then answer the question.

11 What does the professor mean when he says this: 🎧

   Ⓐ He thinks he's given the student too much information.
   Ⓑ He doesn't want to explain any more about the cactus.
   Ⓒ He wants the student to study the cactus in great depth.
   Ⓓ He believes the student should find evidence to support the claims.

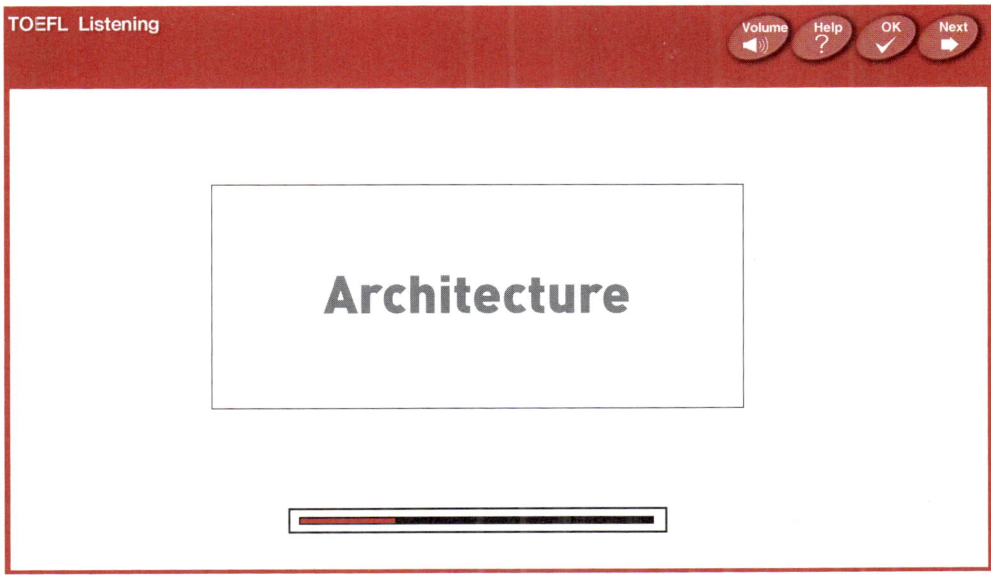

TOEFL Listening
Volume
Help
OK
Next
Architecture

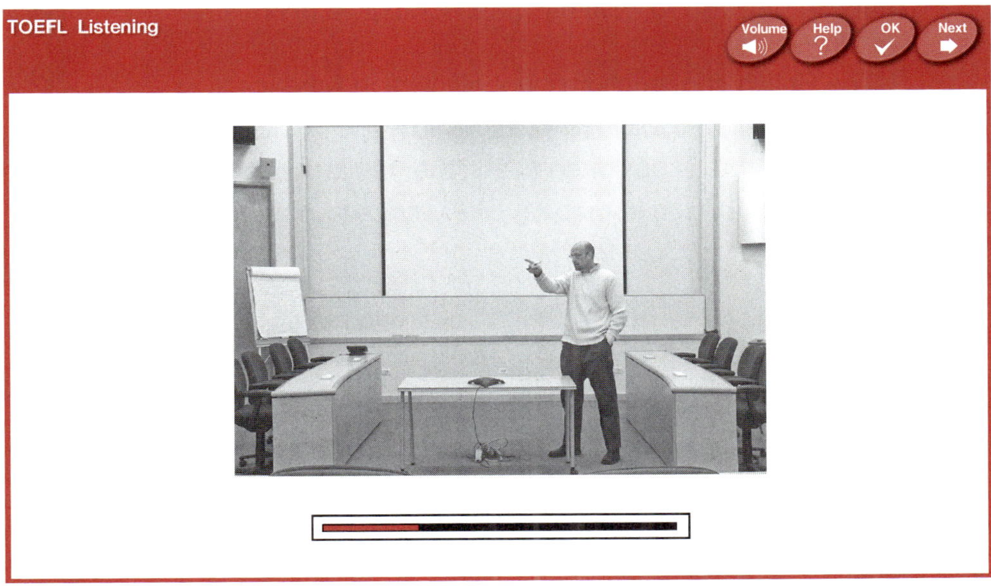

TOEFL Listening
Volume
Help
OK
Next

12   What is the professor mainly talking about?

    Ⓐ The climate of New England
    Ⓑ A particular style of architecture
    Ⓒ The essence of English housing
    Ⓓ Early immigrants in Cape Cod

Listen again to part of the lecture. Then answer the question.

13   Why does the professor say this: 🎧

    Ⓐ The students should know what it's like.
    Ⓑ The students should agree with the professor.
    Ⓒ The students should remember the concept.
    Ⓓ The students should write that down.

14   What can be inferred from the Cape Cod style of house?

    Ⓐ The British construction is not efficient in America.
    Ⓑ It was designed exclusively for use by the English.
    Ⓒ The structure is designed to suit the demand of people.
    Ⓓ It is rarely utilized in modern cities and suburbs.

15   Why was the chimney in the center of the Cape Cod house?

    Ⓐ To reduce expenditure of fuel
    Ⓑ To maximize heat on the main floor
    Ⓒ To heat up the central living room
    Ⓓ To facilitate the heating inside the house

16 Why were the rooftops of the Cape Cod cottage angled?

    Ⓐ Residents could collect water falling off the top for drinking.
    Ⓑ The shape minimized the amount of rain that hit the house.
    Ⓒ The design was purely an ornamental facade.
    Ⓓ Rainwater fell off and did not collect on top.

17 In the lecture, the professor discusses the characteristics of a Cape Cod house. Indicate on the chart below whether each of the following is mentioned as one of the characteristics.

Click in the correct box for each phrase.

	Mentioned	Not Mentioned
Ⓐ An asymmetrical floor plan		
Ⓑ Rectangular windows		
Ⓒ Southern facing structure		
Ⓓ Dormers and shutters		
Ⓔ A steep roof		

www.bansok.co.kr
T.02-2093-3399 F.02-2093-3393

ALL ABOUT JUNIOR TOEFL [Reading]

〈ALL ABOUT JUNIOR TOEFL〉시리즈는 4섹션(Reading, Listening, Speaking, Writing), 3스텝(초, 중, 고급)으로 구성되어 있으며, 예비중학생부터 고등학생들을 대상으로 합니다. (전12권)

리딩교재는 학생들의 어휘력과 개별문장의 해석 및 문장 간의 관계와 각 단락의 중심생각을 정확하게 유추할 수 있게 구성했습니다. 학생들이 반드시 알아야 할 각 섹션별 기초스킬들에 대한 충분한 예제와 연습문제를 제공하고 있으며, 강의준비에 바쁜 강사들을 위해 모든 예제와 문제(Mini Test, Actual Test, Vocabulary Review 등)를 자세하게 설명(해석, 해설 포함)하고 있습니다.

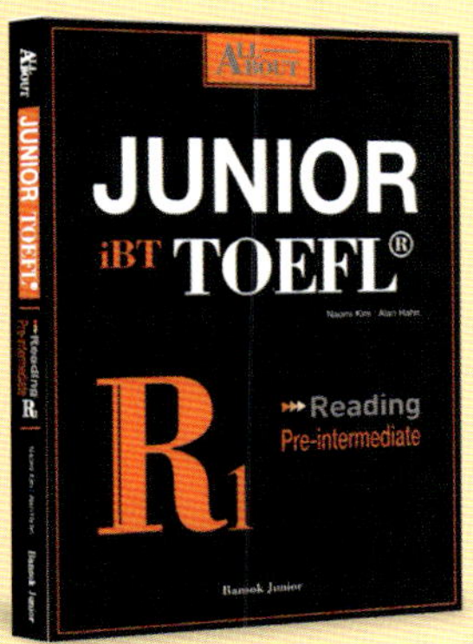

ALL ABOUT JUNIOR TOEFL
Reading
[R1 : Pre-intermediate Course]

대상 : 예비중학생 ~ 중 1, 2학년
판형 : 4×6배판 / 12,000원

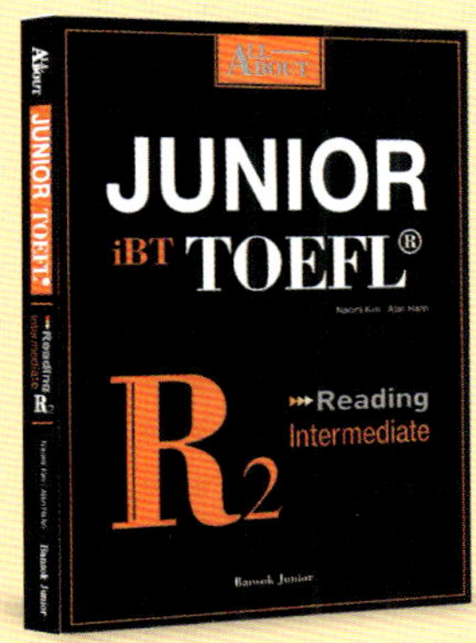

ALL ABOUT JUNIOR TOEFL
Reading
[R2 : Intermediate Course]

대상 : 중 1, 2학년 ~ 중 2, 3학년
판형 : 4×6배판 / 12,000원

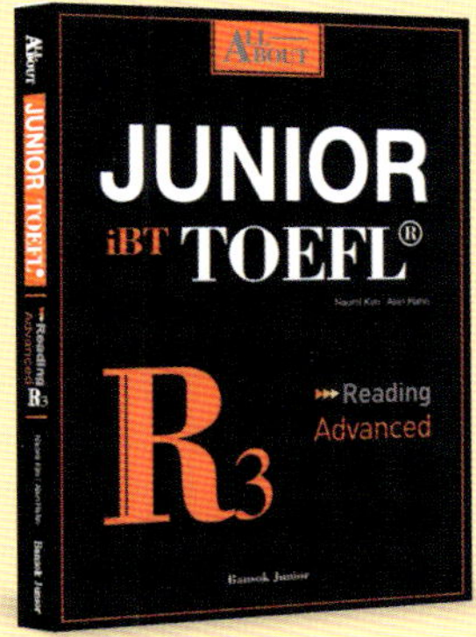

ALL ABOUT JUNIOR TOEFL
Reading
[R3 Advanced Course]

대상 : 중 2, 3학년 ~ 고 1, 2학년
판형 : 4×6배판 / 12,000원

>>>> 목 차

Chapter 1 Sentence Simplification 문장 간단화 ‖ Chapter 2 Fact 세부사항
Chapter 3 Category Chart 범주표 완성 ‖ Chapter 4 Reference 지시어
Chapter 5 Insertion 문장 삽입 ‖ Chapter 6 Vocabulary 어휘
Chapter 7 Inference 추론 ‖ Chapter 8 Rhetorical Purpose 수사적 의도 파악
Chapter 9 Summary 요약표 완성 ‖ Answer / Translation

www.bansok.co.kr
T.02-2093-3399 F.02-2093-3393

iBT Find TOEFL Series

iBT Find TOEFL [Reading]

Steven Oh 저
4×6배판
본책 600쪽(별책 156쪽)
22,000원(mp3 CD포함)

리딩 고득점을 위한 테마별, 레벨별 공략 프로그램 제시!

- 방대하고 다양한 독해지문
- iBT 토플유형에 대한 친절한 해설
- 복습을 위해 활용할 수 있는 Vocabulary Check-Up
- 지문별 주요 어휘 영영한 사전식 설명
- 권말 실전 테스트 수록
- 문제를 풀기 전에 들어야 할 원어민이 녹음한 CD제공

iBT Find TOEFL [Listening]

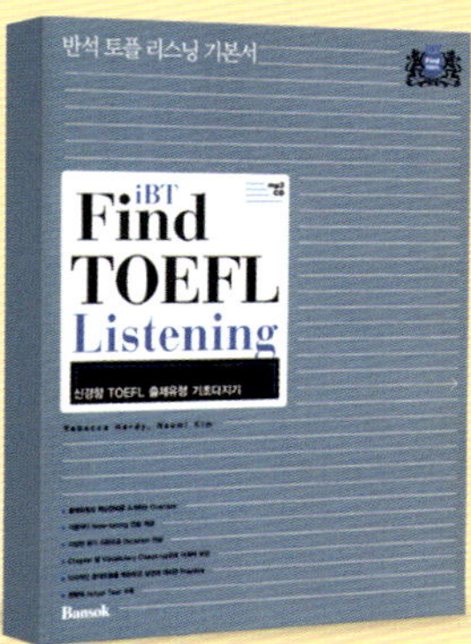

Rebecca Hardy, Naomi Kim 저
4×6배판
368쪽
19,000원(mp3 CD포함)

리스닝 고득점을 위한 최적의 전략과 문제 제공!

- 유형공략에 앞서 풀어보는 샘플문제
- 체계적인 문제유형 학습
- 미니 테스트의 핵심내용을 적는 노트 테이킹 박스 마련
- 어휘와 표현에 대한 정확한 발음과 스펠링 훈련
- 유형공략 학습 후 풀어보는 실전문제
- 실전과 유사한 문제 난이도와 형식 반영

iBT Find TOEFL [Speaking]

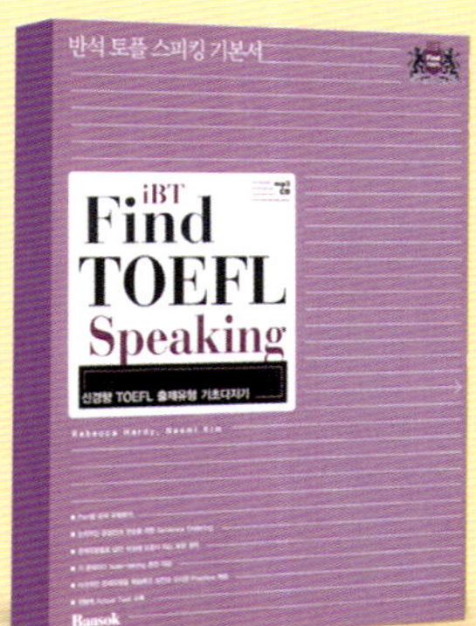

Rebecca Hardy, Naomi Kim 저
4×6배판
379쪽
15,000원(mp3 CD포함)

스피킹 고득점을 위한 6주간 프로그램 제시!

- 스피킹 섹션의 각 파트별 문제유형 상세 분석
- 논리적 문장전개를 위한 센텐스 오더링 훈련
- 문제유형별로 답안작성에 도움이 되는 표현정리
- 문제해결에 필수인 노트 테이킹 훈련
- 실전감각을 익히기 위한 실전 테스트
- 문제와 해답 내용 mp3 CD 제공

iBT Find TOEFL [Writing]

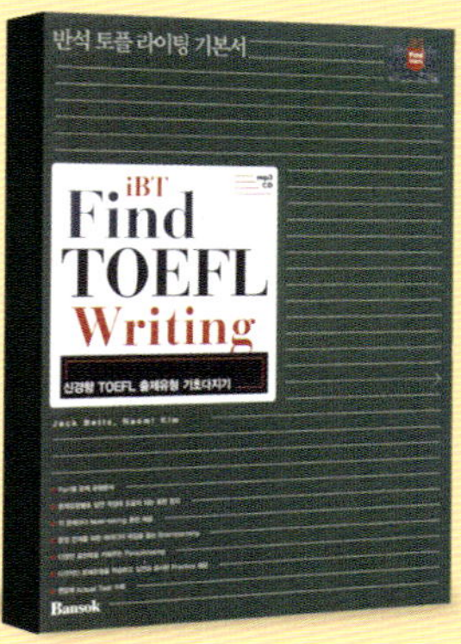

Jack Betts, Naomi Kim 저
4×6배판
332쪽
15,000원(mp3 CD포함)

라이팅 고득점을 위한 공략 프로그램 제시!

- 라이팅 섹션의 각 파트별 문제유형 상세 분석
- 각 문제마다 문제 해결에 필수인 노트 테이킹 훈련
- 문장전개를 위한 아이디어 채집을 돕는 브레인스토밍 훈련
- 문제유형별 답안작성에 도움이 되는 표현정리
- 실전감각을 익히기 위한 실전 테스트
- 문제와 해답 내용 mp3 CD 제공

ALL ABOUT

JUNIOR iBT TOEFL®

Answer / Script / Explanation

L₃

Bansok Junior

ALL ABOUT JUNIOR TOEFL
[LISTENING]

Advanced Course

Answer / Script / Explanation

Bansok Junior

Chapter 1 Main Idea

1. Ⓓ **2.** Ⓒ **3.** Ⓒ **4.** Ⓑ

Dictation: Office Hours

1. 1. for the extension 2. a retirement party 3. as a matter of fact 4. taking care of that
5. some important books and papers

2. 1. it was supposed to be 2. an original film 3. edit it down to 4. do your best 5. make
sense

3. 1. having trouble 2. drop the class 3. stick with it 4. during the second half 5. bring up
your grade

4. 1. sort out something 2. hurt my grade 3. always absent 4. any ideas or suggestions
5. move on 6. due in a week 7. on my own 8. assign me to one of them 9. solve the
problem

01

여 : Blair 교수님, 여기 제 리포트입니다. 늦어서 죄송해요. 기한을 연장해주셔서 다시 한 번 감사 드립니다. 음,
가기 전에요, 혹시 Murakami 교수님의 퇴직 기념 파티가 있을 건가요?

남 : 그렇단다. 기말 고사 직전에 열릴 거야. 너도 참석하고 싶니?

여 : 실은, 파티 준비를 도와드리고 싶어서요. Murakami 교수님은 제가 정말 좋아하는 교수님이시기 때문에 도
와드리고 싶어요.

남 : 아, 그럴 필요는 없단다. 학과에서 준비하고 있어.

여 : 그렇지만 뭔가 꼭 하고 싶어요, 네?

남 : Shirley, 네가 학생 신문에 글을 쓰고 있지?

여 : 네, 왜 그러시는데요? 좋은 생각이라도 있으세요?

남 : 신문에 Murakami 교수님의 경력에 관해서 글을 써보는 건 어떠니? 그 분은 훌륭한 책과 논문을 여러 편
저술하셨잖니. 그렇게 하면 교수님께서 더 고마워하실 거야.

여 : 정말 좋은 생각이에요!

어휘 extension 연장, 연기 retirement 은퇴 as a matter of fact 사실 organize 조직하다 favorite 좋아하는
take care of ～를 돌보다 career 경력, 생애 appreciate 고마워하다, 인정하다

1. 화자들은 주로 무엇에 관해 이야기 하고 있는가?
   Ⓐ 여자의 강의 리포트
   Ⓑ Murakami 교수 강의의 기말 고사
   Ⓒ 학교 신문에 글 쓰기
   Ⓓ 다른 교수의 은퇴 기념 파티

02

여 : 기말 영화 프로젝트에 대해 몇 가지 질문이 있습니다.

남 : 그래. 궁금한 점이 무엇이지?

여 : 그게요, 강의 계획서에는 영화를 12분 길이로 찍으라고 되어 있는데요, 교수님께서 수업 시간에는 20분이라
고 말씀하셨거든요. 이해가 안됩니다.

남 : 아, 그것 말이구나. 이 프로젝트는 편집이 주가 되는 과제물이지. 20분 길이로 영화를 찍어서 12분 길이로 편집을 하면 된단다.

여 : 그럼 중간 프로젝트와 기말 프로젝트의 관계 같은 건가요?

남 : 그렇지. 20분짜리 영화를 중간고사로 생각해봐. 영화 제작에 관해 배운 각종 기법을 이용해서 최선을 다해 만들어야지. 학기 후반부에는 편집에 관해 더 배우게 되잖니. 네가 찍었던 영화를 12분 길이로 줄이되, 앞뒤 연결은 자연스럽게 이어져야 하지.

여 : 이제 무슨 말인지 알겠어요! 감사합니다!

2. 왜 학생은 교수를 찾아가는가?

　Ⓐ 편집 기법에 관한 정보가 더 필요하다.

　Ⓑ 12분짜리 영화 대신 20분짜리 영화를 만들기를 원한다.

　Ⓒ 프로젝트로 만들어야 하는 영화의 길이 때문에 헷갈려 하고 있다.

　Ⓓ 영화 프로젝트로 어떤 주제를 잡아야 할지 조언을 구하고 있다.

03

여 : 시간 좀 있으세요? 교수님의 철학 개론 수업에 대해 드릴 말씀이 있어요.

남 : 그래, 무슨 일이니?

여 : 음, 수업 내용을 따라가기가 너무 힘들어요. 책 내용이 너무 어려워서 읽어도 무슨 말인지를 모르겠어요. 수강 신청을 취소해야 할까 봐요.

남 : 그렇구나. 사실 첫 부분이 가장 어렵단다. 아직 평균 C 학점을 받고 있으니, 수업을 계속 듣는 편이 더 좋을 것 같구나. 앞으로는 집단 토론도 더 많이 하고 개별 활동도 더 많아질 거란다. 학생들은 보통 강의 후반부에 더 좋은 성과를 나타내는 편이야.

여 : 정말이요?

남 : 그래. 일단 기본적인 개념에 대해서 공부한 후에는, 학생들이 직접 흥미를 느끼는 주제와 철학자들에 관해 탐구해보도록 하고 있어.

여 : 다행이네요.

남 : 그래. 다시 한 번 잘 생각해보렴, 내가 보기엔 성적을 올릴 가능성이 높은 것 같으니까.

여 : 그렇게 하겠습니다!

3. 여자는 왜 교수를 찾아가는가?

　Ⓐ 학생은 수업 시간에 유명한 철학자에 관해 배우기를 원한다.

　Ⓑ 학생은 그 강의에서 C 학점을 받고 있으며 성적을 올리기를 원한다.

　Ⓒ 학생은 철학 강의를 수강 취소하는 것을 고려하고 있다.

　Ⓓ 학생은 철학을 전공하는 것에 대해 생각하고 있다.

04

여 : 제가 문제가 좀 있는데 도와주시겠어요? 교수님의 화학 실험 수업에 관해서인데요, 제 점수가 깎일까 봐 걱정이 되어서요.

남 : 그래. 실험 파트너 때문인 것 같구나, 그렇지?

여 : 어떻게 아셨어요?

남 : 그 학생의 이름을 잊어버렸네… 뭐였더라?

여 : Justine이에요. 그 애는 맨날 결석을 해요! 어떻게 생겼는지 기억도 안 날 정도에요!

남 : 그래, 무슨 말인지 알겠다. 출석률 좀 한 번 보도록 하자… 음, 내가 생각한 게 맞구나. 실험실에 4번 밖에 오지 않았어.

여 : 그럼 제가 찾아온 이유를 아시겠네요.

남 : 그래, 알겠다. 어떻게 할 지 생각해 둔 것이라도 있니? Justine에게 기회를 한 번 더 주겠니, 아니면 파트너를 그만두겠니?

여 : 더 이상 기회를 주기 싫어요. 첫 과제를 일주일 후에 제출해야 하는데, 그 애가 할 수 있는 게 없을 거에요. 저 혼자 하고 싶어요.

남 : 알겠다. 필요하다면 이틀 정도 시간을 더 줄 수 있어. 어찌됐든, 네 잘못은 아니니까.

여 : 수업에 새로 들어온 학생들이 몇 명 있는 것 같은데요. 다음 번에는 그 학생들과 함께 조를 짤 수 있을까요?

남 : 그래. 세 명이 한 조가 될 수도 있겠지.

여 : 네. 그렇게 하면 되겠네요. 감사합니다!

어휘 sort out 해결하다 chemistry 화학 absent 결석한 attendance 출석 on one's own 스스로 fault 잘못

4. 학생이 교수와 대화를 나누고 있는 이유는 무엇인가?
　　Ⓐ 화학 실험 수업 성적이 안 좋다.
　　Ⓑ 실험 파트너가 수업을 너무 자주 빠진다.
　　Ⓒ 교수가 자신에게 기회를 한 번 더 주기를 원한다.
　　Ⓓ 첫 과제를 완성하는데 며칠이 더 필요하다.

Service Encounters
1. Ⓒ　2. Ⓒ　3. Ⓐ　4. Ⓑ

Dictation: Service Encounters

1. 1. having trouble concentrating 2. all the noise 3. being renovated 4. so far away from 5. it stayed open late

2. 1. can't sleep 2. dorm supervisor 3. practices guitar 4. so late in the semester 5. keeps disturbing you

3. 1. in charge of 2. than it used to be 3. is going up 4. costs you an arm and a leg 5. discourage waste

4. 1. is closed down 2. some special occasion 3. every meal in restaurants 4. to compete with 5. sign me up

01

여 : 저 좀 도와주시겠어요? 컴퓨터실에서 집중을 못하겠어요.

남 : 무슨 일이죠? 괜찮아요?

여 : 컴퓨터실에서 들리는 소음 때문이에요. 소리가 너무 커서 리서치에 집중 할 수가 없어요. 수요일에 제출해야 할 리포트가 있는데, 정말 집중해야 해요.

남 : 아, 무슨 이야기인지 알겠군요. 컴퓨터실이 있는 건물이 수리 중이거든요. 바닥도 새로 하고, 페인트칠도 새
　　로 하고요. 아마 지금 굉장히 시끄러울 거에요.
여 : 네, 그래서 무얼 해야 할지 모르겠어요. 다른 컴퓨터실들은 기숙사에서 너무 멀고 항상 사람들이 가득 차 있
　　거든요.
남 : 밤 늦게나 아침 일찍 가는 편이 좋을 거에요. 낮에만 인부들이 있으니까요.
여 : 어머, 늦게까지 문을 여는 줄은 몰랐어요. 그럼 그 때 가야겠네요. 도와주셔서 감사합니다!

어휘　concentrate 집중하다　renovate 수리하다

1. 여자는 왜 남자와 이야기 하고 있는가?
　　Ⓐ 컴퓨터실이 기숙사에서 멀리 떨어져 있다.
　　Ⓑ 컴퓨터실이 낮 시간에는 너무 붐빈다.
　　Ⓒ 컴퓨터실이 너무 시끄러워서 집중을 할 수가 없다.
　　Ⓓ 컴퓨터실이 수리 때문에 폐쇄되어 있다.

02

여 : 안녕하세요. 제 기숙사 방을 바꿀 수 있는지 여쭤보고 싶어요.
남 : 무슨 일이죠?
여 : 음, 룸메이트랑 약간의 문제가 있어요. 너무 시끄럽게 해서 잠을 잘 수가 없어요.
남 : 어떤 종류의 소음을 말하는 건가요? 룸메이트와 그 문제에 관해 이야기 해보았어요?
여 : 네, 이야기를 나누어봤어요. 사감도 그 애랑 이야기를 해봤는데요, 계속 그래요. 제 룸메이트가 밴드 활동을
　　해서 기타 연습을 해요. 방에서 음악도 많이 듣고요.
남 : 그렇군요. 보통은 학기 중에 이렇게 늦게 방을 바꿀 수는 없지만, 지금 학생의 사감에게 전화를 해봐야겠군
　　요. 학생의 룸메이트와 여기 내 사무실에서 만나봐야겠어요. 계속해서 학생에게 피해를 주면 큰 곤경에 처할
　　겁니다.
여 : 안심되는 말이네요.

어휘　dorm supervisor 사감　disturb 방해하다　relief 안심

2. 학생은 왜 기숙사 사무실을 찾아가는가?
　　Ⓐ 여자의 룸메이트가 여자의 가구를 망가뜨렸다.
　　Ⓑ 여자는 기숙사에 있는 연습실을 사용하고 싶어한다.
　　Ⓒ 여자는 룸메이트와 더 이상 함께 살 수 없다.
　　Ⓓ 여자는 사감과 문제가 있다.

03

남 : 저, 컴퓨터 실습실 담당자이신가요?
여 : 네, 제가 컴퓨터 실습실 총관리자입니다. 도와줄 일이 있나요?
남 : 네. 새로 바뀐 프린트 출력비에 대해 말씀 드리고 싶습니다. 전보다 너무 비싸서 좀 문제가 될 정도에요.
여 : 문제가 될 정도라니 유감이네요. 하지만 이용료를 올린 이유는 아주 간단합니다. 종이 가격이 오르고 있어서
　　어떻게든 그 비용을 충당해야 하니까요.
남 : 이해는 되지만, 그래도 너무 비싸요!
여 : 음, 학생에게 엄청난 비용이 드는 정도는 아닌 것 같은데요. 이용료를 올린 또 다른 이유는 낭비를 줄이자는
　　겁니다. 많은 학생들이 꼭 필요하지도 않은 것들을 출력하기도 하고, 별 신경을 안 쓰기도 해요. 매우 많은

양의 종이를 낭비하고 있죠.
남 : 알겠습니다. 그렇게 하는 것이 환경에도 더 좋겠네요.

어휘　in charge of ~을 담당하고 있는 general manager 총지배자 fee 요금 printout 출력정보 expensive 비싼
go up (가격이) 오르다 cost an arm and a leg 엄청나게 비용이 많이 들다 discourage 말리다, 단념시키다
waste 낭비 environment 환경

3. 학생은 왜 여자를 찾아갔는가?
　　Ⓐ 문서 출력 요금에 대해 불만을 제기하려고
　　Ⓑ 실습실에 프린터가 부족한 것에 대해 불만을 제기하려고
　　Ⓒ 프린터에 사용되는 종이 종류에 대해 불만을 제기하려고
　　Ⓓ 실습실에 있는 프린터 가격에 대해 불만을 제기하려고

04

여 : 안녕하세요, 혹시 다른 기숙사에 있는 조리실을 사용할 수 있을까요? 저희 기숙사 조리실은 수리에 들어가
　　서 지금 폐쇄되어 있거든요.
남 : 그렇군요, 특별한 일이라도 있나요?
여 : 네, 이번 주말에 저와 함께 지낼 친구들이 있는데요, 지금 제가 있는 기숙사에서는 요리를 할 공간이 없어요.
　　요리는 제가 가장 좋아하는 거고, 식당에서 모든 끼니를 때우고 싶지는 않아요.
남 : 알겠어요. 학생 기숙사 양 옆에 있는 기숙사 조리실을 예약할 수 있어요. 영양학과에 있는 강습용 조리실 중
　　한 곳을 예약할 수도 있습니다.
여 : 학생들이 사용할 수가 있는 건가요?
남 : 다른 사람들이 사용하지 않으면 주말에는 사용이 가능해요. 그렇지만 사용 후에는 반드시 뒷정리를 말끔히
　　해야 하고, 캠퍼스 구내 식당에 피해가 갈만한 간이식당 영업은 금지되어 있어요.
여 : 음식을 팔면 안 된다는 거군요. 그 부분은 걱정 마시고 신청해주세요!

어휘　close down 폐쇄하다 renovation 수리 occasion 경우, 행사 favorite 좋아하는 next to ~ 옆에 nutrition
영양학 clean up 정돈하다 compete with ~와 경쟁하다

4. 화자들은 주로 무엇에 관해 이야기 하고 있는가?
　　Ⓐ 학생은 수리를 하고 있지 않는 기숙사에 살고 싶어한다.
　　Ⓑ 학생은 친구들을 위해 요리를 해주려고 조리실을 사용하고 싶어한다.
　　Ⓒ 학생은 캠퍼스에 간이 식당을 열고 싶어한다.
　　Ⓓ 학생은 영양학과에서 공부하고 싶어한다.

Lectures

1. 1. Ⓑ 2. Ⓓ **2.** 1. Ⓒ 2. Ⓑ 3. Ⓑ

Dictation: Lectures

1. 1. set up a business 2. a not-for-profit organization 3. an outline of the services 4. the type
and number of staff 5. a strong management team 6. financial projections 7. government
regulatory agencies 8. goals and objectives 9. reposition itself 10. toward the ultimate goal
2. 1. reduce our energy consumption 2. both humans and the environment 3. emit toxic
gases 4. fewer illness-related absences 5. old buildings are demolished 6. in the heat
island effect

01 마케팅 수업

P : 모두 자리에 앉았으니, 수업을 시작하도록 할까요? 사업 계획서가 무엇인지 말해볼 사람 있어요?

S : 사업을 시작할 때 필요한 것 아닌가요? 서류 작업 해야 할 것이 많잖아요?

P : 맞아요, 비슷해요. 사업 계획서는 영리 사업체던 비영리 단체던 사업을 시작할 때 준비해야 하는 첫 단계 가운데 하나죠. 사업 계획서에는 사업의 목표가 명확하게 드러나야 하며, 비영리 단체를 세우는 경우라면 앞으로 제공하게 될 서비스에 대한 개요가 제시되어 있어야 해요. 이러한 것들 말고도 잘 수립된 사업 계획서에는 어떤 내용들이 들어있어야 할까요?

S : 재무 데이터가 포함되어야 하지 않나요? 혹은 채용 예정인 직원들의 직무별 유형과 인원이라던가요?

P : 맞아요. 보통 사업 계획서에는 직원들에 대한 기본 정보가 들어있는데, 이미 사업에 관여하고 있는 사람이나 앞으로 채용 예정인 사람들이 모두 포함됩니다. 그런 점에서 유능한 경영팀이 필요하죠. 현실적인 재무 예측 또한 중요하며, 상세한 시장 조사와 경쟁사 조사 역시 중요하죠. 사업 계획서는 대외용으로 작성되기도 하는데, 이는 조직의 외부 사람들에게 중요한 의미를 갖는 목표에 초점을 맞추는 걸 의미해요. 재정상의 투자자나 정부 규제 기관 등이 이에 해당하죠. 내부 사업 계획서는 기업이 정한 목표에 중점을 둔 것이지요. 누가 예를 한 번 들어보겠어요?

S : 신제품을 개발하거나 출시할 때 사업 계획서가 필요하겠죠?

P : 바로 그렇죠. 혹은 시장에서 자사 브랜드를 재정립하거나 이미지 전환을 꾀하는 경우에도 필요하죠. 방향을 정하고 최종 목표에 도달하기 위해 충족되어야 하는 모든 세부 목표를 정립하는 등의 목적으로 사업 계획서가 이용될 수도 있죠. 자, 보다 구체적으로 사업 계획서에 관해 살펴보기 전에, 질문 있는 사람 있어요?

어휘 set up 시작하다, 착수하다 paperwork 서류 작업 for-profit 영리 목적의 not-for-profit 비영리 목적의 hire 채용하다 realistic 현실적인 projection 예측 detailed 상세한 competitor 경쟁자 externally 외부적으로 stakeholder 투자자, 이해 관계자 regulatory 규제의 internal 내부의 launch 출시하다, 발사하다 chart 정하다 path 방향, 길 meet 충족시키다 ultimate 궁극적인, 최종의

1. 강의의 주제는 무엇인가?
   Ⓐ 영리 사업체와 비영리 단체
   Ⓑ 사업 계획서의 구성 요소
   Ⓒ 창업 준비 과정의 단계
   Ⓓ 신제품 개발

2. 사업 계획서의 두 가지 유형은 무엇인가?
   Ⓐ 각종 서식과 서류 작업
   Ⓑ 재무 예측과 시장 조사
   Ⓒ 투자와 고용
   Ⓓ 대내적과 대외적 사업 계획서

02 건축학 수업

P : 지구 기후 변화가 두드러지는 요즘 시대에 우리는 에너지 소비를 줄일 수 있는 방법을 생각해볼 필요가 있어요. 이를 위해서는 새롭고 보다 환경 친화적인 건설 기법들이 중요한 자리를 차지해요. 여러분은 '친환경 건물'이라는 말을 들어봤을 겁니다. 무슨 뜻일까요? 친환경 건물 기법은 인간과 환경 모두를 위해 더 건전한 건물을 만들려는 것이에요. 친환경 건물은 단순히 건물을 에너지 효율성이 더 높아지도록 만든다는 것은 아니에요. 건설 자재와 위치, 햇볕을 받는 방식, 냉난방 기술과 같은 것을 정할 때부터 세심하게 주의를 기울이죠. 하지만, 유독 가스를 배출하지 않는 페인트와 단열재, 바닥재를 선택함으로써 친환경 건물 내의 공기의 질이 기존의 방법과 자재를 이용해 지어진 건물에서보다 훨씬 더 향상되었어요. 실내 공기가 더 좋아진다는 것은

건강이 더 좋아지고, 아파서 결근을 하게 되는 일이 줄어든다는 것이죠.

친환경 건물에는 혁신적인 기법들이 많이 이용되죠. 예를 들어, 기존의 단열재는 섬유 유리로 만들어지죠. 하지만, 새롭게 등장한 단열재는 재활용 된 데님과 옷으로 만들어져요. 페인트는 우유와 기타 안전한 유기질로 만들어지기도 하죠. 빨리 자라서 심은 지 6년 후에 활용할 수 있는 대나무는 생장 속도가 더 더딘 나무로 만들어지는 목재를 효율적으로 대체하는 품목이죠. 건축상의 재화 구출 역시 친환경 건물 디자인에서 장려되는 부분이죠. 오래된 건물을 헐 때, 많은 양의 쓸만한 목재와 유리, 금속이 남게 됩니다. 옥상 정원은 여름에는 건물을 시원하게 하고, 겨울에는 지붕을 단열시킬 겁니다. 이러한 것들은 주변 도시에서 열섬 현상이 일어나는 것을 줄여주게 되죠.

어휘 reduce 줄이다 consumption 소비 environmentally-friendly 친환경의 term 용어 energy-efficient 에너지 효율적인 location 위치 face 향하다, 마주하다 insulation 단열 emit 배출하다 toxic 독성의 absence 결근 innovation 혁신 fiberglass 섬유 유리 organic 유기적인 bamboo 대나무 substitute 대체품 salvage 구조 demolish 헐다, 부수다

1. 교수는 주로 무엇에 관해 이야기 하는가?
   Ⓐ 현재의 기후 변화 추세
   Ⓑ 에너지 소비 감축의 중요성
   Ⓒ 친환경 건물의 이점
   Ⓓ 혁신적인 건설 기술

2. 다음 중 친환경 건물 기법의 주요 장점은?
   Ⓐ 비용 절감
   Ⓑ 실내 공기 향상
   Ⓒ 건설 기간 감소
   Ⓓ 더 나은 실내 디자인

3. 왜 건축상의 재화 구출이 친환경 건물 철학의 중요한 부분을 이루는가?
   Ⓐ 대나무가 신축 건물의 많은 부분에 사용될 수 있다.
   Ⓑ 예전 건물의 구성 요소들이 재활용 될 수도 있다.
   Ⓒ 신축 건물이 예전 건물보다 더 멋있게 보인다.
   Ⓓ 건축상의 재화 구출은 도심 온도를 내려가게 한다.

> **Practice**
>
> [1-5] 1. Ⓑ 2. Ⓓ 3. Ⓒ 4. Ⓐ 5. Mentioned – Ⓑ, Ⓓ, Ⓔ Not Mentioned – Ⓐ, Ⓒ
> [6-11] 6. Ⓓ 7. Ⓐ 8. Ⓒ 9. Basic Types – Ⓑ, Ⓒ, Ⓔ Herbal Tea – Ⓐ, Ⓓ 10. Ⓓ 11. Ⓑ

[문제 1–5] Listen to part of a conversation between a student and a professor.

W : Hi, are you busy? I'm trying to register, and several of the classes I want are already full... including one of yours.

M : I'm fine. Come on in. So one of my classes is booked up already? I haven't checked the enrollment system today. Which class is it?

W : Second Language Acquisition. I'd really been looking forward to that one.

M : Hmm, interesting. I didn't think it would fill up so early in the registration period. Would you consider putting your name on the waiting list?

W : Yes. I've already done that, but after this semester, I'll only have one semester left. I'd rather not take any chances. I can't afford to delay graduation.

M : That's a good point, and I'm not teaching it the following semester. I understand why you wouldn't want to wait.

W : Is there another course that's reasonably similar in content?

M : Well, you could take Bilingualism. It's similar enough. I don't know who's teaching it this semester-either Tetsuji or Drinnan. You'll have to check, if you're interested.

W : 🎧 Then I should check it out. I'd actually been thinking about Bilingualism, but not as an alternative to Second Language Acquisition. Are there any other courses you'd recommend?

M : 3.Well, no, not at the master's level. The undergraduate courses aren't as advanced, obviously. Uh, I'm supposed to be teaching a new course, Languages of Asia, next semester...

W : Really? That's great, since I'm planning to take a job in Taiwan after I graduate. I've been studying Chinese for a few years, as well.

M : Good. I think you'll benefit from that class, then. The thing is I was also going to teach one of the core linguistics courses, either Intro to Applied Linguistics or Comparative Linguistics. We're hiring a new professor next semester, and we're thinking of starting that person out with the two basic courses. If that happens, then I'd be available to teach Second Language Acquisition.

W : How likely is that?

M : It's pretty likely. Why don't you check with me in about a month? In the meantime, just register for the classes you want....

W : That sounds great. Thank you for your time.

여 : 안녕하세요, 지금 바쁘세요? 제가 수강신청을 하려고 하는데, 듣고 싶은 과목들이 벌써 마감되었어요… 그 중에 교수님의 강의도 있고요.

남 : 그래. 들어오렴. 내 강의 중 한 과목이 벌써 마감되었단 말이지? 오늘 수강신청 시스템을 확인해보지 않아서 말이야. 어떤 과목이지?

여 : '제 2 언어 습득' 과목입니다. 그 수업을 꼭 듣고 싶었어요.

남 : 그렇구나. 수강신청 기간에 그렇게 빨리 마감 되리라고는 생각지 못했는데. 그럼 대기자 명단에 이름을 올려놓겠니?

여 : 네. 벌써 그렇게 했는데, 이번 학기가 지나면 한 학기 밖에 안 남아요. 운에 맡겨두는 건 좀 위험할 것 같아요. 졸업을 미룰 수 있는 상황도 아니고요.

남 : 그렇지, 그리고 다음 학기에는 내가 그 과목을 가르칠 계획이 없단다. 왜 대기자 명단에 이름을 올려놓고 기다리고 싶어하지 않는지 이해한단다.

여 : 혹시 비슷한 내용을 다루는 다른 과목이 있을까요?

남 : 음, '2개 국어 상용' 과목이 있단다. 상당히 비슷한 내용을 다루지. 이번 학기에 누가 가르치는 모르겠는데, 아마 Tetsuji 교수니 Drinnan 교수일거야. 한 번 확인해보도록 하렴.

여 : 그럼 확인해봐야겠네요. '2개 국어 상용' 과목을 생각해보긴 했는데, '제 2 언어 습득' 과목 대신은 아니었어요. 권해주실 만한 과목이 또 있으세요?

남 : 글쎄다, 석사 과정에는 없는 것 같은데. 학부 과정은 그만큼 높은 수준을 다루지는 않는단다. 다음 학기에 '아시아 언어' 라는 새로운 과목을 가르칠 계획인데…

여 : 정말이요? 잘됐네요, 제가 졸업 후에 대만에서 취직할 계획이거든요. 몇 년 동안 중국어도 배우고 있어요.

남 : 잘됐구나. 그 수업이 너에게 아주 유익할 것 같구나. 그런데 내가 핵심 언어학 강의 중 하나를 맡을 예정이었어, 응용 언어학 개론이나 비교 언어학 말이야. 다음 학기에 신임 교수를 채용할 예정인데, 그 교수에게 이 기초 과목 두 개부터 맡길 예정이야. 그렇게 되면, 내가 '제 2 언어 습득' 과목을 가르치게 될 수도 있지.

여 : 그럴 가능성이 얼마나 되나요?

남 : 가능성이 아주 높지. 한달 정도 후에 다시 들러서 확인해 보는 것이 어떻겠니? 그 동안에는 네가 듣고 싶은 수업에 등록을 하도록 하고…

여 : 그게 좋겠네요. 시간을 내주셔서 감사합니다.

어휘 be booked up (예매가) 매진되다 enrollment 등록 look forward to ~를 고대하다 take chances 위험을 무릅쓰다, 운에 맡기다 delay 연기하다, 미루다 master 석사 advanced 고등 과정의 benefit from ~로부터 이익을 얻다 core 핵심 likely ~할 것 같은 in the meantime 그 사이에

Note-taking

Topic: Register for class 수강신청

1. Student: want to take SLA '제 2 언어 습득' 과목을 수강하고 싶어함
   – already full 이미 등록이 마감되었음
2. Prof.'s suggestions 교수의 제안
   – waiting list ➡ risky 대기자 명단에 이름을 올리기 ➡ 약간 위험함
   – similar course: Bilingualism 비슷한 과목 수강: '2개 국어 상용' 과목
   – take next semester when it is decided who teaches
     누가 가르치는지 결정된 후 다음 학기에 수강하기

1. 학생은 왜 교수와 이야기 하고 있는가?
   Ⓐ 그녀는 언어학 연구 프로젝트를 수행하고 싶어한다.
   Ⓑ 그녀는 교수가 가르치는 과목들 중 한 과목을 듣고 싶어한다.
   Ⓒ 그녀는 졸업 후의 계획에 대해 논의하고 싶어한다.
   Ⓓ 그녀는 신임 교수로 채용되길 원한다.
   해설 그녀는 교수의 '제 2 언어 습득' 과목을 수강하고 싶어하는데, 이미 등록이 마감되어버린 상황이다.
   정답 Ⓑ

2. 교수가 '제 2 언어 습득' 과목 대체로서 추천하는 강의는 무엇인가?
   Ⓐ 아시아 언어
   Ⓑ 비교 언어학
   Ⓒ 응용 언어학 개론
   Ⓓ 2개 국어 상용
   해설 교수에 따르면 '2개 국어 상용' 과목이 학생이 원래 수강하고자 했던 '제 2 언어 습득' 과목과 상당히 유사한 내용을 다룬다고 하였다.
   정답 Ⓓ

대화의 일부를 다시 들으시오. 그러고 나서 질문에 답하시오.

3. 교수가 이것을 말할 때 의미하는 것은 무엇인가? 
   M : Well, no, not at the master's level.

Ⓐ 학생은 학부 과정 강의를 알아보는 편이 좋다.

Ⓑ 학생은 석사 과정 강의를 수강할 자격이 없다.

Ⓒ 학생은 언어학 석사 과정을 밟고 있다.

Ⓓ 학생은 언어학 분야에서 전문가로 성장할 것이다.

해설 학생이 교수에게 권해줄 만한 다른 과목이 또 있냐고 묻자, 교수가 석사 과정에는 없는 것 같다고 하였다. 그리고 학부 과정은 그만큼 높은 수준의 강의가 아니라는 말을 통해 학생이 현재 석사 과정에 있다는 것을 짐작할 수 있다.

정답 Ⓒ

4. 학생이 '아시아 언어' 강의에 관해 암시하는 것은 무엇인가?

Ⓐ 학생은 다음 학기에 그 강의를 수강하는데 관심을 보이고 있다.

Ⓑ 그 강의는 고등 과정이 아니다.

Ⓒ 학생은 이미 그 과목을 수강했다.

Ⓓ 그 강의는 아시아 학생들을 대상으로 한다.

해설 교수가 다음 학기에 '아시아 언어'라는 새로운 과목을 가르칠 예정이라고 하자, 학생이 매우 긍정적인 반응을 보이고 있다. 졸업 후 대만에서 일자리를 구할 것이라는 내용과 중국어를 몇 해 동안 공부했다는 내용을 통해 학생이 다음 학기에 그 과목을 들을 가능성이 높다고 예상할 수 있다.

정답 Ⓐ

5. 대화에서, 교수는 학생에게 문제 해결책을 몇 가지 제시하고 있다. 아래 표의 각 보기가 이러한 해결책에 속하는지 표시하시오. 각 보기에 맞는 칸에 클릭하시오.

	Mentioned	Not Mentioned
Ⓐ 다른 학교의 똑같은 강의를 온라인으로 수강하기		
Ⓑ 대기자 명단에 이름을 올려 놓기		
Ⓒ 학과장님께 편지를 쓰기		
Ⓓ 누가 가르치는지 확실해지게 되면 나중에 수강하기		
Ⓔ 다른 과목으로 대체하여 수강하기		

해설 교수는 학생에게 원래 듣고 싶었던 과목의 수강 대기자 명단에 이름을 올려 놓을 것과, 비슷한 과목으로 대체하여 듣기, 원하던 과목을 다음 학기에 누가 가르칠 것인지가 결정되고 나면 그 후에 그 과목을 수강할 것을 제안하고 있다.

정답 Mentioned – Ⓑ, Ⓓ, Ⓔ Not Mentioned – Ⓐ, Ⓒ

[문제 6–11] Listen to part of a lecture in a botany class.

P(W) : Well, I imagine everybody here has drunk tea before. Am I right? Would anybody like to tell me what kinds of tea you've drunk?

S(M) : Iced tea? Or Green tea?

P : Those are probably the forms of most common to Americans nowadays. When we think of hot tea, we tend to think of black tea and not other varieties. Green tea has become familiar to us only in the last ten or fifteen years. Although people in Asia have been drinking it for thousands of years, it's still a new arrival here in the United States. So, uh, first of all, a definition: What is tea, exactly?

S : A hot drink made with leaves of the tea tree?

P : You're on the right track, but it's important to be careful with terms regarding tea tree. When we talk about tea tree oil, which is used as an antiseptic, we're talking about the oil derived from a totally different species, *Melaleuca*. That isn't the tea that we drink. That would be *Camellia sinensis*. *Sinensis* means China in Latin. So tea is a beverage made by steeping the leaves of *Camellia sinensis* or other plants in hot water for a short period of time. Some teas need to be steeped for only 30 seconds; others, like some of the herbal teas, are best if they're steeped for a few minutes. It depends on the form of tea.

S :

P : 8.If I tried to list them all, we'd be here all day. So I'll keep it to just the basics: black tea, oolong tea, green tea, white tea, yellow tea, and dark green tea. They are a little different from each other in their making. All other forms of tea tend to be lumped together under the umbrella term of herbal tea. Chamomile tea, rooibos, peppermint, lemon verbena, you name it: those would be considered types of herbal tea.

Uh, tea has been cultivated for millennia in the parts of Asia including China, India, and northern Myanmar. In fact, tea has been a part of these cultures for so long that there are various creation myths in existence to explain it. You want to know some of them? One Chinese legend suggests that about 5000 years ago, an emperor was drinking a bowl of boiling water and some leaves from a tree fell into the bowl. The water changed color. The emperor was curious, took a sip, and liked it. A slightly different version of the story gives the credit to Buddha. However people were first motivated to soak tea leaves and drink the stuff, the Chinese quickly realized its uses as a mild stimulant.

The British are probably the people we think of next, with regard to tea cultivation and consumption. England's history with tea begins in the 17th century. A Portuguese princess who had married into the British Royal Family brought her fondness for tea with her. It didn't take long before the British East India Company was shipping immense quantities of tea out of Canton, which is now Guangzhou. Well, the history of sugar is closely linked to the history of tea, but we're running a little low on time; shall we continue this tomorrow?

P : 자, 모두들 차(茶)를 마셔본 적이 있을 거라 생각되는군요. 그렇죠? 어떤 차를 마셔보았는지 말해볼 사람 있어요?

S : 아이스티나 녹차요?

P : 그 둘이 현재 미국인들에게 가장 잘 알려진 차 종류일 거에요. 뜨거운 차라고 하면, 홍차만 생각하고 다른 차 종류는 생각하지 않는 경향이 강하죠. 우리가 일상적으로 녹차를 즐기게 된 것은 고작 10년~15년 밖에 안되었어요. 아시아인들은 녹차를 수천 년간 즐겨왔지만, 미국에서는 여전히 새로운 제품으로 인식되고 있죠. 자, 그럼 먼저, 차가 대체 무엇인지 그 뜻을 말해보겠어요?

S : 차나무 잎으로 만든 뜨거운 음료요?

P : 잘 알고 있네요, 그런데 차나무와 관련하여 용어를 구분하여 이해해야 해요. 소독제로 쓰이는 티트리오일은 완전히 다른 나무 종인 멜라유카(Melaleuca)에서 짜낸 오일을 말해요. 멜라유카는 우리가 마시는 차가 아니에요. 우리가 마시는 차는 카멜리아 시넨시스(Camellia sinensis) 나무에요. 시넨시스는 라틴어로 중국을 의미해요. 따라서 차는 카멜리아 시넨시스 나무나 기타 식물의 잎을 따서 뜨거운 물에 짧은 시간 동안 우려내어 마시는 음료라고 할 수 있죠. 30초간 짧게 우려내야 하는 차도 있고, 몇몇 허브차의 경우에는 몇 분간 우려내야 맛이 제대로 나는 차도 있어요. 차의 종류에 따라 달라지는 거죠.

S : 슈퍼마켓에 가면 수십 종의 차가 판매되는 걸 볼 수 있어요.

P : 차 이름을 모두 열거하자면, 하루 종일이 걸릴 거에요. 그러니 아주 기본적인 차종만 언급하도록 하겠어요. 대표적으로 홍차와 우롱차, 녹차, 백차, 황차, 흑차가 있어요. 만드는 방식은 조금씩 다르죠. 그 외에는 대개 허브차라

는 포괄적 용어에 포함됩니다. 카모마일차, 루이보스차, 페퍼민트차, 레몬버베나차 등 그 밖에도 여러 종류가 있는데, 모두 허브차에 속하죠.

차는 중국과 인도, 미얀마 북부 지방을 포함하여 아시아 지역에서 수천 년간 재배되어 왔어요. 아주 오랜 세월 아시아 문화권의 일부를 이루어왔기 때문에 차를 언제부터 어떻게 마시게 되었는지에 관한 이야기들이 많이 전해져 내려오고 있죠. 궁금한가요? 중국 전설에 따르면 지금으로부터 약 5000년 전에 황제가 끓인 물을 마시고 있었는데, 나뭇잎이 사발에 떨어졌다고 해요. 그러자 물 색깔이 바뀌었죠. 황제는 호기심이 발동해서 그 물을 한 모금 마셔보았는데, 아주 맘에 들어 했다고 하는군요. 이와는 약간 다른 이야기로 부처와 관련된 것도 있어요. 맨 처음 어떻게 나뭇잎을 물에 우려내어 차를 마시게 되었는지는 잘 모르지만, 중국인들은 차에 각성 효과가 있다는 것을 곧바로 알게 되었죠.

차 재배와 소비에 관해서라면, 영국인들 역시 빠지지 않죠. 영국인들이 차를 즐기기 시작한 것은 17세기부터입니다. 영국 왕실과 혼인을 맺은 포르투갈 공주가 차 애호가였죠. 그 후로 영국 동인도 회사가 지금의 광저우(Guangzhou)에 해당하는 광둥(Canton) 지방에서 엄청난 양의 차를 수입하기까지 그다지 오랜 시간이 걸리지 않았어요. 음, 설탕의 역사와 차의 역사는 밀접한 연관이 있는데, 오늘은 시간이 거의 다 된 것 같네요. 내일 다시 수업을 진행하도록 할까요?

어휘 nowadays 요즘 definition 정의 antiseptic 소독제 steep 담그다, 깊이 스며들게 하다 lump together 일률적으로 다루다 umbrella term 포괄적 용어 myth 신화 legend 전설 emperor 황제 sip 한 모금 stimulant 각성제 fondness 애호 immense 엄청난

Note-taking

Topic: Tea 차

1. Def. 정의
   - different from tea tree oil: antiseptic, *Melaleuca* tree
     티트리오일과는 다름: 소독제, 멜라유카 나무
   - C.S. tree leaves 카멜리아 시넨시스 나뭇잎
   - steep leaves in hot water 잎을 뜨거운 물에 우려냄
2. Many types 차종이 다양함
   - basics: black, oolong, green, white, yellow, dark green
     기본 종류: 홍차, 우롱차, 녹차, 백차, 황차, 흑차
   - others: herbal tea 그 외: 허브차
3. Tea culture in Asia 아시아의 차문화
   - Chinese legend: emperor found by accident 중국의 전설: 황제가 우연히 발견했음
   - used as stimulant 각성제로 즐김
4. The British 영국인
   - begin 17th C. 17세기에 차를 즐기기 시작함
   - import tea 차를 수입함

6. 강의의 주제는 무엇인가?
   Ⓐ 허브차의 종류
   Ⓑ 영국 동인도 회사
   Ⓒ 티트리오일의 효능
   Ⓓ 차와 그 역사

해설 차의 정의와 종류, 역사 등에 관해 강의가 진행되고 있다.

정답 Ⓓ

7. 다음 중 어느 것이 티트리오일에 관해 맞는가?

    Ⓐ 약으로 쓰인다.

    Ⓑ 카멜리아 시넨시스 나무에서 짜낸다.

    Ⓒ 주로 중국에서 제조된다.

    Ⓓ 구하기가 어렵다.

해설 티트리오일은 소독제로 쓰인다고 하였으므로 약용이라고 할 수 있다. 카멜리아 시넨시스 나무는 우리가 차를 끓여 마시는 종이므로 보기 Ⓑ는 오답이다.

정답 Ⓐ

강의의 일부를 다시 들으시오. 그러고 나서 질문에 답하시오.

8. 교수가 이것을 말할 때 암시하는 것은 무엇인가: 

    P : If I tried to list them all, we'd be here all day.

    Ⓐ 차 목록은 슈퍼마켓에서 찾아볼 수 있다.

    Ⓑ 차는 일상에서 쉽게 즐기는 품목이 아니다.

    Ⓒ 차의 종류가 매우 다양하다.

    Ⓓ 차 이름은 읽기 어렵다.

해설 차의 종류가 너무 많아서 모두 열거하기에는 시간이 아주 오래 걸린다는 뜻이다.

정답 Ⓒ

9. 강의에서, 교수는 차의 기본 종류와 허브차의 종류에 대해 언급하고 있다. 아래 표의 각 보기가 어떤 것과 관련되어 있는지 표시하시오. 각 보기에 맞는 칸에 클릭하시오.

	Basic Types	Herbal Tea
Ⓐ 루이보스차		
Ⓑ 우롱차		
Ⓒ 백차		
Ⓓ 카모마일차		
Ⓔ 홍차		

해설 차의 기본 종류로 홍차와 우롱차, 녹차, 백차, 황차, 흑차의 6종이 언급되었다. 루이보스차와 카밀레차는 허브차이다. 따라서 **Basic types**에 해당하는 것은 보기 Ⓑ, Ⓒ, Ⓔ이고, 보기 Ⓐ, Ⓓ는 **Herbal tea**의 종류이다.

정답 Basic Types – Ⓑ, Ⓒ, Ⓔ   Herbal Tea – Ⓐ, Ⓓ

10. 중국인들이 차를 즐겨 마시게 된 이유 가운데 하나는 무엇이겠는가?

    Ⓐ 차는 황제가 좋아하던 음료였다.

    Ⓑ 차를 끓이기가 쉽다.

    Ⓒ 차는 다양한 색깔을 낸다.

    Ⓓ 차는 각성제 효과를 낸다.

해설 차는 일종의 각성제 작용을 하기 때문에 중국인들의 기호품으로 자리잡게 되었다.

정답 Ⓓ

11. 교수가 영국인들의 차 소비에 관해 암시하는 것은 무엇인가?
    Ⓐ 차를 구입하기 위허 설탕을 이용했다.
    Ⓑ 수입에 의존한다.
    Ⓒ 차에 설탕을 첨가하여 달게 마시는 것을 좋아했다.
    Ⓓ 설탕과 차를 같은 곳에서 재배했다.
    해설 영국인들이 차를 즐기기 시작하면서 동인도 회사가 광동 지방에서 많은 양의 차를 배로 수송하게 되었다고
       하였는데, 이를 통해 차 소비를 수입에 주로 의존했다는 것을 추론할 수 있다.
    정답 Ⓑ

Chapter 2 Detail

Office Hours

1. Ⓒ **2.** Ⓐ, Ⓒ **3.** Ⓑ, Ⓒ **4.** Ⓑ, Ⓒ

Dictation: Office Hours

1. 1. on the committee 2. kind of overwhelmed 3. what you mean 4. look great
    5. analyzing the results
2. 1. ask for some advice 2. all the concepts 3. ended up chatting 4. get much work done
    5. a free service
3. 1. annual essay competition 2. can't predict 3. a personal statement 4. career goals
    5. submit my transcript
4. 1. To be frank 2. what's the matter 3. why I'm attracted to the idea 4. how to sort the
    cities 5. the relationship between them 6. help me get started.

01

남 : 축하해, 네가 교수 심사 위원회의 위원으로 선출되었다는 소식을 들었단다!

여 : 네, 감사합니다… 실은 위원회의 학생단 대표로도 선출되었어요.

남 : 그럼 두 배로 축하해줘야겠네!

여 : 감사합니다. 그런데 좀 벅차기도 해요. 학교에서 학생들을 가르칠 교수님을 뽑는 것은 정말 대단한 일이잖아
    요. 어쨌든 자격이 없는 분들을 뽑으면 안되니까요.

남 : 무슨 말인지 알겠구나. 그렇지만 네가 잘 해낼 거라 생각해. 너에게 아주 좋은 기회이기도 하고. 이력서를 쓸
    때도 꽤 큰 도움이 될 거야. 위원회에서의 활동 경험을 내 수업 시간에 활용할 수도 있을 거야. 캠퍼스 여론
    조사를 하고 결과를 분석해서 리포트에 첨부할 수도 있지.

여 : 그렇게 말씀해주시니 기분이 좋아지는 것 같아요!

어휘 elect 선출하다 faculty 교수단 screen 심사하다, 가려내다 committee 위원회 representative 대표자
    overwhelm 압도하다 definitely 확실히 opportunity 기회 resume 이력서 conduct 수행하다 opinion poll
    여론 조사 analyze 분석하다

1. 학생은 교수 심사 위원회에서 어떤 일을 하게 되는가?
    Ⓐ 교수들의 연구 실적을 평가할 것이다.
    Ⓑ 여론 조사를 실시할 것이다.
    Ⓒ 교수 채용 과정에 참여할 것이다.
    Ⓓ 학생들의 리포트를 검토할 것이다.

남 : 교수님의 미적분학 수업에 관해 조언 좀 구할 수 있을까요?

여 : 그럼, 무슨 일이니?

남 : 미적분학 강의를 공부하는 게 좀 힘들어요. 수업 중에는 개념을 모두 이해하겠는데요, 수업이 끝나면 다 잊어버려요.

여 : 미적분학 스터디 그룹에 참여해본 적이 있니? 도서관에서 화요일 저녁마다 모임이 있더구나.

남 : 네, 몇 번 정도요, 하지만 항상 잡담만 하다가 끝나버리는데다가 공부도 별로 못했어요.

여 : 음, 그럼 별로 안 좋겠다. 학교에 있는 개별 지도(과외) 센터는 어떠니? 가본 적이 있니?

남 : 아뇨, 그 곳이 무료로 진행되는 곳인지 잘 모르겠어요. 개별 지도를 받는데 돈을 많이 들일 수 없어요.

여 : 네 말대로 무료는 아니지만, 그렇게 비싸지도 않단다. 한 번 확인해보도록 해. 대학원생들에게 도움을 받을 수 있어. 큰 도움이 될 거란다.

남 : 알겠습니다!

어휘 calculus 미적분학 end up ~ing 결국 ~하게 되다 free 무료의 graduate 대학원생

2. 교수가 학생에게 하라고 제안하는 것은 무엇인가? 2개의 답을 클릭하시오.
   Ⓐ 과외 수업 듣기
   Ⓑ 도서관에서 책 빌리기
   Ⓒ 스터디 그룹 참여
   Ⓓ 대학원 입학

여 : Carlos, 너에게 전해줄 좋은 소식이 있단다!

남 : 그게 뭔데요?

여 : 매년 열리는 작문 대회 기억하니? 영문학과의 작문 심사 위원회에서 네 글을 선정했단다. 네 작품이 전국 작문 대회에 출품될 거야.

남 : 정말 잘됐네요! 믿을 수가 없어요!

여 : 정말이란다. 심사 위원들 모두 네 글이 굉장히 잘 쓰여졌다고 생각했어. 정말 잘 쓰여졌단다. 넌 정말 재능이 많아. 물론, 네 글이 1등을 할 수 있을지는 모르겠지만, 자부심을 가지렴.

남 : 정말 굉장해요! 그럼 이제 뭘 해야 하죠?

여 : 음, 자기 소개서를 써내야 해. 읽는 사람이 네가 누구인지를 알 수 있도록 글을 써야 해. 네 가족과 장래 목표, 관심사 등… 네가 보기에 중요하다고 생각되는 것들에 관해 쓰면 된단다.

남 : 네! 언제까지 제출하면 되죠?

여 : 이번 주 금요일까지 나에게 가져올 수 있겠니?

남 : 그럼요! 또 다른 건 없나요?

여 : 사실은 필요한 게 있단다. 추천서가 필요한데, 그건 걱정할 필요 없어. Frederick 교수에게 내가 한 부를 써 달라고 부탁 드렸단다.

남 : 정말 감사 드려요! 아, 성적 증명서 같은 것은 제출 안 해도 되나요?

여 : 아니, 그럴 필요는 없단다.

어휘 committee 위원회 talent 재능 personal statement 자기 소개서, 이력서 a letter of recommendation 추천서

3. 학생이 에세이와 함께 대회에 제출해야 하는 것은 무엇인가? 2개의 답을 클릭하시오.
   Ⓐ 사진
   Ⓑ 추천서
   Ⓒ 자기 소개서
   Ⓓ 성적 증명서

04

남 : 논문 계획서는 잘 되어가고 있니?

여 : 어, 제가 조언을 좀 구할 수 있을까요? 솔직히 말씀 드리면, 잘 되어가고 있지는 않아요.

남 : 그래, 무슨 문제니?

여 : 제가 하고 싶은 건 미국 중소 도시의 임금을 살펴보고 부동산 가격과 비교해보는 거에요.

남 : 올해 부동산 시장에서 일어나고 있는 일들을 고려해보면, 참 흥미로운 계획이구나.

여 : 그래서 그 아이디어에 관심을 갖게 되었어요. 그런데 도시들을 어떻게 분류해야 할지 잘 모르겠어요.

남 : 그럼 두 가지 방향으로 잡아보렴. 인구와 성장률로 분류하는 거지. 서로 아주 다른 결과가 나오겠지만, 둘 사이의 관계를 파악할 줄도 알아야 해. 대도시 지역의 통계도 알아보도록 해.

여 : 명심하겠습니다. 시작하는데 큰 도움이 될 것 같아요.

어휘 wage 임금 real estate 부동산 sort 분류하다 growth rate 성장률 statistics 통계 metropolitan 대도시의

4. 도시를 분류하기 위해 학생은 어떤 데이터를 참조해야 하는가? 2개의 답을 클릭하시오.
   Ⓐ 도시의 평균 임금
   Ⓑ 도시의 인구
   Ⓒ 도시의 성장률
   Ⓓ 도시의 부동산 가격

Service Encounters
1. Ⓑ **2.** Ⓓ **3.** Ⓑ, Ⓓ **4.** Ⓒ

Dictation: Service Encounters
1. 1. drop off 2. any computer-related courses? 3. its hiring policies 4. not likely 5. make any exceptions

2. 1.request permission 2. arranging a movie night 3. wasn't a limit 4. public bulletin boards 5. confirm your permission

3. 1. in the reference section 2. lend them out 3. make copies of the pages 4. run out of time 5. out of print

4. 1. pick up 2. coming for the performance 3. aren't far from 4. knee surgery 5. get towed 6. should have gotten

01

남 : 안녕하세요, 지원서를 제출하러 왔습니다.

여 : 컴퓨터 센터 근무를 지원하는 건가요?

남 : 네. 학교 웹사이트에 보니까 모집 공고가 났던걸요?

여 : 맞아요, 그럼 학생 전공은 무엇인가요?

남 : 영문학을 전공하고 있습니다.

여 : 영문학이라… 컴퓨터 관련 강의는 들어본 적 있나요?

남 : 아뇨, 강의를 수강한 적은 없지만, 컴퓨터에 대해서는 잘 알아요. 무슨 문제라도 있나요?

여 : 음, 센터에서 고용 정책을 얼마 전에 바꾸었어요. 학생 직원들은 이 곳에서 일하기 전에 초급 강의를 수강하고 통과해야 해요.

남 : 그건 몰랐어요. 하지만 컴퓨터에 관해 이미 잘 알고 있는 사람은 어떡해요? 다른 방법은 없나요?

여 : 별 가망성이 없을 것 같아요. 새로 시행되는 정책이라 센터장님께서 예외를 두고 싶어하시지는 않을 것 같아요. 그렇지만 학생의 지원서는 받아두도록 할게요.

남 : 어쨌든 도와주셔서 감사합니다.

어휘 application 지원서 hire 고용하다 major 전공 policy 정책 exception 예외

1. 컴퓨터 센터에서 일하기 위해 필요한 것은 무엇인가?
   Ⓐ 학교에 풀타임 학생으로 등록하는 것
   Ⓑ 기초 컴퓨터 강의를 듣는 것
   Ⓒ 컴퓨터 관련 과목을 전공하는 것
   Ⓓ 센터장과 이야기 하는 것

02

여 : 제가 제대로 찾아온 건지 잘 모르겠는데요, 캠퍼스에 포스터를 붙이려고 하는데 승인을 받으려고요.

남 : 아, 무슨 행사인가요?

여 : 영화 행사를 준비하고 있어요.

남 : 그렇군요, 서류 양식을 작성해야 하는데, 학생 이름과 단체 이름, 포스터의 종류와 매수, 포스터 부착 기간을 적도록 해요.

여 : 알겠습니다.

남 : 포스터를 모두 인쇄해놓았나요?

여 : 이제 하려고요. 포스터 매수에 제한에 있는지 먼저 확인하고 싶었어요. 만약 50장만 붙일 수 있는데 100장을 인쇄하는 건 말이 안 되잖아요.

남 : 잘 생각했어요. 그리고 학생 예상대로 제한이 있어요. 캠퍼스에 공용 게시판이 27개 밖에 없으니까, 100장이나 인쇄하면 안 되겠죠!

여 : 알려주셔서 감사합니다. 여기 양식을 다 적었어요. 이제 무얼 하면 되죠?

남 : 학생에게 이메일을 보내서 승인 결과를 알려줄 거에요.

여 : 감사합니다!

어휘 put up 붙이다 occasion 행사, 경우 arrange 준비하다 fill out 작성하다 bulletin board 게시판

2. 다음 중 어느 것이 학생이 알려주어야 하는 정보가 아닌가?
   Ⓐ 게시 기간
   Ⓑ 주최 단체
   Ⓒ 이메일 주소
   Ⓓ 전화 번호

03

남 : 실례지만, 아이슬란드어 사전과 무용담 책에 대해 질문이 있습니다. 두 개 모두 관내 열람 도서 섹션에 있는

데요, 제가 지금 리포트를 쓰고 있는 중이라 자료 조사를 위해 꼭 필요해요.

여 : 이해는 가지만, 참고 도서기 때문에 대출이 불가능해요.

남 : 하지만 정말 필요하단 말이에요! 어쩌면 좋죠?

여 : 다른 학생들이 하는 것과 똑같이 해야죠. 도서관에서만 책을 이용하고, 만약 시간이 부족하다면 필요한 페이지를 복사하도록 해요.

남 : 그렇지만 이제 도서관이 문 닫을 시간인걸요!

여 : 그럼 내일 오전 일찍 다시 오도록 해요. 미안하지만, 학생이 요청한 책들은 교환해서 비치해두기가 쉽지 않아요. 무용담 책은 절판된 상태이기도 하고요. 이 책들이 도서관 밖으로 반출되어서는 안 됩니다.

남 : 알겠습니다. 그럼 내일 다시 올게요.

어휘 Icelandic 아이슬란드어의 saga 무용담, 전설 reference 참고 도서(대출 금지의 관내 열람 도서) run out of ~을 다 써 버리다, ~이 떨어지다

3. 필요로 하는 책을 이용하기 위해 학생은 무엇을 할 것인가? 2개의 답을 클릭하시오.

　Ⓐ 자료 조사를 위하 대출한다

　Ⓑ 도서관에서 읽는다

　Ⓒ 무용담 책을 프린트한다

　Ⓓ 일부 페이지를 복사한다

04

남 : 안녕하세요, 저희 부모님께서 사용하실 주차 허가증이 필요해서 왔습니다.

여 : 학교에 학생을 방문하러 오시는 건가요?

남 : 네. 제가 오케스트라 단원인데요, 이번 주말에 있을 공연을 관람하러 오시는 거에요.

여 : 그럼 일반 방문객 주차장을 이용하시면 될 텐데요? 연주회장에서도 그리 멀지 않고요.

남 : 아, 저희 아버지께서 지난 주에 무릎 수술을 받으셔서 아직 먼 곳까지 잘 걷지 못하세요.

여 : 어머, 그럼 진작 말해주지 그랬어요? 학생 부모님께서 공인 허가증을 가지고 계시면 장애인 주차 구역에 주차하실 수 있어요. 주차하실 때 자동차 계기반 위에 허가증을 놓아두시라고 말씀 드리도록 해요. 그렇게 하면 주차 위반 딱지를 떼일 일도 없고, 견인되는 일도 없을 거에요.

남 : 제가 특별 허가증 같은 것을 발급받아야 하는 줄 알았어요.

여 : 학생이 장애인이라 장애인 주차 구역을 이용해야 한다면, 허가증을 발급받아야 해요. 하지만 학생 부모님께서는 단지 공연을 보러 오시는 거니까요…

남 : 실은 주말 내내 계실 거에요.

여 : 그래요, 주말이요. 병원이나 운전면허시험 관리 공단에서 발급받은 공인 허가증만 지참하시면 됩니다. 아주 간단하죠.

남 : 정말 간단하네요!

어휘 permit 허가증 knee 무릎 surgery 수술 handicapped 장애가 있는 dashboard 자동차 계기반 tow 견인하다

4. 학생의 부모는 왜 학교로 찾아오는가?

　Ⓐ 학생이 부모님을 보고 싶어 한다.

　Ⓑ 학생이 최근어 무릎 수술을 받았다.

　Ⓒ 학생이 공연을 할 것이다.

　Ⓓ 학생이 퇴원할 것이다.

Lectures
1. 1. ⓒ 2. Ⓐ **2.** 1. Ⓐ 2. ⓒ 3. Ⓑ

Dictation: Lectures
1. 1. far from the only species 2. to be exact 3. native to South America 4. they generate electricity 5. an evolutionary standpoint 6. disrupt the functioning 7. stun their prey 8. harm a human being
2. 1. children acquire language 2. learn vocabulary 3. not memorize lists of words 4. in such a short time 5. an association is made 6. figure out the meaning 7. each new exposure to

01 어류학 수업

P : 내 생각에 우리 모두 전기뱀장어에 관해 어느 정도 잘 알고 있을 것 같군요. 수족관에 가본 적이 있는 사람이나 생물학을 공부한 사람이라면, 본 적도 있을 거에요. 사진을 통해서 보았을 수도 있고 실물을 본 적도 있겠죠. 전기뱀장어가 전기 물고기 가운데 가장 잘 알려져 있지만, 그렇다고 해서 전기를 발산하는 유일한 물고기는 아니에요. 먼저 전기뱀장어는 뱀장어가 아니라는 것부터 짚고 넘어가야겠군요. 전기뱀장어는 엄밀히 말하자면 뒷날개고기의 일종이에요. 전기 물고기는 남아메리카에 서식하는 어류입니다. 이 물고기들이 공통적으로 가지고 있는 특징은 바로 전기를 일으키는 능력이에요. 발전 기관을 통해 전기를 일으키는데, 이 기관에는 방전에 쓰이는 특수 근육과 신경 세포가 들어있어요. 발전 기관은 대개 몸의 꼬리 쪽에 있죠. 만약 이 발전 기관이 머리에 있다면 뇌의 기능을 방해할 수 있으니, 진화론적인 관점에서 보자면 이해가 가는 부분이죠. 매번 전기를 일으킬 때마다 의식을 잃게 된다면, 포식자의 위험에서 벗어날 수도 없잖아요?

먹잇감을 기절시킬 수 있을 만큼 강한 전류를 발생시키는 전기 물고기는 몇 종에 불과해요. 전기뱀장어는 이런 강한 전류를 발생시킬 수 있고, 전기메기와 전기가오리도 마찬가지에요. 전기뱀장어는 특히 몸의 약 80%가 발전 기능에 사용된다는 점에서 특이하죠. 극판을 통해 전기를 발생시키는 배터리와 마찬가지로, 전기뱀장어는 electroplaques라는 세포를 가지고 있어요. 전기뱀장어는 인간을 해칠 수 있을 정도의 강한 전류를 흘려 보내는데, 호주를 포함한 일부 국가는 사실상 전기뱀장어 종을 법으로 금지시켰어요. 너무 위험하다는 것이죠.

어휘 species 종 aquarium 수족관 biology 생물학 point out 지적하다 to be exact 엄밀히 말하면 have in common 공통점을 가지다 generate 발생시키다 specialized 특수화된 muscle 근육 nerve cell 신경 세포 emit 방출하다 electric discharge 방전 tail 꼬리 evolutionary 진화론적인 standpoint 관점, 견지 disrupt 방해하다 predator 포식자 unconscious 무의식의 stun 기절시키다 prey 먹이 devoted to ~에 할애한 plate 전극 outlaw 불법화하다

1. 다음 중 어느 것이 전기 물고기의 발전 기관에 관해 맞는가?
   Ⓐ 물고기가 의식을 잃게 만든다.
   Ⓑ 먹이를 공격하는데 쓸모가 없다.
   ⓒ 몸의 끝부분 가까이에 있다.
   Ⓓ 뇌 기능을 저하시킨다.

2. 전기뱀장어 몸의 어느 정도가 전기 생산에 이용되는가?
   Ⓐ 4/5(80%)
   Ⓑ 20%
   ⓒ 절반(50%)
   Ⓓ 18%

02 심리학 수업

P : 발달 심리학에서 흥미로운 주제 중 하나가 바로 언어 습득 과정입니다. 아이들이 언어를 습득하는 방법에 대한 연구가 수십 년간 광범위하게 진행되었고, 그 결과 매우 흥미로운 것들을 알게 되었죠. 언어학자들과 심리학자들은 특히 '빠른 어휘 습득 전략(fast mapping)' 이란 분야에 관심을 두고 있는데, 이 전략은 아이들이 언어를 배우는 한 방법이다. 여러분들도 알다시피, 아이들은 주변 환경에서 대부분의 어휘를 습득해요. 후에 초등학교에 들어가면, 수업을 통해서 어휘를 배우죠. 하지만, 어린 아이들이 어휘 목록을 암기하는 것은 아니에요. 그렇다면, 아이들이 어떻게 그 많은 어휘들을 그렇게 짧은 시간 안에 습득할 수 있는 걸까요? '빠른 어휘 습득 전략' 으로 이 과정을 설명할 수 있어요.
어린 아이가 자신의 어휘 목록에 있는 단어들과는 다른 단어인 새로운 단어를 처음으로 듣게 되면, 연상작용이 일어납니다. 아이는 그 새로운 단어가 무엇을 의미하는지 추측을 하게 되죠. 즉, 아이는 다른 물체와 그 단어를 관련 지어서 한 번 그 단어를 들은 후에 그 의미를 이해할 수 있어요. '빠른 어휘 습득 전략' 에서는 딱 한 번, 한 번만 들으면 되죠. 나중에, 아이가 똑같은 단어를 다시 들을 때, 단어의 의미가 더 명확해지게 됩니다. 아이는 기본적인 의미를 바로 이해할 수 있고, 곧 그 단어를 완벽하게 이해할 수 있게 되는 거죠.

어휘 subject 주제 acquisition 습득 decade 십년 linguist 언어학자 memorize 암기하다 lexicon 어휘 목록
association 연상 작용 hypothesis 가설, 추측 exposure 노출 clarify 명확하게 하다

1. 발달 심리학자들은 왜 '빠른 어휘 습득 전략' 에 관심을 가지는가?
   Ⓐ 아이들의 빠른 어휘력 증대를 설명하기 때문에
   Ⓑ 초등학교 시기에 일어나는 현상이기 때문에
   Ⓒ 아이들의 암기력이 얼마나 좋은지를 보여주기 때문에
   Ⓓ 언어학에서도 중요한 분야이기 때문에

2. 어린 아이들은 어휘의 대부분을 어디에서 배우는가?
   Ⓐ 학교에서
   Ⓑ 지도에서
   Ⓒ 주변 환경에서
   Ⓓ 어휘 목록에서

3. 어린 아이가 새로운 단어를 들으면 무슨 일이 일어나는가?
   Ⓐ 그 단어가 정확히 무슨 의미인지 즉시 이해한다.
   Ⓑ 그 단어와 이미 알고 있는 것을 관련시켜 생각한다.
   Ⓒ 그 단어와 자신의 어휘 목록에 있는 단어를 혼동한다.
   Ⓓ 처음에는 그 단어를 암기하려고 하지 않는다.

Practice

[1-5] **1.** Ⓓ   **2.** Ⓒ   **3.** Ⓒ   **4.** Ⓐ   **5.** Mentioned – Ⓑ, Ⓓ Not Mentioned – Ⓐ, Ⓒ
[6-11] **6.** Ⓓ   **7.** Ⓒ   **8.** Ⓓ   **9.** Ⓑ   **10.** Ⓑ   **11.** Copyright – Ⓐ, Trademark – Ⓓ,
   Patent – Ⓑ, Trade secret – Ⓒ

[문제 1-5] Listen to part of a conversation at a cafeteria.

W : Mr. Harford, uh, I need to switch my day off next week. Do you think it's OK?

M : What's going on? I just posted the schedule for the next two weeks.

W : I know, and when I gave you my schedule, I thought it would be all right.

M : So is there any emergency or something?

W : Um, I'm doing a group project in my sociology class, and we have to visit two community organizations. Monday's the only day most people can go.

M : I see. The thing is Monday is our busiest day. You know that, too. Both lunch and dinner are always frantic.

W : I'm aware of that. But can I ask if someone would switch with me?

M : We're a little short-staffed right now. I'm not sure anyone is available for that.

W : Um, well, couldn't you hire someone?

M : 3.In a perfect world, yes. But the semester's three-quarters over, and most students aren't looking for jobs right now. Plus, isn't it a little bit much to ask? Hire somebody just so you can have the day off?

W : I'm sorry. This is an important project, though. It counts for a fourth of our grade for the semester.

M : Well, what am I supposed to do about it? I want to help you, but I have a cafeteria to run. I understand your situation, but can't give you the day off if it's not an emergency. There's no one to cover for you.

W : Well, can I at least post a notice asking for people to switch shifts with me?

M : All right. I also think you should talk to the people in your group. Maybe you need to do the project over a couple of different days, instead of all going together at the same time.

W : Yeah, you've got a point there. There are four of us, and one other person has to reschedule something that day. I'll think it over.

여 : Harford씨, 제가 다음 주에 쉬는 날을 바꾸어야 할 것 같아요. 그렇게 해도 될까요?

남 : 무슨 일이니? 방금 전에 다음 2주간 근무시간표를 붙였는데.

여 : 알고 있는데요, 제 스케줄을 알려 드릴 때는 아무 문제가 없을 거라 생각했어요.

남 : 무슨 급한 일이라도 있는 거니?

여 : 그게 말이죠, 제가 사회학 시간에 그룹 프로젝트를 하고 있는데요, 지역사회단체 2 곳을 방문해야 해요. 팀원들 대부분이 갈 수 있는 날이 월요일 밖에 없어서요.

남 : 그렇구나. 문제는 월요일이 가장 바쁜 날이라는 거야. 너도 그 점은 잘 알고 있잖니. 점심 시간과 저녁 시간 모두 정신 없이 바쁘잖아.

여 : 잘 알고 있어요. 그렇지만 저랑 근무 날을 바꿀 사람이 있을지 여쭤봐도 될까요?

남 : 지금 일손이 좀 부족해서 말이지. 바꿔줄 사람이 있을지 잘 모르겠다.

여 : 사람을 더 고용할 수는 없었나요?

남 : 완벽한 세상이라면 그럴 수 있었겠지. 하지만 학기도 이미 3/4이나 지나갔고, 현재 일자리를 구하는 학생도 거의 없어. 그리고, 그건 좀 지나친 요구 같지 않니? 네가 근무를 쉴 수 있도록 새로운 사람을 채용하라고?

여 : 죄송해요. 그렇지만 정말 중요한 프로젝트에요. 이번 학기 성적의 1/4이나 차지하는 걸요.

남 : 그래서 나보고 어떡하라는 말이니? 도와주고는 싶지만, 카페테리아를 운영해야 하잖니. 네 상황은 이해하지만, 긴급 상황이 아니라면 쉽게 해 줄 수 없을 것 같구나. 너 대신에 일할 사람이 없어.

여 : 저와 교대 시간을 바꾸어 줄 사람이 있을지 게시판에 공고물을 붙여도 될까요?

남 : 그렇게 하렴. 그리고 팀원들과도 이야기를 해보도록 해. 모두 같은 시간에 한꺼번에 가는 대신, 다른 날에 나누어 갈 수도 있지.

여 : 네, 맞는 말씀이에요. 모두 4명인데, 저 말고도 그날 다른 일이 있는 아이가 있었어요. 한 번 생각해볼게요.

어휘 switch 바꾸다 post 붙이다, 게시하다 emergency 급한 일, 응급 사태 sociology 사회학 organization 단체 frantic 광란의 short-staffed 직원 부족의 count for 가치가 있다, 수가 ~이 되다 notice 공고, 게시물

  ALL ABOUT JUNIOR TOEFL

Topic: Switch day off 비번 바꾸기

1. Student: want to take Monday off 학생: 월요일에 쉬고 싶음
   – group project in sociology 사회학 수업 그룹 프로젝트
   – visit com. org 지역 단체를 방문해야 함
2. Manager: X allowed 매니저: 허락해 줄 수 없음
   – Mon is busiest 월요일이 가장 바쁨
   – short-staffed 일손이 부족함
3. Suggestion 제안
   – student: post notice for switching shift 학생: 교대 시간을 바꿀 수 있는지 게시물 부착
   – manager: reschedule project trip 매니저: 프로젝트 수행 날짜를 재조정하기

1. 학생이 카페테리아 매니저와 이 대화를 나누는 이유는 무엇인가?
   Ⓐ 학생은 지역 단체에서 일자리를 구할 것이다.
   Ⓑ 학생은 함께 일하는 친구를 대신하여 일하기를 원한다.
   Ⓒ 학생은 매니저가 일하는 사람을 더 채용하기를 원한다.
   Ⓓ 학생은 수업 프로젝트를 위해 근무를 하루 쉬고 싶어한다.
   해설 학생은 지역 단체에서 사회학 수업 프로젝트를 수행하기 위해 월요일 근무를 바꾸고 싶어한다.
   정답 Ⓓ

2. 왜 매니저는 학생이 월요일에 쉬도록 허락해주지 못하는가?
   Ⓐ 학생은 이미 며칠을 쉬었다.
   Ⓑ 매니저에게 그 문제를 결정할 권한이 없다.
   Ⓒ 월요일에는 카페테리아가 사람들로 상당히 붐빈다.
   Ⓓ 근무 스케줄이 바뀌는 일은 없다.
   해설 매니저에 따르면 월요일이 가장 바쁜 날이기 때문에 허락해줄 수 없다. 스크립트의 our busiest day가 보기에서 heavily crowded로 paraphrase 되어 있다. 학생과 근무 시간을 바꿀 사람이 있으면 바꾸어도 되기 때문에 보기 Ⓓ는 오답이다.
   정답 Ⓒ

대화의 일부를 다시 들으시오. 그러고 나서 질문에 답하시오.

3. 남자가 이것을 말할 때 암시하는 것은 무엇인가? 

   M : In a perfect world, yes.
   Ⓐ 학생의 생각이 훌륭하다.
   Ⓑ 남자는 기꺼이 일하는 사람을 채용할 것이다.
   Ⓒ 현재 사람을 고용하는 것이 불가능하다.
   Ⓓ 세상은 완벽한 곳이다.
   해설 매니저가 일손이 부족해서 학생의 요구를 받아줄 수 없을 것 같다고 하자 학생이 직원을 더 채용할 수는 없었냐고 물었다. 이에 매니저가 완벽한 세상에서라면 그럴 수 있었을 것이라고 답했는데, 이는 현재 직원을 더 뽑을 수 없다는 것을 돌려서 말하고 있는 것이다.
   정답 Ⓒ

4. 왜 매니저는 신규 직원을 뽑는데 곤란을 겪을 것 같은가?
  Ⓐ 학기말에는 학생들이 프로젝트와 시험으로 바쁘다.
  Ⓑ 학생들 사이에 카페테리아 근무가 인기가 없다.
  Ⓒ 학생들은 방학 때 쓸 돈이 필요한데, 카페테리아 보수가 별로 좋지 않다.
  Ⓓ 카페테리아의 근무 조건이 안 좋다.
  해설 학기가 이미 3/4이나 지났고 이맘때는 학생들이 일자리를 구하지 않는다고 하였다. 이를 통해 학기말에는
      학생들이 각종 과제물과 시험으로 바쁠 것임을 알 수 있다.
  정답 Ⓐ

5. 대화에서, 화자들은 스케줄 문제에 대한 해결책에 대해 이야기를 나누고 있다. 아래 표의 각 보기가 이러한 해결
  책에 속하는지 표시하시오. 각 보기에 맞는 칸에 클릭하시오.

	Mentioned	Not Mentioned
Ⓐ 교수에게 프로젝트 수행 연장을 요청하기		
Ⓑ 그룹 프로젝트 수행 날짜를 조정하기		
Ⓒ 학생의 친구가 하룻동안 대신 일하도록 하기		
Ⓓ 교대 시간을 바꾸어 줄 사람이 있는지 게시판에 메모를 붙이기		

  해설 학생이 교대 시간을 바꾸어줄 사람이 있는지 알아보기 위해 게시물을 붙여도 되는지를 물었고, 매니저는 지
      역 단체에 같은 날 한꺼번에 가는 대신, 다른 날에 나누어 갈 것을 제안하고 있다.
  정답 Mentioned - Ⓑ, Ⓓ Not mentioned - Ⓐ, Ⓒ

[문제 6-11] Listen to part of a lecture in a law class.

P(M) : Today I'm going to introduce the concept of intellectual property rights, or IP. This is an
       important concept, because it touches on so many areas that we take for granted. We'll talk
       a little about the pros and the cons, as well. There are some interesting arguments against
       the current framework of IP laws. First of all, let's have a quick overview. IP – somebody tell
       us what it means.

S(W) : It's got something to do with copyrights and patents, right?

P : Yes, those are a big part of it. Copyrights and patents are two legal rights we would consider
    intellectual property. Basically, IP pertains to the ways ideas and information can be put to
    use.

S : So IP is the issue in all the controversy about illegal movie and music downloading?

P : Good observation. That's right. Who really owns that music? As you probably know, when
    an author writes a book, the money goes to several places. The author gets a percentage.
    So does the publisher. The distributor who transports the books from the publisher to the
    bookstore gets a cut, and of course the bookstore keeps some of the money as well. But if
    you download a book off the Internet, none of these people earn the money they're
    depending on. The same goes for music, movies, software, and anything else of this nature.
    All these things are protected by copyright, meaning that there is a legal restriction on who
    can reproduce and distribute them.

    A patent is similar, but it pertains to inventions and processes. 8·Think of all the
    wonderful things Thomas Edison invented: electricity generation and distribution systems,
    light bulbs, and so on. He held over 1000 patents in the United States alone. Each patent

represents an invention or some unique, new type of process. It can even be a reproducible improvement to an existing invention or system. Again, as we discussed with the copyright, the idea behind a patent is to protect the inventor's work.

Now, if you think about the competitive nature of Western capitalism, can anyone see the slight contradiction in the reasoning behind IP laws?

S : Aren't they creating monopolies?

P : Excellent! Yes, that is the argument against existing IP laws. Normally, governments whose policies are based on the principles of capitalism do not like monopolies. But those laws give the inventor, the author, and the musician a sort of monopoly. In this case, the U.S. government calls it a *limited monopoly*. This is different from a regular monopoly in one important way: in a true monopoly, one company is controlling the entire market, its competitors, for a product or service. In an IP situation, there is no real competition, because the product or service is unique. After all, two different people can't write and sell the same book, right? Or make the exact same movie?

There are a few other examples of IP rights. There's the trademark, which is a symbol used to identify a product or to distinguish one business from the next. Industrial design rights protect the design of manufactured items. And trade secrets are recognized as the information that businesses use in order to conduct their operations. If that information is stolen, it could harm the business, so it enjoys legal protection. Any questions?

P : 오늘은 IP라고도 하는 지적재산권의 개념에 관해 알아보는 시간을 갖겠어요. 지적재산권은 그동안 우리가 당연시해왔던 많은 부분과 관련이 있기 때문에 꼭 알아두어야 할 중요한 개념이죠. 또한 지적재산권에 관한 찬반 견해에 관해서도 알아보겠어요. 현재의 지적재산권법 구조에 대한 반대론도 있죠. 먼저, 이 지적재산권이란 것이 무엇인지 짚고 넘어가도록 합시다. 지적재산권이 무엇인지 누가 한번 말해보도록 해요.

S : 저작권과 특허와 관련이 있는 것이죠?

P : 맞아요, 그 둘이 지적재산권을 구성하는 일부죠. 저작권과 특허는 우리가 지적재산권으로 간주하는 법적 권리에 해당해요. 원래 지적재산권은 아이디어와 정보가 사용 가능하게 되는 방식과 관련이 있어요.

S : 그럼 지적재산권은 영화와 음악의 불법 다운로드에 대한 모든 논쟁의 중심에 있겠네요?

P : 좋은 지적이군요. 맞는 말이에요. 실제로 음악을 소유하고 있는 사람은 누구일까요? 여러분도 알고 있겠지만, 작가가 책을 쓰면, 그로 인해 생기는 이익은 여러 곳으로 가게 되죠. 작가는 일정 퍼센티지를 갖게 됩니다. 출판사도 마찬가지고요. 출판사에서 책을 공급받아 서점으로 배포하는 유통업자 역시 이윤을 남기고, 서점 역시 이익을 챙기죠. 하지만 여러분이 인터넷에서 책을 다운로드 하게 되면, 이들은 아무도 자신들의 몫을 챙기지 못하게 됩니다. 음악과 영화, 소프트웨어, 그 밖에 이런 종류의 모든 경우에도 마찬가지죠. 이 모든 것들이 저작권의 보호를 받게 되는데, 바로 이러한 자료들을 복제하고 배포하는데 법적인 제한이 뒤따른다는 말이죠.

특허도 이와 비슷한데, 특허는 발명 및 만들어내는 방법과 관련이 있어요. Thomas Edison(토마스 에디슨)이 발명한 위대한 발명품들을 생각해봐요. 전력 생산과 배전 시스템, 백열 전구와 그 외 많은 것들 말이에요. 에디슨은 미국에서만 1000개 이상의 특허를 냈어요. 각각의 특허는 발명품 또는 이 세상에 유일한 새로운 제작 방식을 나타내요. 이미 존재하는 발명품이나 시스템을 재현 가능한 방식으로 개량하는 것 역시 특허라고 할 수 있어요. 저작권을 설명하며 언급했듯, 특허를 인정해주는 것은 발명가의 연구를 보호하기 위해서입니다.

그렇다면, 서구 자본주의의 본질을 이루는 경쟁 원리를 생각해볼 때, 지적재산권법이 가지고 있는 모순점에 대해 말해볼 사람이 있나요?

S : 독점이 생겨나지 않나요?

P : 그렇죠! 바로 그 점이 현행 지적재산권법을 반대하는 사람들의 주장이에요. 일반적으로 자본주의 원리를 따르는 국가는 독점을 좋아하지 않아요. 하지만 지적재산권법은 발명가와 작가, 음악가들에게 일종의 독점을 허용해줘

요. 이 경우를 미국 정부는 '제한적인 독점'이라고 부르고 있어요. 이는 일반 독점과는 큰 차이점을 보이는데, 본래의 독점에서는 한 회사가 그들이 제공하는 제품이나 서비스에 대해 시장 전체, 즉, 경쟁사를 장악하죠. 지적 재산권의 경우에는 경쟁이 존재하지 않는데, 바로 해당 제품과 서비스가 이 세상에서 유일한 것이기 때문이에요. 2명의 다른 사람이 똑같은 책을 써서 팔게 되는 일은 없잖아요? 똑같은 영화를 만드는 것도 그렇겠죠?

지적재산권에는 또 다른 것들도 있어요. 제품을 식별 가능하게 해주고 한 회사를 다른 회사와 구별하게 해주는 상표권이 있죠. 산업디자인권은 제조 물품의 디자인을 보호해줘요. 기업 비밀은 기업이 영업 활동을 하기 위해 사용하는 정보로 인정되는 거에요. 이러한 정보가 유출되면 기업이 막대한 피해를 입기 때문에 이 역시 법의 보호를 받고 있어요. 질문 있는 사람?

어휘 intellectual property rights 지적재산권 take A for granted A를 당연하게 여기다 pros and cons 찬반 argument against ~에 대한 반대론 current 현재의 overview 개관 copyrights 저작권 patent 특허 pertain to ~와 관련이 있다 put to use 이용하다 controversy 논쟁 author 작가 distributor 유통업자, 배급업자 restriction 제한 reproduce 복제하다 invention 발명 light bulb 백열 전구 improvement 개량, 개선 competitive 경쟁에 의한 capitalism 자본주의 contradiction 모순, 부정 monopoly 독점 trademark 상표 distinguish 구별하다 conduct 수행하다

Note-taking

Topic: IP 지적재산권

1. Copyright 저작권
   - illegal download 불법 다운로드
   - book, music, movie, software, etc. 책, 음악, 영화, 소프트웨어 등
   - legal restriction on repro. & distr. 복제와 배포에 법적 제한
2. Patent 특허
   - invention & process 발명과 제작 방법
   - e.g. Edison 예. 에디슨
3. Cons 반대
   - limited monopoly 제한적인 독점
   - X competition ← unique 경쟁 대상이 없음
4. Others 기타 지적재산권
   - trademark: symbol 상표권: 심벌
   - indus. design 산업 디자인
   - trade secret 기업 비밀

6. 오늘 강의의 주제는 무엇인가?
   Ⓐ 저작권과 특허
   Ⓑ 불법 다운로드
   Ⓒ 제한적인 독점
   Ⓓ 지적재산권

해설 교수는 지적재산권의 개념과 종류 등에 관해 강의를 하고 있다. 강의의 앞부분만 잘 들어도 답을 쉽게 고를 수 있다. 보기 Ⓐ의 저작권과 특허는 지적재산권에 해당하는 법적 권리로 언급한 것으로서, 지적재산권에 속하는 개념이다. 주제로는 부족하다.

정답 Ⓓ

7. 책이 출간될 때, 수익을 올리지 못하는 사람은 누구인가?
   Ⓐ 유통업자
   Ⓑ 작가
   Ⓒ 독자
   Ⓓ 출판사
   해설 강의에 따르면, 책이 출간될 때의 수익은 작가, 출판사, 유통업자, 서점이 나누어 갖는다.
   정답 Ⓒ

강의의 일부를 다시 들으시오. 그러고 나서 질문에 답하시오.

8. 교수는 왜 토마스 에디슨을 언급하는가? 
Think of all the wonderful things Thomas Edison invented: electricity generation and distribution systems, light bulbs, and so on.
   Ⓐ 에디슨이 위대한 발명가였다는 것을 강조하기 위해
   Ⓑ 역사상 위대한 발명품의 예를 들기 위해
   Ⓒ 에디슨의 발명품이 사람들의 삶을 더 편리하게 만들었다는 것을 나타내기 위해
   Ⓓ 학생들이 특허의 개념을 이해하기 쉽게 하기 위해
   해설 특허 역시 저작권과 비슷한 개념이지만, 특허는 발명이나 만들어내는 방법과 관련이 있다고 하면서, 전기와 같은 에디슨의 발명품을 언급하였다. 이는 학생들이 특허의 개념을 보다 쉽게 하도록 하려는 것이다. 보기 Ⓑ와 같이 단순히 역사상 위대한 발명품들의 예를 들기 위해 언급한 것은 아니다.
   정답 Ⓓ

9. 강의에 따르면, 지적재산권법이 드러내고 있는 분명한 모순점은 무엇인가?
   Ⓐ 경쟁 상대들을 완전히 장악한다.
   Ⓑ 독점이 일어나게 한다.
   Ⓒ 독점이 발생하지 못하게 한다.
   Ⓓ 일반적인 독점을 붕괴시킨다.
   해설 지적재산권을 인정받는 제품이나 서비스, 창작물 등은 이 세상에서 유일한 것이기 때문에 사실상 경쟁이 존재하지 않는데, 그렇기 때문에 독점이 생겨나게 된다고 하였다. 하지만 이러한 독점은 일반적인 독점과는 약간 다른 '제한적인 독점'이다. 보기 Ⓓ처럼 일반적인 독점을 붕괴시키는 것이 아니라, 이와는 다른 형태의 독점이다.
   정답 Ⓑ

10. 제한적인 독점은 일반 독점과 어떻게 다른가?
   Ⓐ 자본주의를 옹호한다.
   Ⓑ 경쟁이 없다.
   Ⓒ 정부의 규제를 받는다.
   Ⓓ 보편적으로 지켜진다.
   해설 제한적인 독점은 발명품이나 저작물 등 세상에 하나 밖에 없는 것에 대해 존재하는 것이기 때문에 경쟁 대상이 없다고 하였다.
   정답 Ⓑ

11. 강의에서, 교수는 지적재산권의 종류에 대해 이야기 하고 있다. 이를 각 보기의 관련 있는 것에 연결하시오.

지적재산권	특징
저작권	
상표권	
특허	
기업 비밀	

Ⓐ 책이나 음악

Ⓑ 새로운 발명품

Ⓒ 기업의 기밀 정보

Ⓓ 다른 것과 구별되는 심벌

해설 저작권은 보기 Ⓐ의 책이나 음악에 대한 권리이고, 상표권은 보기 Ⓓ의 다른 제품과 구별되는 심벌을 말하고, 특허는 보기 Ⓑ의 새로운 발명품에 대한 권리이고, 기업 비밀은 보기 Ⓒ의 기업의 기밀 정보를 말한다.

정답 저작권 − Ⓐ, 상표권 − Ⓓ, 특허 − Ⓑ, 기업 비밀 − Ⓒ

Chapter 3 Inference

Office Hours

1. Ⓓ **2.** Ⓒ **3.** Ⓑ **4.** Ⓑ

Dictation: Office Hours

1. 1. trying to launch 2. than we expected 3. in addition to the ones 4. every two months

2. 1. give me a reference letter 2. guarantee anything 3. presenting a paper 4. spring break coming up

3. 1. get the instruction sheet 2. specified a couple of things 3. either of those things 4. referring to handwritten notes

4. 1. running in the door now 2. how much time is left 3. expects to review each case 4. appeal to the dean 5. disrupting the other students

01

여 : 사진 클럽에서 창간 준비 중인 잡지에 관해 조언 좀 해주시겠어요?

남 : 그래, 무슨 문제라도 있니?

여 : 정말로 뛰어난 사진이 많지 않다는 것이 문제에요. 사진이 더 많을 거라 생각했는데요, 예상했던 것보다 학생들이 사진을 많이 제출하지 않았어요.

남 : 그렇구나. 얼마 간격으로 잡지를 간행할 계획이었니?

여 : 월간이요?

남 : 그런 경우라면, 두 가지 선택의 여지가 있을 것 같구나. 첫 번째는, 아주 훌륭한 사진들 말고도 그냥 보기에 괜찮은 사진들도 넣는 거야. 두 번째는 격월이나 학기당 1회 잡지를 출간하는 것이지. 대학에서 발행되는 출판물들은 주로 그런 식으로 이루어지지.

여 : 월간 잡지를 내는 것은 너무 큰 욕심이었나 봐요… 다른 아이들과 이야기를 해봐서 어떻게 생각하는지 알아보도록 할게요. 조언 주셔서 감사합니다!

남 : 그래. 뭐 도움이 될 일이 있으면 또 얘기하렴.

어휘 launch 시작하다, 발사하다 in addition to ~이외에 ambitious 야심이 큰, 의욕적인

1. 다음 중 어느 것이 사진 클럽에 관한 사실처럼 보이는가?
    Ⓐ 클럽에 재능 있는 사진가들이 많다.
    Ⓑ 대학이 주는 자금이 필요하다.
    Ⓒ 계획대로 잡지를 발행할 것이다.
    Ⓓ 출판 경험이 있는 회원이 거의 없다.

02

여 : 안녕하세요, 추천서를 좀 써주실 수 있으세요? 제가 B&G 인턴에 지원하는데요, 마감일이 얼마 안 남았어요.
남 : 그럼, 써줄 수 있지. 그러고 보니 지금 그 회사에서 근무하고 있는 졸업생 몇 명을 알고 있어.
여 : 감사합니다!
남 : 그렇지만 경쟁이 매우 치열하다는 것을 알아두도록 해. 많은 경험을 가진 사람을 비롯해서 많은 사람들이 지
    원한단다. 확신할 수는 없을 것 같구나.
여 : 네.
남 : 그런데 Douglas 교수가 너의 지도 교수 아니니? 그 분께 요청 드려 보았니?
여 : 저희 지도 교수님은 맞으시지만, 지금 Kyoto(교토) 학회에서 논문 발표 중이세요.
남 : 아, 그렇지. 이제 곧 봄방학이라 일본에 계속 머무신다고 하더구나. 행복한 분이시지. 네가 내 수업을 들어서
    아니까, 별 문제는 없을 거란다. 언제까지 필요하니?
여 : 금요일까지 가능하신가요?

어휘 reference letter 추천서 competitive 경쟁이 센 academic advisor 지도 교수

2. 추천서를 쓰는 것에 관해 교수가 암시하는 것은 무엇인가?
    Ⓐ 학생이 적어도 2통의 추천서가 필요하다고 생각한다.
    Ⓑ 학생을 잘 모른다.
    Ⓒ 지도 교수가 추천서를 쓰기에 적임자라고 생각한다.
    Ⓓ 추천서에 무슨 말을 써야 할지 잘 모르고 있다.

03

여 : 수업이 끝나고 저를 보자고 하셨죠?
남 : 그래. 오늘 발표에 관한 가이드라인을 받았었니? 23일 수업 시간에 나누어주고, 웹사이트에도 자료를 올려
    놓았는데.
여 : 네… 받았어요. 무슨 문제라도 있나요?
남 : 가이드라인을 보면 지켜야 할 사항들이 구체적으로 적혀있지. 발표를 하는 것 외에도, 파워포인트를 이용해
    서 준비를 하고 학생들에게 프린트를 나누어주어야 했어. 보니까 둘 다 안 한 것 같은데.
여 : 저, 그게…
남 : 그리고 발표를 하면서 메모를 너무 자주 보고 말하더구나. 이 수업에서 낙제하지 않으려면, 앞으로 남은 발
    표 두 개는 더 잘해야 할 거야. 무슨 말인지 알겠니?
여 : 죄송합니다.
남 : 말하고 싶었던 건 그게 다야. 즐거운 오후 보내도록 해.

어휘 pass out 나누어주다 specify 상술하다

3. 학생에 관해 교수가 암시하는 것은 무엇인가?
   Ⓐ 학생은 가장 뛰어난 수강생 중 한 명이다.
   Ⓑ 학생은 발표 준비가 완전히 되어 있지 않았다.
   Ⓒ 학생은 다른 수업 발표 때문에 바빴다.
   Ⓓ 학생은 컴퓨터 소프트웨어 프로그램에 대해서는 잘 모른다.

04

남 : 지금 와서 정말 죄송해요! 지각해서 정말 죄송합니다! 지금이라도 시험을 볼 수 없나요?
여 : 20분 내로 다 끝낼 수 없으면 안 된단다. 지금 남아있는 시간이 20분이야.
남 : 이런. 죄송해요. 그게… 늦잠을 잤어요. 저기… 추가 시험을 볼 시간을 정할 수 있을까요?
여 : 그럴 수는 없어. 학과장님께서 그 부분에 대해서는 아주 완고하시단다. 의사 진단서가 없는 한, 모든 경우를 직접 검토하시지. 결정에 따를 수 없으면, 학적부장님께 이의를 제기하도록 해.
남 : 지금까지 늦은 적이 한 번도 없었어요! 제발요… 그냥 시간을 정할 수는 없나요?
여 : 다른 학생들에게 방해가 되고 있잖니. 남은 시간 동안 할 수 있는 만큼 하고 나서 나중에 이야기 하도록 하자, 알겠니?
남 : 아… 다 망쳐버린 것 같아요.

어휘 oversleep 늦잠 자다 doctor's note 진단서 appeal to ~에 이의 제기하다 disrupt 방해하다

4. 학생은 이제 무엇을 할 것 같은가?
   Ⓐ 다음에 시험 전체를 다시 볼 것이다.
   Ⓑ 남은 20분 동안 문제를 최대한 많이 풀 것이다.
   Ⓒ 시험을 포기하고 답안을 채우지 않고 남겨놓을 것이다.
   Ⓓ 진단서를 제출할 것이다.

Service Encounters
1. Ⓒ **2.** Ⓐ **3.** Ⓒ **4.** Ⓑ

Dictation: Service Encounters
1. 1 stand this 2. closed for renovations 3. relocate to the new dorm 4. an extra fee 5. at a reduced rate
2. 1. the exchange program 2. be eligible for credit 3. a couple of simple documents 4. update our list
3. 1. it can't be turned down 2. go to the library 3. in the dorms are overflowing 4. who want to take a rest 5. turn down the volume 6. turn it off
4. 1. write down the title 2. look it up 3. how it works 4. in luck 5. out of print

01

남 : 더 이상은 못 참겠어요!
여 : 무슨 일이죠?
남 : 보수 공사 때문에 폐쇄된 기숙사 옆에 사는데요. 그게…
여 : 아, 무슨 일인지 알겠네요, 공사 소음이 너무 심하죠.

남 : 그러니까요, 게다가 그 빌딩과 붙어 있는 쪽에 제 방이 있어요. 그리고 다음 주부터 중간 고사인데, 공부하기
　　가 힘들어요. 어떡하면 좋죠?

여 : 이해해요. 학교 측에서 공사 소음으로 인해 영향을 받는 학생들이 새로운 기숙사로 옮길 수 있도록 하기로
　　했어요. 원래 계획은 다음 학기에 기숙사를 개관하는 것이었는데, 현재 보수 공사 소음이 예상 외로 너무 커
　　서요.

남 : 새 기숙사로 옮기는 데에 추가 비용이 들까요?

여 : 아뇨, 물론 없어요. 공사가 시끄러운 것이 학생 잘못은 아니니까요. 중간 고사 기간에 이 일로 인해 피해를
　　보는 학생들이 있을 거라는 걸 알기 때문에, 할인된 가격으로 이삿짐 센터를 이용할 수 있게 해줄 거에요.

남 : 잘 됐네요! 룸메이트에게 문자 메시지를 보내야겠어요.

여 : 도움이 됐다니 다행이네요.

어휘　stand 참다, 견디다　text 문자 메시지를 보내다

1. 앞으로 무슨 일이 일어날 것 같은가?
　　Ⓐ 학생들 대부분은 공부해야 하기 때문에 자기 방에 있을 것이다.
　　Ⓑ 많은 학생들이 중간 고사에서 안 좋은 성적을 받을 것이다.
　　Ⓒ 소음이 심한 쪽에 살고 있는 학생들 일부는 새 기숙사로 옮길 것이다.
　　Ⓓ 학교 측에서 기존의 기숙사에서 진행 중인 보수 공사를 중단시킬 것이다.

02

남 : 안녕하세요, 제가 교환 학생으로 뽑혀서 한 학기 동안 멕시코로 갈 예정이에요.

여 : 아, 기대하고 있는 것 같네요. 방금 소식을 들은 건가요?

남 : 네! 그런데 조금 전에 멕시코 대학의 웹사이트를 찾아보았는데, 제가 듣고 싶어하는 과목 몇 개가 우리 학교
　　에서는 학점 인정이 안 되는 것 같아요.

여 : 그게 어떤 강의들이죠?

남 : 고급 스페인어 강좌와 고급 문학 강좌 2개요. 신규 개설된 강의 같아요. 이 강의들을 들으면 무슨 문제가 있
　　을까요?

여 : 아뇨, 그러면 안 되죠. 그 강의들이 신규 개설 된 것이라면, 멕시코 대학 측에서 몇 가지 간단한 서류를 받아
　　학점 인정을 해 줄 수 있어요.

남 : 제가 대학교에 직접 연락해야 하나요?

여 : 아뇨, 수강 가능 강의 목록을 업데이트 해야 하니까 우리가 연락을 할게요. 이런 문제를 알려줘서 고마워요!

남 : 천만에요(De nada).

어휘　be eligible fo´ ~에 적격이다, 적합하다　document 서류

2. 스페인어 구절인 *de nada*가 의미하는 것은 무엇이겠는가?
　　Ⓐ 천만에요.
　　Ⓑ 이해해요.
　　Ⓒ 참 안됐네요.
　　Ⓓ 나중에 봐요.

03

남 : 학생 휴게실에 문제가 약간 있습니다.

여 : 뭔가 잘못되었나요? 누가 다쳤어요?

남 : 아뇨, 그런 건 아닙니다. 응급 상황은 아니에요. 그게, TV 소리가 너무 커서 줄이고 싶은데요, 리모컨이 없으면 줄일 수가 없어요. 공부를 하려고 하거든요.

여 : 음… 도서관에서 하면 안되나요?

남 : 도서관도 사람이 가득 찼어요. 다음 주부터 기말고사라 모두들 도서관에서 공부하고 있어요. 기숙사 휴게실도 학생들이 넘쳐나요. 공부 장소로 찾을 수 있는 곳이 여기 밖에 없었어요.

여 : 그렇지만, 휴게실에서 휴식을 취하길 원하는 학생들도 있어요.

남 : 오늘은 아무도 TV를 안 봐요.

여 : 알겠어요, 그럼 리모컨을 가져가서 볼륨을 줄이도록 할게요. 볼륨을 줄일까요, 아니면 그냥 TV를 끌까요?

남 : 끄져도 될 것 같아요.

여 : 알겠어요.

남 : 감사합니다!

어휘 emergency 비상 사태, 응급 loud 시끄러운 turn down 소리를 줄이다 remote control 리모컨 overflow 가득 차다, 넘쳐 나다 take a rest 휴식을 취하다 turn off 끄다

3. 남자가 학생 휴게실에 있는 학생들에 관해 암시하는 것은 무엇인가?

   Ⓐ 학생들은 TV 보는 것을 매우 좋아한다.

   Ⓑ 학생들은 도서관에서 공부하는 것을 좋아하지 않는다.

   Ⓒ 학생들은 지금 열심히 공부하고 있다.

   Ⓓ 학생들은 평소에는 휴게실을 이용하지 않는다.

04

남 : 실례합니다, 제가 책을 잃어버렸는데요, 앞으로 어떻게 해야 하는 건지 잘 모르겠어요.

여 : 네. 책 제목과 저자 이름을 적어주겠어요? 여기 종이와 펜이 있어요.

남 : 아, 감사합니다. 그런데 이름이 기억나질 않아요. 세 명이었던 것 같은데. 찾아봐주실 수 있는 거죠?

여 : 네, 기본 정보만 있으면 보통 찾기 쉬워요. 학생증도 필요해요.

남 : 저기, 제가 벌금을 내거나 새 책으로 사놓던가 해야 하는 건가요? 어떻게 되는 건지 잘 모르겠어요.

여 : 책을 잃어버린 것이 확실한 건가요?

남 : 네. 방도 구석구석 뒤져보고 제가 그동안 갔던 곳을 모두 찾아봤는데요. 책이 어디에도 없어요.

여 : 그렇군요… 아, 학생은 운이 좋았네요.

남 : 네? 책을 잃어버린 게 좋은 일은 아닌 것 같은데요.

여 : 그게 말이죠, 다행히 책이 절판된 상태가 아니에요. 학생이 새 책을 가져다 놓으면 될 거에요, 비싼 책도 아니니까요. 그래서 운이 좋다고 말한 거였어요.

남 : 네. 다행이네요. 책 값이 얼마나 들까요?

여 : 24.95달러에요.

어휘 look up 찾아보다 fine 벌금 absolutely 확실히 retrace 되돌아가다, 거슬러 올라가 조사하다 out of print 절판된 replace 대체하다 relief 안심

4. 학생에 관해 추론할 수 있는 것은 무엇인가?

   Ⓐ 집 안에서 책을 찾아볼 것이다.

   Ⓑ 책값을 물어내야 할 것이다.

   Ⓒ 앞으로 다른 책들도 대출할 수가 없을 것이다.

   Ⓓ 책 저자와 이야기를 나누어볼 것이다.

Dictation: Lectures

1. 1. only in operation 2. a rapid mail service 3. the western end of the line 4. bound for cities farther 5. run an overland shipping service 6. change horses regularly 7. everything has its end 8. both ending and beginning a new chapter

2. 1. aware of the sensation 2. stop noticing 3. when the stimulus changes 4. learned to tell the difference 5. replace it with another 6. process everything in its environment equally 7. be able to concentrate

01 미국 역사 수업

P : 여러분이 미국의 역사에 대해 어느 정도 잘 알고 있다면, 아마도 포니 익스프레스(조랑말 속달 우편)에 관해 들어본 적이 있을 거예요. 1860년 4월부터 1861년 10월까지 1년 6개월 정도 밖에 운영되지 않았지만, 포니 익스프레스는 전설로 남아있죠. 아주 짧은 시간이었죠? 포니 익스프레스는 서부의 여러 주와 준주를 가로질러 우편물을 빠르게 배달하기 위해 세워졌는데, 대륙횡단 우편회사의 진짜 목적은 정부의 우편 계약을 따내는 것이었어요. 동부의 시발역이자 회사의 본사는 미주리(Missouri) 주의 세인트 조셉(St. Joseph)에 소재했고, 서부의 종착역은 캘리포니아(California) 주의 새크라멘토(Sacramento)에 있었어요. 샌프란시스코(San Francisco)와 오클랜드(Oakland)처럼 더 서쪽에 위치한 도시로 운송되는 우편물은 새크라멘토에서 증기선에 실려 수송되었어요.

자, 포니 익스프레스는 여러 면에서 그전과는 다른 새로운 시스템이었고, 그게 바로 우리가 오늘날에도 기억하는 이유기도 하죠. 포니 익스프레스가 도입되기 이전에는 대륙을 횡단하여 우편물을 배달할 수 있을 거란 생각을 한 사람이 아무도 없었어요. 우편물은 남미대륙 아래를 돌아 배편으로 수송되던가, 파나마를 통해 수송되던가, 아니면 애리조나(Arizona) 주와 뉴멕시코(New Mexico)주와 같은 남부 지역을 통과하여 수송되어야만 했었죠. 이 수송로들이 빠른 배달을 보장해줄 리 만무했죠. 가령, 배를 이용하면 우편물을 보내는데 6개월 이상이 걸렸어요! 하지만 포니 익스프레스 운송 역은 거의 10마일마다 세워졌고, 그에 따라 배달부들은 정기적으로 말을 바꿔 타고 달릴 수 있었어요. 이런 식으로 배달부들이 열흘 내지 열 하루 이내에 우편물을 배달하게 되었는데, 그 당시로서는 아주 획기적인 일이었어요. 더군다나 포니 익스프레스는 겨울에도 이용 가능하다는 것이 증명되었죠. 안타깝게도, 모든 일에는 그 끝이 있듯, 포니 익스프레스 역시 전보선이 솔트레이크시티(Salt Lake City)까지 설치된 지 이틀 후에 이제 더 이상 사업을 계속 할 수가 없다고 발표했죠… 어떻게 보면, 이는 미국 역사의 한 챕터가 끝나는 동시에 새로운 챕터가 열리는 순간이었어요.

어휘 legend 전설 operation 운영, 운행 state 주 territory 준주, 영토 contract 계약 terminus 시발역, 종착역 headquarters 본사 bound for ~행의, ~로 가는 pioneering 선구적인, 개척자의 outfit 조직, 회사 overland 육상의 upward of ~보다 이상, 약 regularly 정기적으로 unheard of 전례가 없는, 전대 미문의 telegraph 전신, 전보 extend 확장하다 announce 발표하다

1. 다음 중 어느 것이 포니 익스프레스에 관해 맞지 않는가?
    Ⓐ 서부의 모든 도시에 연결된 것은 아니었다.
    Ⓑ 우편물이 배달되는데 보통 열흘 가량 걸렸다.
    Ⓒ 전보시스템의 약점을 보완했다.
    Ⓓ 18개월간 운용되었다.

2. 포니 익스프레스 운송 역이 10마일마다 세워졌다면, 다음 중 어느 것이 사실이겠는가?

    Ⓐ 10마일 간격으로 역을 짓는 것이 포니 익스프레스 회사 측에 가장 비용이 적게 드는 옵션이었을 것이다.

    Ⓑ 10마일이 말이 너무 지치지 않고 계속 달릴 수 있는 최장거리이다.

    Ⓒ 역을 더 가깝게 짓기 위한 토지가 없었다.

    Ⓓ 배달원들이 달리는 말 위에서 10마일 이상을 버틸 수 없었다.

02 심리학 수업

P : 습관화는 심리학에서 중요한 개념이고, 여러분은 이 습관화라는 작용을 바로 지금 경험하고 있어요. 여러분이 지금 입고 있는 옷을 느낄 수 있나요? 잠깐만 생각해보면, 여러분은 아마 '뭐, 약간요' 같은 대답을 할 거에요. 옷을 입을 때는 피부에 닿는 옷의 촉감을 느낄 수 있어요. 하지만 시간이 조금 지나면, 더 이상 인지하지 않게 되죠. 입고 있는 옷이 체중이 조금 늘어서 불편하다던가, 바지가 너무 꽉 끼어서 불편하다던가 하면 계속 신경이 쓰이겠죠.

습관화는 자연적인 현상이에요. 원생동물문을 포함한 모든 동물들에게서 관찰되는 형상이죠. 특정한 자극이 오랫동안 작용하면, 더 이상 인지하지 않게 되요. 자극이 바뀔 때만 다시 신경을 쓰기 시작해요. 예를 들어, 새가 들어있는 새장에 이 새들의 포획자인 박제한 올빼미를 넣으면, 새들은 놀라 기절하겠죠. 하지만 시간이 지나면, 이 박제 올빼미에 대한 반응을 완전히 멈춰버려요. 새가 진짜 올빼미와 가짜 올빼미의 차이를 구별하는 것을 배웠다던가 하는 것은 아니에요. 박제 올빼미를 꺼내고 다른 것을 다시 집어 넣으면, 새는 다시 반응을 나타내죠.

이로 볼 때, 습관화는 자극에 있어서의 변화와 관련된 것이란 걸 알 수 있어요. 말하자면 여과기 같은 작용을 한다는 건데요, 주변의 자극에 무관심하게 해주죠. 뇌는 주변에서 일어나는 모든 것을 똑같이 처리할 수 없어요, 그래서 우리가 이미 경험한 자극을 차단하기 위해 습관화 작용을 발달시킨 것이죠. 이 습관화는 여러 면에서 도움이 되는 작용이에요. 예를 들어, 습관화 작용 때문에 시간이 흐르면 우리가 더 이상 냄새를 못 맡게 되는 거에요. 강의실에 들어가면, 처음에는 먼지 냄새나 청소용품 냄새를 맡겠죠, 하지만 계속 그 냄새를 맡고 있으면, 더 이상 그 냄새에 집중하지 않게 되죠. 이런 능력에 감사해야겠죠!

어휘 gain weight 체중이 늘다 phenomenon 현상 protozoa 원생동물문 stimulus 자극 stuffed 박제한 cage 우리 predator 포획자 false 가짜의 filter 여과기 tune out ~에 무관심 하게 되다, 무시 하다 odor 냄새 dust 먼지

1. 강의의 주제는 무엇인가?

    Ⓐ 변하지 않는 조건에 대한 반응의 감소

    Ⓑ 심리학에서의 다양한 개념

    Ⓒ 인간에 대한 습관화 작용 관찰

    Ⓓ 습관화의 좋은 점

2. 박제 올빼미와 새에 대한 실험에 관해 결론지을 수 있는 것은 무엇인가?

    Ⓐ 새는 처음부터 박제 올빼미가 살아있는 것이 아니라고 알아본다.

    Ⓑ 새는 박제 올빼미에 익숙해지지 못한다.

    Ⓒ 새는 결국 박제 올빼미를 공격할 것이다.

    Ⓓ 새는 시간이 지나면서 박제 올빼미를 위협이라고 생각하지 않는다.

3. 습관화의 또 다른 예로는 무엇이 있겠는가?

    Ⓐ 남의 눈에 띄지 않는 곳에서 단 둘이 이야기 하는 것

    Ⓑ 운전하면서 라디오를 듣는 것

    Ⓒ 토론에 참여하는 것

    Ⓓ 조용한 방에서 책을 읽는 것

[1-5] **1.** Ⓑ **2.** Ⓒ **3.** Ⓒ **4.** Mentioned – Ⓑ, Ⓒ, Ⓔ Not Mentioned – Ⓐ, Ⓓ **5.** Ⓐ
[6-11] **6.** Ⓑ **7.** Ⓑ **8.** Ⓓ **9.** Ⓒ **10.** Ⓒ **11.** Yes – Ⓐ, Ⓓ, Ⓔ No – Ⓑ, Ⓒ

[문제 1–5] Listen to part of a conversation at a housing office.

M : Good afternoon, I'd like to get some more information about housing options for next year.

W : Sure, what are you looking for? I mean, do you want to stay in one of the dorms, or would you like information about off-campus housing?

M : I'd like to stay in one of the dorms, actually. I'd prefer one closer to main campus, not the ones so far away that I'll need to ride the shuttle bus.

W : I understand. What type of room do you want?

M : I'd like a single room.

W : Hmm, there aren't many of those left. I can tell you there are still a lot of semi-singles, where your bedroom is private but you share living areas and a bathroom. Those aren't so bad.

M : Well, I'm really trying to keep my grades up, because I'm on scholarship. I spend a lot of time studying, and I don't want to be distracted by a roommate. Especially if the other guy turns out to be a slob or something.

W : I know what you mean. All right, let me check the system... just one moment...

M : Are there any left?

W : Yes, as a matter of fact, there are. In the two buildings on main campus, we have five singles left. In Buchanan Hall, the single rooms have private bathrooms, by the way.

M : Good, I was hoping for a private bathroom, too. Um, do I have to put down a deposit to get one of those rooms?

W : Yes. Here's the list of charges for the semester.

M : 🎧 Thanks. Um, how soon do I have to pay the deposit?

W : The deadline is two weeks away.

M : My scholarship funds won't be disbursed by then, I don't think. 5·Could I get a letter from somebody?

W : That's fine. There are a few students in the same situation. Get a letter from your professor, from the financial aid office, or from the foundation that gave you the scholarship. When you come back with the letter, the room is yours. How does that sound?

M : Great! Thanks!

남 : 안녕하세요, 내년 숙소에 대한 정보 좀 얻으려고 왔습니다.

여 : 네, 어떤 걸 찾고 있죠? 음, 기숙사를 알아보는 건가요, 아니면 교외 숙소를 알아보는 건가요?

남 : 기숙사에서 살고 싶어요. 메인 캠퍼스와 가까운 곳이면 좋겠어요, 너무 멀리 떨어져 있어서 셔틀 버스를 타고 다녀야 하는 곳 말고요.

여 : 그렇군요. 어떤 방을 원하나요?

남 : 1인실이 좋겠어요.

여 : 아, 1인실은 남은 게 별로 없어요. 세미싱글룸은 아직 많이 남아있는데, 침실은 혼자 쓰지만 거실과 욕실은 함께 써야 해요. 그렇게 나쁘진 않아요.

남 : 그게 말이죠, 제가 장학금을 탔기 때문에 성적을 높게 유지해야 하거든요. 주로 공부하면서 시간을 모두 보내는 편이라, 룸메이트의 방해를 받고 싶지 않아요. 룸메이트가 게으르다거나 지저분하면 골치 아프잖아요.

여 : 무슨 말인지 알겠어요. 그럼, 한 번 확인해볼게요… 잠깐만요…

남 : 자리가 남아있나요?

여 : 네, 남아있네요. 메인 캠퍼스에 있는 건물 두 개에 1인실이 5개 남아있어요. 그리고 뷰캐넌홀에 있는 1인실은 개인 욕실도 딸려 있네요.

남 : 잘됐네요, 개인 욕실이 있었으면 했거든요. 그 방을 사용하고 싶으면 예약금을 내야 하는 건가요?

여 : 네. 여기 한 학기 요금표를 참고하세요.

남 : 감사합니다. 예약금은 언제까지 납부해야 하죠?

여 : 2주 후가 마감이에요.

남 : 그 때까지 장학금이 지급될 것 같지 않아요. 확인서 같은 걸 받아와도 될까요?

여 : 네. 학생과 같은 상황에 처한 학생들이 몇 있어요. 교수님이나 학자금 대출과 직원, 또는 장학 재단의 확인서를 받도록 해요. 확인서를 가져오면, 학생이 원하는 방을 갖게 됩니다. 어때요?

남 : 좋아요! 감사합니다!

어휘 scholarship 장학금 distract 혼란시키다 slob 게으름뱅이 disburse 지불하다 foundation 재단

Note-taking

Topic: Housing options 숙소에 대한 정보

1. Want a dorm 기숙사에 살고 싶어함
    – closer to main campus 메인 캠퍼스와 가까운 곳일수록 좋음
    – single room 1인실을 원함
    – private bathroom 개인 욕실이 딸려 있는 방
2. Deposit 예약금
    – in 2 weeks 2주 후까지 내야 함
    – scholarship fund coming later than that 장학금은 그 후에 지급될 예정임
    – W's suggestion: get a letter 여자의 제안: 확인서 받아오기

1. 대화에서 화자들은 주로 무엇에 관해 이야기 하고 있는가?
    Ⓐ 교외 숙소로 이사 가기
    Ⓑ 기숙사 방을 예약하기
    Ⓒ 기숙사 방을 바꾸기
    Ⓓ 새로운 룸메이트를 구하기
    해설 학생은 내년에 거주할 기숙사를 알아보기 위해 기숙사 사무실을 찾아왔다.
    정답 Ⓑ

2. 학생은 왜 룸메이트를 원하지 않는가?
    Ⓐ 넓은 방을 혼자 쓰고 싶어한다.
    Ⓑ 다른 사람들과 잘 어울리지 못한다.
    Ⓒ 게으르고 지저분한 사람을 좋아하지 않는다.
    Ⓓ 룸메이트의 방해를 받지 않고 공부하고 싶어한다.
    해설 학생이 장학금을 계속 받기 위해서는 높은 성적을 유지해야 하는데, 룸메이트와 방을 함께 쓰면 공부에 지장을 받을까 걱정하고 있다. 보기 Ⓒ와 같이 단순히 게으르고 지저분한 사람이 싫어서 룸메이트를 원하지 않는 것이 아니다.
    정답 Ⓓ

3. 여자가 뷰캐넌홀에 관해 암시하는 것은 무엇인가?

Ⓐ 건물이 상당히 크다.

Ⓑ 수용인원이 적다.

Ⓒ 메인 캠퍼스에 있다.

Ⓓ 1인실이 없다.

해설 여자의 말에 따르면, 메인 캠퍼스에 있는 두 개의 기숙사 건물에 1인실이 5개 남아있다고 하였는데, 그 중에
서도 뷰캐넌홀에 있는 1인실에는 개인 욕실도 딸려 있다고 하였다. 이 말을 통해 뷰캐넌홀이 메인 캠퍼스에
있다는 것을 짐작해낼 수 있다.

정답 Ⓒ

4. 대화에서, 학생은 자신의 숙소에 대한 몇 가지 조건을 언급하고 있다. 아래 표의 각 보기가 이 조건에 해당하는지
표시하시오. 각 보기에 맞는 칸에 클릭하시오.

	Mentioned	Not Mentioned
Ⓐ 버스 정류장과 가까운 기숙사		
Ⓑ 개인 욕실		
Ⓒ 룸메이트가 없는 방		
Ⓓ 혼자 사용하는 공부방		
Ⓔ 메인 캠퍼스에서 멀지 않은 기숙사		

해설 학생이 원하는 기숙사는 메인 캠퍼스에서 가까워야 하고, 룸메이트가 없는 1인실에 개인 욕실이 딸려 있어
야 한다. 기숙사에서 캠퍼스까지 셔틀 버스를 타고 싶지 않다고 했으므로 보기 Ⓐ는 언급하지 않았다. 또한
조용히 공부하기 위해 1인실이 필요하다고 한 것이지, 개인 공부방을 요구하지는 않았으므로 보기 Ⓓ 역시
언급하지 않았다.

정답 Mentioned – Ⓑ, Ⓒ, Ⓔ Not Mentioned – Ⓐ, Ⓓ

대화의 일부를 다시 들으시오. 그러고 나서 질문에 답하시오.

5. 남자가 이것을 말할 때 암시하는 것은 무엇인가: 

M : Could I get a letter from somebody?

Ⓐ 학생은 기한 내에 예약금을 내지 못할 것 같아 걱정하고 있다.

Ⓑ 학생은 은행 계좌에 예금이 충분히 들어있는지 확인하고 싶어한다.

Ⓒ 학생은 예약금을 납부한 후에 마음이 바뀔지도 모른다고 생각한다.

Ⓓ 학생은 교수님에게 예약금을 빌려달라고 부탁할 것이다.

해설 학생은 2주 후인 마감일까지 장학금이 지급되지 않아 기한 내에 기숙사 예약금을 내지 못할 것 같자, 곧
장학금이 지급될 것이라는 사실을 확인해 줄 수 있는 사람에게서 장학금 지급 확인서를 받아와도 되는지를
묻는다. 이는 학생이 기한 내에 예약금을 납부하지 못할 것 같아 걱정하고 있음을 보여준다.

정답 Ⓐ

[문제 6-11] Listen to part of a lecture in a modern art class.

P(W) : All right, we've discussed several of the earlier periods in American art, and now I'd like
us to move on to the more modern period. I'd like to talk about Georgia O'Keeffe to get us
started on this topic, because she had quite a long career and was associated with some of
the most important figures in American art. Not only that, but she was also very emblematic

of the changes going on in American society, with regard to the role of women. Can anyone tell us a little bit about O'Keeffe and her work, to get things started? What do you already know?

S1(M) : She's seen as an important feminist artist, I think.

S2(W) : She's best known for her work from the American Southwest. She lived in New Mexico for more than half her life, and many of her most famous paintings were inspired by the things she saw there, like flowers and rock formations and animal bones.

P(W) : 🎧 Also true. Bear in mind that her career had its start in 1917, and she came to prominence during the 20s. 9.That's not quite a hundred years ago, but it's close enough. The fact that she was a highly prominent woman artist was remarkable in itself.

Now, uh, let's go back to the beginning... I guess many of you have heard of the very well-known photographer Alfred Stieglitz. He was the first to exhibit her work, back in 1917. This came about without O'Keeffe's knowledge. Her college classmate brought several of her paintings to Stieglitz's gallery. They were a series of abstract charcoal drawings and he loved them. This was all arranged without O'Keeffe finding out, and when she did, she went to New York to confront Stieglitz. He was married at the time, but he and O'Keeffe soon became romantically involved. He divorced his wife, married O'Keeffe, and did a great deal to advance her career.

During the 1920s, living in New York, she focused mostly on large-scale depictions of flowers and architectural images like churches. In 1928, a group of her paintings of calla lilies sold for $25,000, which was a record: it was the most a living American artist had ever been paid for their work. But for some personal reasons, O'Keeffe was becoming restless, and she went looking for inspiration. She made many trips back there, looking out at splendid vistas, and in Santa Fe, Albuquerque, and Taos, she found it.

S1(M) : I've once visited The Georgia O'Keeffe Museum located in Santa Fe.

P(W) : Oh, you did? Well, the work she did during that time was extremely successful, and her popularity increased during the 1930s and 40s. In 1946, the Museum of Modern Art in New York held a one-woman show, to celebrate her work. This was the first time this had been done for a female artist. That year, Stieglitz passed away, and not long after that, O'Keeffe left New York and settled in a fairly remote part of New Mexico, to focus on her work. Her New Mexico period began. She depicted a view of mountains, cliffs, hills, and lakes there.

P : 자, 미국의 초기 미술사조에 대해 살펴보았는데요, 다음으로 미국의 현대 미술에 대해 알아보도록 합시다. 이 주제를 다루면서 먼저 Georgia O'Keeffe(조지아 오키프)에 대해 이야기하고 싶은데, 오키프가 화가로서의 오랜 경력을 갖고 있었을 뿐만 아니라 미국 미술사에서 빼놓을 수 없는 중요한 인물들과도 관련이 있기 때문이에요. 그 뿐만 아니라, 오키프는 미국 사회에서 일어나고 있던 변화를 상징하는 인물이기도 했는데, 특히 여성의 역할과 관련된 사회적 시각의 변화를 상징했어요. 자, 오키프와 그녀의 작품에 대해 이야기해 볼 사람 있어요? 오키프에 대해 어떤 것들을 알고 있나요?

S1 : 오키프는 페미니스트 화가로 인식되고 있어요.

S2 : 오키프는 미국의 남서부 지역에서 창조해낸 작품들로 가장 널리 알려져 있어요. 뉴멕시코에서 반평생을 넘게 살았고, 그녀의 유명한 작품들 가운데 상당수는 그 지역에서 관찰했던 것들, 예를 들면, 꽃이나 암석, 동물의 뼈 등에서 영감을 얻어 그려졌어요.

P : 그것도 맞는 얘기에요. 그녀의 화가로서의 삶이 1917년에 시작되었다는 것과 1920년대에 두각을 나타내며 이름을 날리기 시작했다는 사실을 기억해 두도록 해요. 100년까지는 아니지만, 거의 그 정도 전의 일이죠. 오키프가

상당히 중요한 여성 화가였다는 사실 그 자체도 대단한 일이죠.

자, 처음으로 다시 돌가가서… 여러분 대부분이 유명한 사진작가인 Alfred Stieglitz(알프레드 스티글리츠)에 대해 들어본 적이 있을 텐데요. 1917년에 오키프의 작품을 처음으로 전시했던 사람이 바로 스티글리츠였어요. 전시회는 오키프가 모르는 상태에서 진행되었어요. 그녀의 대학 동창생이 오키프의 작품 몇 점을 스티글리츠의 갤러리로 가져갔어요. 목탄 추상화 그림들이었는데, 스티글리츠는 그 그림들을 매우 마음에 들어 했어요. 오키프는 이 일에 대해 전혀 도르고 있었는데, 이러한 사실을 알게 되자 뉴욕으로 가서 스티글리츠를 만났어요. 스티글리츠는 당시에 결혼한 상태였는데, 둘은 곧 애정 관계로 발전하게 되었어요. 스티글리츠는 부인과 이혼을 한 후 오키프와 결혼을 했고, 그녀가 화가로서 성장하는데 큰 도움을 주었어요.

1920년대에는 뉴욕에 살면서 주로 큰 꽃 그림과 교회와 같은 건축 이미지를 그렸어요. 1928년에는 칼라릴리 연작이 25,000 달러에 팔렸는데, 당시로서는 최고가였어요. 미국의 생존 화가 가운데 가장 큰 액수였죠. 하지만 뭔가 개인적인 이유로 오키프는 불안감을 느끼고 있었고, 작품의 영감을 찾아 뉴멕시코로 향했어요. 그 곳에서 뛰어난 경관을 내려다보며 여행도 많이 했고, 샌타페이, 앨버커키, 타오스에서 그녀는 결국 영감을 얻게 되었어요.

S1 : 전 샌타페이에 있는 조지아오키프 미술관을 가본 적이 있어요.

P : 그랬어요? 음, 오키프가 이 시기에 그린 작품들은 큰 성공을 거두었고, 1930년대와 1940년대에는 사람들의 관심과 사랑을 더 많이 받게 되었죠. 1946년에는 뉴욕 현대미술관에서 오키프 단독전이 열렸어요. 여성 화가로서는 최초의 일이었죠 그 해에 스티글리츠가 세상을 떠났고, 그 후 얼마지 않아 오키프는 뉴욕을 떠나서 뉴멕시코의 외딴 지역에 자리를 잡고 작품 활동에 전념했어요. 뉴멕시코 시기가 시작된 것이었죠. 그녀는 그 곳의 산, 절벽, 언덕, 호수의 풍경을 그려냈죠.

어휘 prominence 두드러짐, 탁월 be associated with ~와 연관된 figure 인물 emblematic of ~를 상징하는 with regard to ~에 관해서 bear in mind 명심하다 prominent 유명한, 중요한 remarkable 대단한 exhibit 전시하다 confront 대면하다 depiction 묘사 restless 불안한 inspiration 영감 splendid 뛰어난 vista 경관 pass away 죽다 fairly 꽤 remote 외딴

Note-taking

Topic: Georgia O'Keeffe 조지아 오키프

1. Represent changes in society regarding woman role
   여성의 역할과 관련하여 사회에서 일어나던 변화를 대변함
   - feminist artist 페미니스트 화가
2. Work from New Mexico 뉴멕시코에서 생활하며 작품 활동
   - painted natural things 자연에서 발견한 것들을 그림
3. 1st exhibit by Stieglitz 스티글리츠가 첫 전시회를 열어줌
   - charcoal drawing 목탄화
   - she didn't know 오키프는 몰랐음
   - married him 스티글리츠와 결혼했음
4. 1920s, 30s, 40s, NY 1920, 30, 40년대, 뉴욕
   - mainly painted flowers and buildings 주로 꽃과 건축물을 그림
   - calla lilies sold for $25,000 칼라릴리 연작이 25,000 달러에 팔림
   - success & popularity → MoMA exhibit 성공과 인기 → 뉴욕 현대미술관 전시회
5. Stieglitz's death → New Mexico 스티글리츠가 사망 후 뉴멕시코로 떠남
   - got inspiration 영감을 얻음
   - landscape paintings 풍경화
   - The Georgia O'Keeffe Museum 조지아오키프 미술관이 있음

6. 강의의 주제는 무엇인가?
   Ⓐ 유명한 여성 화가들
   Ⓑ 조지아 오키프와 그녀의 작품 세계
   Ⓒ 조지아 오키프와 알프레드 스티글리츠
   Ⓓ 조지아 오키프 박물관
   해설 미국의 유명한 여성 화가인 조지아 오키프와 그녀의 작품 세계에 대해 강의가 진행되고 있다.
   정답 Ⓑ

7. 조지아 오키프가 미국의 미술사에서 중요한 인물로 평가 받고 있는 이유는 무엇인가?
   Ⓐ 오키프의 그림이 뉴욕 현대미술관에 전시되었다.
   Ⓑ 오키프는 여성에 대한 사회적 인식의 변화를 상징했다.
   Ⓒ 오키프의 작품에는 강인함과 우아함이 내재해 있었다.
   Ⓓ 오키프는 세계적으로 유명한 사진작가와 결혼했다.
   해설 오키프는 여성의 역할과 관련된 미국 사회에서의 변화를 상징하는 인물이라고 하였고, 당시 현존하고 있던
        화가로서는 최초로 작품의 일부가 최고가에 팔렸다고 하였다. 보기 Ⓐ에서와 같이 단순히 작품이 뉴욕 현
        대미술관에 전시되었다는 사실 때문에 오키프에 대한 평가가 높은 것은 아니다.
   정답 Ⓑ

8. 남서부 지방 생활은 오키프의 삶에 어떤 영향을 주었는가?
   Ⓐ 전시회를 수 차례 열 기회를 얻었다.
   Ⓑ 남편과 여생을 그 곳에서 보냈다.
   Ⓒ 조지아오키프 미술관을 설립할 부지를 찾았다.
   Ⓓ 그 곳의 자연 풍경으로부터 작품의 영감을 얻었다.
   해설 오키프는 미국의 남서부 지방에 있는 뉴멕시코에서 반평생 이상을 살았고, 그 곳의 풍경에서 영감을 받아
        많은 작품을 그렸다. 미술관을 직접 세웠다고는 언급되지 않았으므로 보기 Ⓒ는 오답이다.
   정답 Ⓓ

강의의 일부를 다시 들으시오. 그러고 나서 질문에 답하시오.

9. 교수는 왜 이것을 말하는가: 
   That's not quite a hundred years ago, but it's close enough.
   Ⓐ 오키프가 아주 일찍이 그림을 그리기 시작했다는 것을 나타내기 위해
   Ⓑ 오키프가 가장 유명한 여성 화가였다는 것을 강조하기 위해
   Ⓒ 당시 사회가 지금과 어떻게 달랐을 지를 학생들이 생각해보도록 하기 위해
   Ⓓ 오키프와 현재 활동하고 있는 화가들을 비교하기 위해
   해설 여권이 크게 신장된 지금과는 다르게 100년 전만 해도 활발한 활동을 하는 여성 화가가 별로 없었는데, 오
        키프는 1920년대에 이미 세상에 자신의 이름을 알리며 두각을 나타냈다. 교수는 지금과는 사회 분위기가
        달랐던 당시 사회에서 이것이 상당히 대단한 일이었다는 것을 알려주기 위해 그 말을 한 것이다.
   정답 Ⓒ

10. 강의에서 알프레드 스티글리츠가 열었던 오키프의 첫 전시회에 대해 암시되어 있는 것은 무엇인가?
   Ⓐ 오키프는 스티글리츠의 명성과 평판을 이용했다.
   Ⓑ 오키프는 스스로의 힘으로 사람들의 관심을 끌어냈다.
   Ⓒ 오키프는 결국 스티글리츠가 자신의 작품을 전시하는 것을 승낙했다.
   Ⓓ 오키프는 전시회를 통해 큰 돈을 벌었다.

해설 자신도 모르는 상태에서 전시회가 열렸다는 사실에 항의하기 위해 스티글리츠를 찾아갔는데, 그 후로 스티글리츠가 오키드의 작품 활동에 큰 도움을 주었다는 사실을 통해 보기 ⓒ와 같이 결국 작품 전시를 승낙했을 것이라고 추론할 수 있다. 오키프가 모르는 상태에서 스티글리츠가 전시회를 열었던 것이므로 보기 Ⓐ의 내용은 오답이다.

정답 ⓒ

11. 강의에서, 교수는 오키프가 그림에서 그려낸 대상들을 언급하고 있다. 아래 표의 각 보기가 이러한 그림 주제에 속하는지 표시하시오. 각 보기에 맞는 칸에 클릭하시오.

	Yes	No
Ⓐ 동물 해골		
Ⓑ 숯		
ⓒ 뉴욕의 거리		
Ⓓ 꽃		
Ⓔ 뉴멕시코 풍경		

해설 오키프는 주로 꽃과 돌, 동물의 뼈, 자연 풍경들을 그림으로 그려냈다. 보기 Ⓑ의 숯(charcoal)은 그림의 주제가 아니라 그림의 도구(목탄화)였다.

정답 Yes – Ⓐ, Ⓓ, Ⓔ No – Ⓑ, ⓒ

Chapter 4 Connecting Information

Office Hours

1. Mentioned – Ⓑ, ⓒ, Ⓔ Not Mentioned – Ⓐ, Ⓓ **2.** Suggested – Ⓐ, ⓒ, Ⓓ
Not Suggested – Ⓑ, Ⓔ **3.** Mentioned – Ⓑ, Ⓓ, Ⓔ Not Mentioned – Ⓐ, ⓒ
4. 2:00~2:45 – Ⓑ, Ⓓ 3:00~3:45 – Ⓐ, ⓒ, Ⓔ

Dictation: Office Hours

1. 1. lined up for the summer 2. neat and organized 3.any other responsibilities 4. basic weekly reports
2. 1. creative writing advice 2. as much as you can 3. from my experience 4. draw upon in your work
3. 1. to get the process started 2. it collapsed last year 3. came short of funds 4. planning a trip to 5. things would go hectic
4. 1. at the symposium 2. during the main presentation 3. being given to composition 4. social networking technologies 5. major recording contract 6. along with traditional CDs

01

남 : 수업 후에 남아주어서 고맙구나. 여름에 할 일은 구해 놓았니?
여 : 아뇨, 아직 못 구했어요.
남 : 잘됐구나, 내 말은 나에게 잘 됐다는 뜻이야. 네가 어학 실습실에서 일하는데 관심이 있었으면 했거든.
여 : 좋아요! 어떤 일을 하게 되는데요?
남 : 아주 간단해. 여름 계절 학기 강의를 듣는 학생들의 튜터가 되어 주는 거야. 숙제도 도와주고. 그리고 실습실

을 정리 정돈하는 것도 도와주어야 하고.

여 : 네. 다른 건요?

남 : 음, 얼마나 많은 학생들이 실습실을 이용했고, 얼마나 오래 실습실을 사용했는지에 관한 주간 리포트를 써서
제출하면 된단다.

여 : 좋아요! 제가 나중에 일자리를 구할 때 도움이 될 것 같아요. 제안해주셔서 감사합니다!

어휘 as a matter of fact 사실은 duty 임무, 직무 neat 정돈된

1. 대화에서, 교수는 어학 실습실에서 학생이 해야 할 일을 언급하고 있다. 아래 표의 각 보기가 교수가 언급한 내용
인지 표시하시오. 각 보기에 맞는 칸에 클릭하시오.

	Mentioned	Not Mentioned
Ⓐ 강의하기		
Ⓑ 학생들이 언어를 배우는 것을 돕기		
Ⓒ 실험실을 정돈하기		
Ⓓ 학생들의 집을 방문하기		
Ⓔ 보고서 쓰기		

02

남 : 창작에 관해 조언을 받고 싶습니다. 전에 글쓰기를 해 본 적이 없는데다, 창작 과목이 제가 생각했던 것보다
훨씬 어려워요.

여 : 그래. 글을 효과적으로 쓰기 위해 따라야 할 절차가 있어. 하지만, 여러 테크닉 사용법을 배우기 전에, 글은
자주 쓰니? 그게 작가로서 할 수 있는 가장 중요한 부분이지, 컴퓨터를 앞에 두고 자리에 앉아서 말이야. 그
냥 쓰는 거야.

남 : 음, 글을 쓰는 것, 그게 가장 중요한 부분이라고요? 그 다음이 독서인가요?

여 : 그래. 읽을 수 있는 만큼 많이 읽도록 해. 과제물뿐만이 아니라, 소설이라던가, 신문이라던가, 잡지라던가,
뭐든지 읽어. 그리고 네가 아는 걸 쓰도록 해.

남 : 제 경험에서 나온 걸 쓰라는 말씀이세요?

여 : 그렇지. 글에 담아낼 수 있는 경험을 가지는 것도 중요하단다. 그게 바로 많은 작가들의 처녀작이 자전적 요
소가 강한 이유지.

남 : 정말 도움이 되는 조언들이에요. 감사합니다!

어휘 creative writing 창작 effectively 효과적으로 autobiographical 자전적인

2. 대화에서, 교수는 학생의 창작에 도움이 되는 사항들을 제시하고 있다. 아래 표의 각 보기가 교수가 제시한 내용
인지 표시하시오. 각 보기에 맞는 칸에 클릭하시오.

	Suggested	Not Suggested
Ⓐ 폭넓게 읽기		
Ⓑ 컴퓨터 사용 시간을 줄이기		
Ⓒ 꾸준히 글쓰기 연습을 하기		
Ⓓ 경험을 반영하기		
Ⓔ 다른 작가들의 소설을 모방하기		

03

남 : 잠깐 시간 좀 있니, Carla? 학교에 프랑스어 클럽을 만드는 것에 대해 할 말이 있단다.

여 : 네, 괜찮아요.

남 : 네가 클럽 만드는 일에 적임자일 거라 생각했단다. 음, 네가 Nimes(님) 출신이잖니.

여 : 아, 알고 계셨네요. 음, 염두에 두고 계신 게 어떤 거죠?

남 : 네가 알고 있을 수도 있을 텐데, 캠퍼스 프랑스어 클럽이 전에 있었단다. 대학 측의 재정이 부족하게 되어서 작년에 문을 닫았지. 올해는 다시 재정이 뒷받침될 것 같구나.

여 : 음, 학생들이 관심을 보일까요?

남 : 물론이지. 우리 학교 프랑스어 프로그램이 아주 탄탄하다는 걸 너도 알고 있을 거야. 클럽이 있다면 가입하고 싶어할 학생들이 많이 있을 거야. 그리고 나도 기쁜 마음으로 너희들의 지도 교수가 되어 줄 거고. 재정도 갖추고 있고 클럽 활동을 할 학생들도 있잖니. 그리고 불어학과에서 다음 학기에 프랑스와 스위스로 여행을 갈 계획이라니, 클럽 활동이 잘 되면 함께 여행을 갈 수도 있을 거야.

여 : 정말 좋은 계획이네요, 그렇게 해요! 와, 이제 눈코 뜰 새 없이 바빠지겠어요.

어휘 collapse 와해하다, 좌절시키다 come short of ~이 부족해지다, 떨어지다 restore 회복하다, 복구하다 serve as ~의 역할을 하다 hectic 몹시 바쁜 from now on 앞으로

3. 대화에서, 교수는 프랑스어 클럽을 만들고자 하는 여러 이유를 언급하고 있다. 아래 표의 각 보기가 교수가 언급한 이유에 속하는지 표시하시오. 각 보기에 맞는 칸에 클릭하시오.

	Mentioned	Not Mentioned
Ⓐ 학교에서 가장 인기 있는 외국어가 프랑스어이다.		
Ⓑ 클럽 활동에 참여하고 싶은 학생들이 많이 있을 것이다.		
Ⓒ 작년에 스위스 클럽이 큰 성공을 거두었다.		
Ⓓ 예비 클럽장이 프랑스 도시 출신이다.		
Ⓔ 대학 측에서 클럽 활동을 지원할 재정을 갖추고 있다.		

04

남 : 교수님께서 다음 주에 열릴 심포지엄에서 서로 다른 주제로 2번의 프레젠테이션을 하신다면서요. 맞는지요?

여 : 그래, 그 날 내가 꽤 바쁠 것 같구나.

남 : 어떤 주제에 관해 발표하실 건가요, 그리고 어디서 열리죠? 저도 참석하고 싶어요.

여 : 잘됐구나. 음, 메인 프레젠테이션에서는 작가 워크샵 모델(Writers Workshop model)을 음악 교육에 적용시키는 작업에 관해 발표를 할거란다. 학생들이 작곡 활동을 했으면 해서 기획하게 되었어. 요즘 작곡에 관심을 가지고 있는 사람들이 별로 없어서, 정말이지 음악계로서는 아주 큰 손실이야.

남 : 어디에서 열릴 예정인가요?

여 : 음악관 1172호야. 내가 맡은 부분은 2시부터 2시 45분까지 진행된단다. 음식도 제공되고 말이지.

남 : 그렇게 말씀하시니 더 흥미로운데요! 그리고 다음 프레젠테이션은 뭔가요?

여 : 그 다음에 음악 교육에서의 친목 네트워킹 기술에 관해 발표를 할 예정이야. 너도 알다시피, 페이스북이나 마이스페이스 같은 웹사이트와 블로그가 음악 산업을 변화시키고 있잖니. 이 발표는 음악관 미디어랩에서 3시부터 3시 45분까지 진행될 거란다. 특별 손님도 있어. 밴드를 소개시키는 시간이 있을 거야. 얼마 전에 첫 음반 계약을 맺은 밴드란다. 기술을 이용한 여러 재미있는 음악 활동들을 하고 있는데, 기존의 CD 뿐만 아니라 USB 드라이브를 이용해 음악을 배포할 정도로 기술을 음악에 잘 활용하고 있지.

남 : 와, 정말 기대되네요.

어휘 foster 촉진하다 contract 계약 look forward to ~를 고대하다

4. 대화에서, 화자들은 얼마 후 음악 심포지엄에서 교수가 진행할 예정인 2개의 프레젠테이션에 관해 이야기 하고
   있다. 각 보기가 어떤 프레젠테이션과 관련이 있는지 아래 표에 표시하시오. 각 보기에 맞는 칸에 클릭하시오.

	2:00~2:45	3:00~3:45
Ⓐ 음악관 미디어랩에서 열림		
Ⓑ 다과 제공		
Ⓒ 친목 네트워킹 사이트와 이것이 음악에 끼치는 영향에 관해 발표		
Ⓓ 학생들에게 작곡을 장려하는 연구에 관해 발표		
Ⓔ 독창적인 음악 밴드 소개		

Service Encounters

1. Ⓑ → Ⓔ → Ⓐ → Ⓒ → Ⓓ **2.** Mentioned – Ⓐ, Ⓑ, Ⓓ Not Mentioned – Ⓒ, Ⓔ
3. Mentioned – Ⓐ, Ⓒ, Ⓓ Not Mentioned – Ⓑ, Ⓔ **4.** Ⓓ → Ⓐ → Ⓑ → Ⓒ

Dictation: Service Encounters

1. 1. use the bicycle parking lots 2. register it with us 3. any distinguishing features
   4. take security
2. 1. for up to three weeks 2. a few conditions 3. other contact information 4. you'd just
   give away
3. 1. got a virus 2. affected by the delay 3. extension on your tuition 4. the extension is
   automatic
4. 1. within the refund period 2. a matter of procedure 3. your original receipts 4. write the
   titles and authors

01

남 : 캠퍼스에 있는 자전거 주차 시설을 이용하려면 뭘 해야 하는지 알려주시겠어요?
여 : 네, 아주 간단해요. 먼저, 학교에 자전거를 가져와요.
남 : 오늘 집에서 제 자전거를 가져왔어요. 바깥에 체인으로 묶어 놓았어요.
여 : 좋아요. 그렇다면, 이제 자전거를 등록해야겠네요. 여기 이 양식을 기재해야 하고, 우리가 학생 자전거의 특
    징적인 부분을 디지털 카메라로 찍을 거에요. 도난 당할 때를 대비해서요.
남 : 그런 일이 자주 일어나나요?
여 : 아뇨, 그래도 보안에 신경을 많이 쓰고 있어요. 이런 절차들을 거치고 나서, 그림 스티커를 줄 테니 자전거에
    붙이도록 하세요.
남 : 네. 그런데 이용료도 내야 하나요?
여 : 네, 월 25 달러에요. 마지막에 이용료를 내고 나면, 다 끝나요!
남 : 네, 감사합니다!

어휘 parking lot 주차장 distinguishing 특색 있는 stolen 도난 당한 decal 그림 등의 전사 인쇄 fee 이용료, 요금

1. 여자는 캠퍼스에 자전거를 등록하는 절차를 설명하고 있다. 각 단계를 순서대로 배열하시오.
보기를 표의 해당되는 빈 칸으로 드래그하시오.

	캠퍼스 자전거 등록 절차
1	
2	
3	
4	
5	

Ⓐ 자전거의 특징적인 부분을 사진 찍기
Ⓑ 자전거를 학교로 가져오기
Ⓒ 자전거에 스티커 붙이기
Ⓓ 이용료 25 달러 내기
Ⓔ 신청서 작성하기

02

남 : 안녕하세요. 도와줄 일이 있나요?
여 : 네, 도와주셨으면 좋겠어요. 전 4학년인데, 이 책들을 통상 대출 기간인 10일 이상 빌리고 싶어요. 최대 3주 동안 대출할 수 있는 것이 맞죠?
남 : 맞아요, 학생이 4학년이니까요. 그렇지만 몇 가지 조건이 있어요.
여 : 이런, 모든 일이 이렇게 복잡하다니까요. 그럼, 조건이 무엇이죠?
남 : 장기간 대출하려던 학생이 장기 대출 신청을 해야 해요. 그리고 학생의 휴대 전화 번호와 이메일 주소, 기타 연락처를 우리가 알아두어야 하죠, 책을 꼭 돌려 받아야 하니까요.
여 : 네, 그리고 4학년 장기 대출 신청을 하려면 보증금을 내야 하는 것 아닌가요?
남 : 맞아요, 25 달러라 별로 비싸진 않지만, 지금 바로 낼 수 있는 액수도 아니죠.
여 : 괜찮아요. 신청하고 싶어요!

어휘 senior 4학년 period 기간 condition 조건 extended 연장한, 장기간에 걸친 deposit 예약금, 보증금 give away 거저 주다 남에게 맡기다

2. 대화에서, 사서는 장기 대출 요건을 설명하고 있다. 각 보기가 이 요건에 속하는지 아래 표에 표시하시오.
각 보기에 맞는 칸게 클릭하시오.

	Mentioned	Not Mentioned
Ⓐ 장기 대출 서비스를 신청하기		
Ⓑ 연락처가 정확한지 확인하기		
Ⓒ 빌린 책 목록을 만들기		
Ⓓ 보증금 25 달러를 내기		
Ⓔ 학생증을 사진 복사하기		

03

남 : 안녕하세요, 무엇을 도와 드릴까요?
여 : 음, 제가 이용하는 학자금 융자 회사 컴퓨터 시스템이 바이러스에 걸려서 2주 정도 일 처리가 늦어지게 되었

어요. 그런데 등록금도 내야 하고, 책도 사야 하고…

남 : 아, 너무 걱정 말아요, 같은 문제로 찾아온 학생들이 몇 명 있었어요.

여 : 그래요? 그럼 제가 할 수 있는 일이 있을까요?

남 : 먼저, 학자금 융자 회사의 업무 지연으로 인해 피해를 입었다는 것을 증명할 양식을 작성해야 해요.

여 : 네, 그 다음에는요?

남 : 교재 구입과 기본 경비 충당을 위해 긴급 대출이 필요할 거에요. 그리고 등록금 납부 기한 연장을 신청해야
    할 거에요. 여기 서류 양식이 있어요.

여 : 이미 이 일에 대해 잘 알고 계신다니 다행이에요. 얼마나 걸릴까요?

남 : 긴급 대출 받는데 24시간이 걸리고, 기한 연장은 자동적으로 처리됩니다. 마지막으로 할 일은 바이러스 문
    제가 해결될 때까지 인내심을 갖고 기다리는 겁니다!

여 : 감사합니다, 정말 큰 도움이 되었어요!

어휘 loan 융자, 대출 delay 연기시키다 emergency 긴급 상황 expense 경비 extension 기한 연장 patient 참을
      성 있는

3. 대화에서, 직원은 학생에게 문제 해결을 위해 해야 할 일을 일러주고 있다. 아래 표의 각 보기가 남자가 언급한
   내용인지 표시하시오. 각 보기에 맞는 칸에 클릭하시오.

	Mentioned	Not Mentioned
Ⓐ 학자금 융자 회사의 바이러스로 인한 지체 상황을 보여주는 서류 작성하기		
Ⓑ 학자금 융자 회사에 전화하여 상황을 설명하기		
Ⓒ 등록금 납부 마감일 연장 허가를 받기		
Ⓓ 교재 납부와 기타 경비 충당을 위해 긴급 대출 신청하기		
Ⓔ 교수님에게 학생이 가진 문제에 관해 이야기 하기		

04

여 : 안녕하세요, 이걸 반품하고 싶어요. 아직 환불을 받을 수 있는 기간인 것 같은데요?

남 : 언제 구입했죠?

여 : 4일 전에요.

남 : 그럼 환불 기간은 맞지만, 환불할 물건이 여러 가지라 조금 절차가 복잡합니다.

여 : 음… 무슨 문제라도 있나요?

남 : 그런 건 아니고, 환불 절차가 그래요. 먼저, 학생증 사본 1부를 제출해야 해요. 그리고 물건 구입 영수증도
    있어야 하고요.

여 : 네, 알겠어요. 모두 가지고 있어요.

남 : 좋아요. 그럼 이제 책을 처리하도록 하죠. 이 서류에 책 제목과 저자 이름을 쓰도록 해요, 강의명도 함께요.

여 : 네…

남 : 그리고 마지막으로, 랜턴이 그 박스에 들어있는지 확인해야겠어요. 그리고 학생은 랜턴 환불을 받으려면 다
    른 양식을 작성해야 해요.

여 : 네, 간단하네요. 도와주셔서 감사합니다!

어휘 bring back 반환하다 refund 환불하다 receipt 영수증 author 저자 verify 확인한다

4. 대화에서, 구내 서점 직원은 물품을 환불하는 절차를 설명하고 있다. 아래 보기를 순서대로 배열하시오.
각 보기를 표의 빈칸에 끌어다 넣으시오.

	물품 환불
단계 1	
단계 2	
단계 3	
단계 4	

Ⓐ 구입 물품 영수증 제출
Ⓑ 교재의 저자명과 제목을 적기
Ⓒ 랜턴이 들어있는지 확인하기
Ⓓ 학생증 사본 제시

Lectures

1. 1. Ⓒ 2. Athens – Ⓐ, Ⓒ, Ⓔ Sparta – Ⓑ, Ⓓ
2. 1. Ⓓ 2. Yes – Ⓐ, Ⓑ, Ⓔ No – Ⓒ, Ⓓ

Dictation: Lectures

1. 1. for times of war 2. taught to read and write 3. by a male slave 4. rare and costly
5. what additional subjects 6. military school 7. create an army 8. loyalty to the government 9. survival skills
2. 1. in a series of caves 2. strictly limited 3. date back to 4. in three distinct dialects
5. diverse group of documents 6. discovered by accident 7. chased an animal
8. breaking pottery 9. twisted and full of intrigue

01 유럽사 수업

P : 오늘 오후에는 고대 스파르타와 아테네의 교육에 관해 강의를 하겠어요. 아테네 학교는 시민들에게 인문 교육을 하였고, 전쟁에 대비하여 교육을 시켰을 뿐만이 아니라 평화로운 시기에 대해서도 교육을 시켰어요. 여자 아이들은 학교에 다니지 않았지만, 집에서 읽고 쓸 줄 아는 법을 배우는 여자 아이들이 많았죠. 남자 아이들은 6~7세 때까지는 어머니나 남자 노예에게 집에서 교육을 받았어요. 6~14세 때에는 집 근처의 학교에 다니거나 사립 학교에 보내졌죠. 책이 희귀하고 비쌌기 때문에, 교사들은 학생들이 수업 내용을 크게 따라 읽도록 하고, 수업 내용을 암기하도록 했어요. 남자로만 이루어져 있던 교사들은 추가 과목으로 어떤 걸 가르치고 싶은지를 선택할 수 있었어요. 호메로스(호머)의 시는 필수 교과 과정이었어요. 교사들은 연극이나, 웅변, 윤리, 회화, 독서, 수학과 같은 과목을 선택하기도 했죠. 초등학교를 마친 후에는 상급 학교에 4년간 더 다녔고, 그 후에 2년간 군대 학교에 갔죠.
그와 반대로, 스파르타 교육 제도는 군대를 만들 목적으로 이루어졌어요. 스파르타 사회는 엄격한 규율과 극기, 간단명료함, 정부에 대한 충성을 요구했죠. 따라서, 남자 아이들은 어린 나이에 군대에 들어갔어요. 생존 기술과 군대 생활에 필요한 기타 기술들을 배웠죠. 이러한 과목들은 상당히 어렵고 고통스러운 것이었어요. 학생들은 읽고 쓰는 법도 배웠지만, 고대 스파르타인들에게는 이러한 기술들이 전쟁보다는 중요치 않다고 여겨졌어요. 그 결과 무시무시한 군대가 만들어졌죠.

어휘 citizen 시민 slave 노예 aloud 크게 public speaking 연설 civics 국민 윤리 army 군대 discipline 규율 self-denial 극기 ancient 고대의 warfare 전쟁 terrifying 무서운

1. 강의의 주제는 무엇인가?
   Ⓐ 아테네의 남녀 공학 교육
   Ⓑ 스파르타 사회에서의 군대 교육의 중요성
   Ⓒ 고대 아테네와 스파르타의 교육 제도 비교
   Ⓓ 고대 아테네의 학교 역사

2. 교수는 두 가지 형태의 교육 제도를 설명하고 있다. 아래의 각 보기가 어떤 형태의 특징인지 아래 표에 표시하시오. 각 보기에 맞는 칸에 클릭하시오.

	Athens	Sparta
Ⓐ 교사는 다양한 과목 가운데 학생들을 가르칠 과목을 선택했다		
Ⓑ 군사 훈련이 강조되었다		
Ⓒ 여자 아이들은 집에서 교육 받았다		
Ⓓ 유일한 문과 과목은 기초 읽기와 쓰기였다		
Ⓔ 암기가 공부의 중요한 부분이었다		

02 세계사 수업

P : 오늘은 전세계에서 발견된 역사적으로 큰 의의가 있는 성서들 가운데 사해 두루마리에 관해 알아봅시다. 약 900여 개의 두루마리가 존재한다는 사실을 알게 되면 놀랄지도 모르겠군요. 사해 두루마리는 1947년과 1956년 사이에 웨스트 뱅크(요르단 강 서안 지구)의 사해 인근 동굴에서 발견되었어요. 처음에는 이 문서에 대한 접근이 엄격하게 제한되어 있었죠. 사해 두루마리가 이렇게 중요한 가치를 지니는 이유는 이 문서가 서기 100년 전부터 성서 시대의 기록을 보여주는 유일한 자료이기 때문이에요. 방사성 탄소 연대 측정 결과에 따르면 가장 오래 전에 만들어진 두루마리는 기원전 2세기 이전으로 거슬러 올라가며, 약 200여 년에 걸쳐 제작되었어요. 필사본은 세 개의 서로 다른 히브리 방언으로 쓰여졌고, 아랍어와 고대 그리스 방언으로 쓰여지기도 했죠.

여러분이 꼭 기억해두어야 할 중요한 점은 이 사해 두루마리를 통해 당시의 유대교 문화에 관해 알 수 있다는 겁니다. 실제로 필사본에는 상당히 다양한 내용이 담겨 있어요. 일부는 고대 유대교에 대한 기록처럼 보이고, 또 다른 두루마리에는 당시의 사회상에 관한 설명이 들어있기도 하고, 심지어는 금과 무기, 또 다른 필사본, 그 외 귀중품이 숨겨져 있는 장소를 나타낸 보물 지도처럼 보이는 것도 있어요. 역사적으로 큰 가치를 가지고 있는 많은 발견물들이 그러하듯, 첫 번째 필사본은 우연히 발견되었어요. 들리는 이야기에 의하면, 한 소년이 동물을 쫓던 중에 동굴 입구에 다다르게 되었다고 해요. 이 소년이 어떤 동물이었는지는 확실히 알려져 있지 않지만, 아무튼 이 동물을 몰아내기 위해 동굴 안으로 돌을 던졌어요. 소년은 도자기가 깨지는 소리를 듣고 안에 뭔가 값이 나가는 물건이 있을 거라 생각하게 되었어요. 이렇게 해서 이 소년이 리넨으로 싸여져 있는 필사본을 발견하게 된 거죠. 사해 두루마리는 현재 예루살렘에 소재한 박물관에 소장되어 있는데, 박물관에 보관되기까지 아주 험난한 과정을 거쳐야 했어요. 오늘날 이 필사본을 비교 연구할 수 있는 문서가 극소수에 불과하기 때문에, 이를 완벽하게 이해하기는 어려워요. 그렇다고 해도, 이 사해 두루마리의 가치에 대해 부인하는 사람은 아무도 없죠.

어휘 holy 성스러운 document 문서 approximately 대략 cave 동굴 access 접근 strictly 엄격하게 Biblical 성서의 distinct 독특한, 별개의 dialect 방언, 사투리 Judaism 유대교, 유대 문화 religion 종교 function 기능하다 treasure 보물 map 지도 stash 은닉처, 은닉한 것 weapon 무기 valuable 귀중품 find 발견물 by accident 우연히 chase 쫓다 specify 상술하다 pottery 도자기 wrap 감싸다 linen 리넨, 아마포 intrigue 음모

1. 최초의 사해 두루마리는 어디에서 발견되었는가?
    Ⓐ 고대 사원에서
    Ⓑ 사해 밑바닥에서
    Ⓒ 예루살렘에서
    Ⓓ 동굴에서

2. 교수는 사해 두루마리에 쓰여져 있는 내용에 대해 언급하고 있다. 아래의 각 보기가 이 내용에 속하는지 아래 표
   에 표시하시오. 각 보기에 맞는 칸에 클릭하시오.

	Yes	No
Ⓐ 종교적 내용		
Ⓑ 당시의 사회상		
Ⓒ 도기 제작 과정		
Ⓓ 멸종된 동물		
Ⓔ 보물이 숨겨져 있는 장소		

Practice

[1-5] 1. Ⓑ   2. Ⓓ   3. Ⓓ   4. Ⓒ   5. Suggested – Ⓒ, Ⓓ Not Suggested – Ⓐ, Ⓑ
[6-11] 6. Ⓐ   7. Ⓑ   8. Ⓓ   9. Ⓑ   10. Ⓓ   11. Mentioned – Ⓑ, Ⓒ Not Mentioned – Ⓐ, Ⓓ

[문제 1–5] Listen to part of a conversation between a student and a professor.

W : Professor Mackenzie, could you spare me a few minutes? I could use some perspective on
    something.

M : Sure, what's on your mind?

W : Well, it's about my major. I'm beginning to question whether I've made the right decision.

M : How so? You're an English literature major, right?

W : 🎧 That's right, that's my major, but I've been thinking about changing. Well, I'm concerned
    about the job market, to be honest. I really enjoy reading literature and writing a short story,
    but...

M : But you're worried about how useful it will be. I understand. 3.These days, many students
    who are majoring in the humanities are asking those questions. I think economics and
    accounting are more popular than ever, for that very reason. You are also one of those
    interested in number-related jobs?

W : Well, actually I don't know about that. But I've long been thinking that maybe teaching is my
    thing. Do you know what I mean?

M : Um, are you thinking about that as a career?

W : I guess I am. I'm interested in adult education. Maybe literacy or illiteracy.

M : Good. Uh, are you planning on going to graduate school? I think that might be an important
    question, actually.

W : Yes, I think I should go to graduate school. Many people say it's better to have a master's
    degree if I'm looking for a good job.

M : In that case, I'd keep your major if you're happy with it. You might consider switching to
    education in grad school.

W : That makes sense.

M : What's your minor?

W : Spanish.

M : Oh, you have a linguistic talent. Spanish is useful. What I'd suggest, then, is that if you're interested in adult education, you ought to start looking at graduate programs. A master's in adult education, applied linguistics, or several other disciplines might be the right path for you. Maybe one here will appeal to you.

W : So I don't necessarily have to change my major?

M : Of course not. You just need to investigate your options, and start planning ahead now.

W : All right, thanks!

여 : Mackenzie 교수님, 잠깐 시간 좀 내주시겠어요? 조언을 구하고 싶은 일이 있습니다.

남 : 그래, 무슨 일이지?

여 : 제 전공 때문에요. 옳은 결정을 내린 건지 잘 모르겠어요.

남 : 어떤 점에서? 넌 영문학을 전공하고 있잖니?

여 : 네, 영문학이 제 전공인데요, 전공을 바꾸어야 하지 않을까 생각 중이에요. 솔직히 말씀 드리자면, 취업이 걱정돼요. 문학 작품 읽는 것도 정말 좋아하고 단편도 즐겨 쓰긴 하는데요…

남 : 그렇긴 한데 얼마나 쓸모가 있을지 잘 모르겠다는 말이구나. 이해한단다. 요즘 인문학을 공부하는 학생들 상당 수가 그런 질문을 하고 있어. 그런 이유 때문에 어느 때보다도 경제학과 회계학이 인기가 높은 것 같더구나. 너도 숫자 관련 직업에 관심이 있니?

여 : 사실 잘 모르겠어요. 하지만 오래 전부터 뭔가를 가르치는 일이 저에게 맞는 일일지도 모른다고 생각해왔어요. 무슨 얘긴지 아시겠어요?

남 : 직업으로도 생각하고 있는 거니?

여 : 그런 것 같아요. 전 성인 교육에 관심이 있어요. 문맹 교육 같은 거요.

남 : 그렇구나. 대학원에 진학할 생각도 있니? 이게 결정을 내리는데 중요한 문제가 될 것 같은데.

여 : 네, 대학원에 가야 할 것 같아요. 좋은 직장을 구하려면 석사 학위를 따는 게 좋다고 말하는 사람들이 많아요.

남 : 그런 경우, 지금 전공에 만족하고 있으면 계속 그 공부를 하는 게 나을 것 같구나. 대학원에 진학하면서 교육학으로 전공을 바꿀 수도 있지.

여 : 그럴 수도 있겠네요.

남 : 부전공은 뭐니?

여 : 스페인어요.

남 : 어학적 재능이 있구나. 스페인어도 유용하지. 그럼, 네가 성인 교육에 관심이 있으면, 대학원 프로그램을 한 번 알아보도록 하렴. 성인 교육이나 응용 언어학 같은 분야가 너에게 적합할 것 같구나. 우리학교 프로그램 중에도 맘에 드는 게 있을 거야.

여 : 그럼 제가 굳이 전공을 바꿀 필요는 없다는 말씀이시죠?

남 : 그렇지. 너에게 어떤 선택의 기회가 있을지 알아보고 미리 계획을 세워두면 된단다.

여 : 알겠습니다, 감사합니다!

어휘 perspective 관점 the humanities 인문학 economics 경제학 accounting 회계 literacy 읽고 쓸 줄 앎 illiteracy 문맹 switch 바꾸다 minor 부전공 discipline 학문 분야 path 길, 진로

Topic: Major charge 전공 바꾸기

1. English lit major 영문학 전공
   – concerned about job 취업 걱정
2. Interested in teaching 교육 쪽에 관심이 있음
   – Adult education 성인 교육
   – going to grad school 대학원 진학 계획
3. Prof.'s suggestion 교수의 제안
   – keep major 현재 전공 유지
   – switch to education in grad school 대학원에서 교육학으로 전공 바꾸기

1. 교수와 학생이 이 대화를 나누는 이유는 무엇인가?
   Ⓐ 학생은 경제학을 전공할까 생각 중이다.
   Ⓑ 학생은 전공을 바꾸는 것에 대해 생각하고 있다.
   Ⓒ 학생은 아직 전공을 선택하지 못했다.
   Ⓓ 학생은 대학원 진학에 대해 생각하고 있다.
   해설 학생은 영문학을 전공하고 있는데, 취업 전망을 고려하여 전공을 바꾸어야 할지 고민하고 있다. 보기 Ⓒ의
       내용처럼 아직 전공을 선택 못한 것은 아니다.
   정답 Ⓑ

2. 왜 학생은 현재 전공에 대해 다시 생각해보게 되었는가?
   Ⓐ 글쓰기에 재능이 없다.
   Ⓑ 아이들을 가르치는데 관심이 있다.
   Ⓒ 숫자와 관련된 직업을 가지고 싶어한다.
   Ⓓ 현재 전공이 취직할 때 별로 도움이 안 될지도 모른다.
   해설 학생은 문학 작품 읽는 것도 좋아하고 단편을 쓰는 것도 좋아하지만, 취업에 대해 걱정하고 있다. 영문학이
       취업에 얼마나 도움이 될지 확신을 못하고 있다.
   정답 Ⓓ

대화의 일부를 다시 들으시오. 그러고 나서 질문에 답하시오.

3. 교수가 이것을 말할 때 암시하는 것은 무엇인가?
   *M : These days, many students who are majoring in the humanities are asking those
        questions.*
   Ⓐ 많은 학생들이 전공을 인문학으로 바꾸고 있다.
   Ⓑ 인문학 전공생들은 자신의 선택에 의구심을 품지 않는다.
   Ⓒ 경제학과 회계학이 인문학보다 더 재미있다.
   Ⓓ 인문학 전공자 수가 감소하고 있다.
   해설 영문학이 졸업 후 취업을 할 때 얼마나 유용할지 잘 모르겠다고 학생이 말하자, 교수가 요즘 인문학을 전공
       하는 많은 학생들이 그와 같은 질문을 하고 있다고 말했다. 교수의 이 같은 말을 통해 인문학 전공자 수가
       감소하고 있을 것임을 미루어 짐작할 수 있다.
   정답 Ⓓ

4. 대화에 따르면, 학생의 부전공은 무엇인가?

   Ⓐ 응용 언어학

   Ⓑ 경제학

   Ⓒ 스페인어

   Ⓓ 성인 교육

해설 학생의 현재 전공은 영문학, 부전공은 스페인어, 앞으로 공부하고 싶은 분야는 성인 교육이다.

정답 Ⓒ

5. 대화에서, 교수는 학생이 고려해보아야 할 점들을 제시하고 있다. 아래 표의 각 보기가 이에 해당하는지 표시하시오. 각 보기에 맞는 칸에 클릭하시오.

	Suggested	Not Suggested
Ⓐ 스페인어 사용 국가에서 일하기		
Ⓑ 다른 대학으로 편입하기		
Ⓒ 성인 교육 분야에서 석사 학위 취득		
Ⓓ 현재 전공을 유지하기		

해설 학생이 졸업 후에 하고 싶은 교육 분야의 일이 영문학과도 관련이 있기 때문에, 교수는 학생에게 학부에서는 계속 영문학을 전공하고 대학원 진학시에 전공을 교육 분야로 바꾸라고 조언하고 있다.

정답 Suggested – Ⓒ, Ⓓ Not Suggested – Ⓐ, Ⓑ

[문제 6-11] Listen to part of a lecture in an energy resources engineering class.

P(W) : 🎧 All right, to start our discussion of the benefits of natural gas, let me ask a question: Do you know how much less natural gas costs, per unit of energy it produces, than oil?

S(M) : 7.Umm... half, or 70%?

P : Well, it's hard to say precisely. It depends on variables like the local taxes or the price of oil. Look, oil prices have been rising so fast lately. In general, natural gas produces the same amount of energy for a third the price of petroleum. What's even better about natural gas is that we've got a lot of it. Does anybody know which country has the most natural gas?

S : The U.S.A?

P : Actually, Qatar has the most recoverable gas that we know of right now, although Iran might be in 2nd place. Also, scientists suspect that huge reserves exist in ocean trenches, but obviously there's no feasible technology capable of extracting it from those depths yet.

S : Um, as far as I know, natural gas is also a form of fossil fuels like coal and oil.

P : That's true. It can be produced from the decay of organic material that was buried about 3.5 billion years ago. Methane, a gas composed of one carbon atom and four hydrogen atoms, is the most common ingredient of natural gas. Although both natural gas and petroleum are fossil fuels, natural gas has a number of important benefits compared with petroleum. First of all, it burns more cleanly. For the same amount of heat energy, gas produces 30% less carbon dioxide than petroleum, and 45% less than coal. Almost no ash is left after it is burned, as well. Next, uh, natural gas requires a significant amount of processing in order to purify it, but it's still a lot less expensive and labor-intensive than petroleum. It can also be used to produce hydrogen, which itself can be used as a fuel.

S : What about CNG vehicles?

P : Compressed natural gas can be used instead of gasoline and diesel fuel. It's not in wide use in the U.S. yet, except in public transit vehicles, but in other countries, it's not unusual to find cars that run on CNG. The energy efficiency is about the same as petroleum, although diesel engines still get better mileage. Many predict that biogas will become one of the world's primary sources of energy in the future. Next, why don't we take a brief look at how natural gas is stored and delivered?

P : 자, 천연 가스의 이점에 관한 오늘의 강의를 시작하면서, 질문 하나를 하겠어요. 석유에 비해 에너지 단위당 천연 가스 생산 비용이 얼마나 적게 드는지 알고 있나요?

S : 음... 절반, 아니면 70% 정도요?

P : 정확하게 말하기는 어려워요. 지방세나 석유 가격과 같은 변수들에 따라 달라지죠. 음, 최근에 유가가 급등하고 있죠. 보통 천연 가스는 유가의 1/3에 해당하는 경비로 같은 양의 에너지를 생산해내요. 매장량이 많다는 사실이 천연 가스의 또 다른 이점이죠. 천연 가스 매장량이 가장 풍부한 국가가 어디인지 아는 사람 있어요?

S : 미국이요?

P : 음, 현재 알려진 바로는 카타르(페르시아만 연안의 독립국)에 채굴 가능한 가스 매장량이 가장 풍부하다고 해요, 그 뒤가 이란이고요. 그리고 과학자들은 해구에 엄청난 양의 가스가 매장되어 있다고 생각하고 있는데, 아직 그렇게 깊은 심해에서 가스를 채굴해낼 현실적인 기술이 없는 것이 사실이에요.

S : 제가 알기로는, 천연 가스도 석탄과 석유와 마찬가지로 화석 연료라고 하던데요.

P : 맞아요. 천연 가스는 약 35억년 전에 묻힌 유기물로 만들어집니다. 탄소 원자 1개와 수소 원자 4개로 이루어진 기체인 메탄이 천연 가스의 주성분이죠. 천연 가스와 석유 모두 화석 연료이긴 하지만, 천연 가스는 석유와 비교해 볼 때 이점이 아주 많아요. 첫째로, 천연 가스는 환경에 더 깨끗하게 연소해요. 똑같은 양의 열에너지를 생산한다고 치면, 천연 가스는 석유보다 30% 더 적은 양의 이산화탄소를 배출하고 석탄보다는 45%가 더 적은 양의 이산화탄소를 배출하죠. 연소된 후에 남아있는 재도 거의 없어요. 다음으로, 천연 가스를 정제하기 위해서는 처리 과정이 상당히 복잡하지만, 석유보다는 비용이 훨씬 저렴하고 노동력이 더 적게 들어요. 또한 천연 가스는 수소 생산에도 사용되는데, 이 수소만으로도 연료 이용이 가능하죠.

S : 압축천연가스 차량은요?

P : 압축천연가스는 가솔린과 디젤 연료를 대신하여 사용 가능해요. 미국에서는 대중교통차량을 제외하고는 아직 크게 보편화되어 있지는 않지만, CNG 차량을 쉽게 찾아볼 수 있는 국가들이 여럿 있어요. 연비는 디젤 엔진이 좀 더 우수하지만, 에너지 효율성은 석유와 거의 같은 수준이에요. 앞으로 생물 가스가 전세계의 제 1의 에너지원이 될 것이라고 생각하는 사람들이 많이 있죠. 자, 이제 천연 가스 저장과 수송 방법에 관해 잠깐 살펴볼까요?

어휘 precisely 정확하게 variable 변수 lately 최근에 petroleum 석유 reserves 매장량 ocean trench 해구 feasible 실행 가능한 extract 추출하다 depth 깊이 decay 자연 붕괴, 쇠퇴 organic material 유기물 bury 묻다 methane 메탄 atom 원자 ingredient 성분, 요소 fossil fuel 화석 연료 ash 재 purify 정제하다 labor-intensive 노동 집약적인 efficiency 효율성 mileage 연비

Topic: Natural gas 천연 가스

1. 1/3 of the oil price 석유 가격의 1/3
2. Qatar has the most 카타르에 매장량이 가장 많음
   – Iran: 2nd 이란: 2번째
   – huge reserves in ocean trench, but no tech 해구에 매장량이 많지만 기술이 부족함
3. Fossil fuel 화석 연료
   – Methane: 1st ingredient 메탄: 주성분
4. Benefits compared w/ oil 석유와 비교할 때의 이점
   – burn more cleanly: less carbon dioxide 더 깨끗하게 연소함: 이산화탄소를 더 적게 배출함
   – no ash left 재도 남지 않음
   – purifying: cheaper, less labor 정제 과정: 더 저렴하고 노동력이 더 적게 듦
   – produce hydrogen 수소를 발생시킴
5. CNG vehicles 압축천연가스 차량
   – the same energy efficiency as oil 에너지 효율이 석유와 거의 같음

6. 화자들은 강의 시간에 무엇에 관해 이야기 하고 있는가?
   Ⓐ 천연 가스의 이점
   Ⓑ 화석 연료의 종류
   Ⓒ 에너지 생산
   Ⓓ 압축천연가스 차량
   해설 다른 연료와 비교하여 천연 가스(natural gas)의 이점과 이용에 관해 설명하고 있다.
   정답 Ⓐ

강의의 일부를 다시 들으시오. 그러고 나서 질문에 답하시오.

7. 학생이 이것을 말할 때 의미하는 것은 무엇인가: 

   S : Umm... half, or 70%?
   Ⓐ 교수가 자신에게 답을 알려주기를 원한다.
   Ⓑ 대답이 정확한지 확신하지 못하고 있다.
   Ⓒ 교수가 무슨 말을 하고 있는지 전혀 감을 못 잡고 있다.
   Ⓓ 정확한 수치를 알고 있다.
   해설 석유에 비해 에너지 단위당 천연 가스 생산 비용이 얼마나 적게 드는지 알고 있냐는 교수의 질문에 망설이
        면서 절반이나 70% 정도가 아니냐고 답하고 있다. 이는 학생이 정확한 답을 모르고 있음을 나타낸다.
   정답 Ⓑ

8. 천연 가스 매장량이 가장 많은 나라는 어디인가?
   Ⓐ 이란
   Ⓑ 미국
   Ⓒ 사우디아라비아
   Ⓓ 카타르
   해설 카타르에 채굴 가능한 가스 매장량이 가장 풍부하고 그 다음이 이란이라고 하였다.
   정답 Ⓓ

9. 심해 천연 가스 매장량을 이용하기 위해 필요한 것은 무엇인가?
    Ⓐ 탐사 비용
    Ⓑ 기술 발전
    Ⓒ 인적 자원
    Ⓓ 정부 지원
    해설 현재 해구에 엄청난 양의 천연 가스가 매장되어 있지만, 아직 이곳의 자원을 채굴할 기술이 많이 발달되어
        있지 않다. 따라서 천연 가스 이용량을 증대시키기 위해서는 기술 발전이 우선되어야 한다.
    정답 Ⓑ

10. 천연 가스의 주성분은 무엇인가?
    Ⓐ 질소
    Ⓑ 수소
    Ⓒ 탄소
    Ⓓ 메탄
    해설 천연 가스의 주성분은 메탄이라고 하였다.
    정답 Ⓓ

11. 강의에서, 교수는 쓰유와 비교하여 천연 가스의 여러 이점에 대해 언급하고 있다. 아래 표의 각 보기가 어떤 것
    에 해당하는지 표시하시오. 각 보기에 맞는 칸에 클릭하시오.

	Mentioned	Not Mentioned
Ⓐ 첨단 기술을 이용하여 추출된다.		
Ⓑ 이산화탄소를 훨씬 적게 배출한다.		
Ⓒ 생산비가 더 저렴하다.		
Ⓓ 저장과 수송이 쉽다.		

    해설 보통 천연 가스는 같은 양의 에너지를 석유의 1/3에 해당하는 경비로 생산해낼 수 있다고 하였고, 연소할
        때 비교적 적은 양의 오염 물질을 배출하고, 정제 비용이 석유보다 저렴하고 노동력이 적게 든다고 하였다.
        교수가 천연 가스의 저장과 수송에 대해 알아보자고 하면서 강의가 끝났기 때문에, 저장과 수송이 쉬운지
        에 대해서는 알 수 없다.
    정답 Mentioned – Ⓑ, Ⓒ Not Mentioned – Ⓐ, Ⓓ

Chapter 5 Stance/Function

Office Hours

1. Ⓓ **2.** Ⓒ **3.** Ⓒ **4.** Ⓓ

Dictation: Office Hours

1. 1. at the beginning of the semester 2. in front of other people 3. to some degree 4. raise my hand and ask more questions

2. 1. you're having second thoughts 2. disagree with you 3. simple administrative things 4. when they start new jobs

3. 1. let me put it this way 2. a good reference out of this 3. taking your duties seriously 4. shrug it off 5. act more mature

4. 1. whether t'll influence my grade 2. another commitment 3. to make sure he's ready 4. gave them my word 5. giving extra credit to 6. I'm relieved

01

남 : 교수님, 무슨 일로 보자고 하셨어요?

여 : 이번 학기 너의 수업 참여도에 대해 좀 걱정이 되는구나. 수업 참여도 점수가 전체 성적의 25%를 차지한다는 건 알고 있겠지?

남 : 네, 알고 있어요. 학기 초에 말씀하셨잖아요.

여 : 그런데 네가 우리 수업을 듣는 학생인 것처럼 보이지 않더구나.

남 : 음, 그게 말이죠… 제가 수줍음을 많이 타요, 그리고 다른 사람들 앞에서 말할 때면, 정말 긴장되거든요.

여 : 대부분의 사람들이 어느 정도는 너처럼 그렇게 느낀단다.

남 : 그럼, 제가 안 좋은 점수를 받게 되는 건가요?

여 : 수업에 더 적극적으로 참여하지 않으면, 그렇단다. 넌 매우 똑똑한 학생이고, 과제물도 열심히 해오고 있잖니. 그 부분의 점수는 좋아. 네 수업 참여도가 문제란다. 그것 때문에 점수가 많이 깎이게 될 거야.

남 : 아직 이번 학기가 한 달 정도 더 남았잖아요. 제가 손을 들고 질문을 더 많이 하면, 도움이 될까요?

어휘 shy 수줍음을 타는 get nervous 긴장하다 bright 똑똑한

대화의 일부를 다시 들으시오. 그러고 나서 질문에 답하시오.

1. 교수가 이것을 말할 때 의미하는 것은 무엇인가: 

   W : It'll pull you down.

   Ⓐ 학생은 낙제를 할 것이다.

   Ⓑ 학생은 수줍음을 완전히 극복해야 한다.

   Ⓒ 학생은 숙제를 제쳐 두고 더 적극적이 되어야 한다.

   Ⓓ 낮은 수업 참여도 점수가 학생의 전체 성적에 좋지 않은 영향을 줄 것이다.

02

남 : Catherine 교수님, 조교 일에 관해서 이야기를 나눌 수 있을까요? 다음 주부터 시작하기로 했는데요, 아직 몇 가지 질문이 있어요.

여 : 그래. 그런데 조교 일에 대해 다시 생각해보고 있는 것처럼 보이는구나. 아직 하고 싶은 마음은 있니?

남 : 그런 것 같습니다. 가이드 북을 읽어봤지만, 튜터를 할만큼 과목에 대해 많이 알고 있는 것 같지 않아요.

여 : 음, 네가 듣고 있는 수업에서 아주 잘 하고 있으니까 그 말에는 동의할 수가 없구나. 그렇지만 걱정하지 말도록 해. 가르치는 일은 별로 없을 거니까. 대개는 점수를 매기거나 하는 것처럼 간단한 행정 일을 하게 될 테니까.

남 : 제가 잘 할 수 있을지 정말 모르겠어요!

여 : 난 네가 잘 할 수 있을 거라 믿는단다. 그래서 조교 일을 부탁한 거야. 그리고 이번이 처음이잖아. 사람들은 새로운 일을 시작할 때 모두 긴장하게 마련이야.

남 : 네, 감사합니다. 이제 좀 기분이 나아진 것 같아요.

어휘 TA 조교(teaching assistant) second thought 재고 subject 과목

대화의 일부를 다시 들으시오. 그러고 나서 질문에 답하시오.

2. 교수는 왜 이렇게 말하는가: 

   W : Sure. Well, you look like you're having second thoughts.

Ⓐ 조교 일을 정말 하고 싶어하는 것처럼 보인다.
Ⓑ 조교 일을 하기 위한 준비를 더 많이 해야 한다.
Ⓒ 학생이 조교 일에 대한 생각을 바꾼 것처럼 보인다.
Ⓓ 학생은 돈을 더 벌기 위해 부업을 해야 할 것이다.

03

남 : 음, 저에 대한 평가가 어땠어요? 저에 대해 어떻게 생각하는지 정말 궁금해요…
여 : 이렇게 말해볼게. 네가 미술관을 불태워버리지도 않았고, 소장품을 훼손시킨 것도 아니지…
남 : 무슨 말씀이신지 알겠어요.
여 : Nate, 지금 네가 일하는 곳은 시에서 가장 중요한 미술관이잖니. 좋은 평판을 얻으려면, 반드시 지켜서 해
　　내야 하는 일들이 있어.
남 : 제가 별로라고 생각한대요?
여 : 네가 맡은 일을 진지하게 생각하지 않는 것 같다고 하더구나. 이 문제에 대해 매니저가 너에게 이야기를 하
　　니까, 네가 그냥 대수롭지 않게 넘어갔다고 하고.
남 : 그게 말이죠…
여 : 너에게 아주 솔직하게 말해 주는 거야. 매니저의 평가도 읽어봤고, 직접 이야기도 몇 번 해봤고, 내가 느낀
　　점도 있어. 좀 더 어른스럽게 행동하도록 하렴. 지각도 하지 말고, 복장도 깔끔하게 갖추고, 맡은 일도 제대
　　로 하고. 이 일에 최선의 노력을 다해야 한다는 뜻이야.
남 : 실망시켜드려 죄송합니다.
여 : 괜찮아. 이 일로 뭔가 깨달은 바가 있겠지.

어휘　evaluation 평가　burn down 불태워버리다　collection 소장품　shrug off 무시해버리다　mature 성숙한　give
　　　　one's best shot at ~에 최선을 다하다　let down 실망시키다하다

대화의 일부를 다시 들으시오. 그러고 나서 질문에 답하시오.

3. 교수가 이것을 말할 때 의미하는 것은 무엇인가: 

　　W : Well, let me put it this way. You haven't burned the museum down or damaged anything
　　　　in the collection...
　　Ⓐ 학생은 인턴 근무를 아주 잘 했다.
　　Ⓑ 학생이 재산 피해를 냈다.
　　Ⓒ 학생에 대한 평가가 꽤 안 좋다.
　　Ⓓ 학생은 미술관 소장품을 조심성 있게 다루었다.

04

남 : 잠깐 시간 좀 있으세요, Danes 교수님?
여 : 그래, Jake. 무슨 일이니?
남 : 토요일에 열리는 특별 강연에 대해 여쭤볼게 있습니다. 그 날 참석을 못 할 것 같은데요, 제 성적에 영향이
　　있을 지 알고 싶습니다.
여 : 다른 일이라도 있니?
남 : 네, 제가 개인 과외를 하는데요, 제가 가르치는 학생이 다음 주에 시험을 봐요. 시험에 충분히 대비할 수 있
　　게 특별 공부 시간을 갖기로 되어 있어요. 이번 강연이 중요한 건 줄은 알지만, 제가 그 분들과 약속을 했거
　　든요.

여 : 알겠구나. 참석을 안 해도 괜찮아. 어쨌든 학생들에게 수업 시간 이외에 이런 행사에 참여하라고 강요할 수
는 없는 노릇이니까. 참석하는 학생들에게는 특별 점수를 주긴 하지만, 학기 중에 특별 점수를 받을 기회가
또 있으니까. 걱정 안 해도 될 거야.

남 : 이제 안심이 되네요.

어휘 commitment 약속 give one's word 약속하다 force 강요하다 show up 나타나다 relieved 안심이 되는

대화의 일부를 다시 들으시오. 그러고 나서 질문에 답하시오.

4. 학생은 왜 이것을 말하는가: 

 M : I know this lecture is important, but I gave them my word.

 Ⓐ 무슨 수를 써서라도 강연에 참석할 것이다.

 Ⓑ 강연이 열리든 말든 상관 없다.

 Ⓒ 특별 학점이 선약보다 더 중요하다.

 Ⓓ 학생을 가르친다는 약속을 지켜야 한다.

Service Encounters
 1. Ⓑ **2.** Ⓑ **3.** Ⓓ **4.** Ⓐ

Dictation: Service Encounters
 1. 1. check out the video series 2. kept losing them 3. rather watch by myself 4. evenings
  are busiest
 2. 1. I got lost 2. don't simply give up 3. make a series of appointments 4.from the
  graduate students
 3. 1. hold a conference 2. the president of the campus branch 3. for the keynote speech
  4. a copy of the fee schedule
 4. 1. haven't gotten a reply 2. includes 3 meals a day 3. sleep through breakfast
  4. printed out a copy 5. a deadline for changes

01

남 : 안녕하세요, 제가 스페인어 수업을 듣고 있는데요, 비디오 시리즈를 빌려가고 싶습니다. 어떻게 하면 되죠?
여 : 학생은 이 곳을 이용해 본 적이 한 번도 없죠? 비디오 테이프는 비용이 많이 드는데다, 계속 잃어버리는 경
우가 많았어요. 그러니 이 곳 비디오 부스에서 비디오를 봐야 해요. 아, 지금 학생과 같은 반 학생들이 기초
스페인어를 보고 있는데, 같이 보겠어요?
남 : 고맙지만, 혼자 보는 게 더 좋겠습니다. 언제 부스를 이용할 수 있죠?
여 : 도서관이랑 시간은 같아요. 한 번에 2시간 동안 부스를 예약할 수 있어요. 비디오 시청에 필요한 시간보다는
약간 더 긴 시간이죠.
남 : 어떻게 예약하죠?
여 : 원하는 날짜와 시간을 예약하면 됩니다. 보통은 당일 날 사용할 수 있어요. 저녁 시간은 가장 붐빌 때죠. 오
후에 오는 편이 좋아요.
남 : 네, 고맙습니다!

어휘 by oneself 혼자서 recommend 추천하다

대화의 일부를 다시 들으시오. 그러고 나서 질문에 답하시오.

1. 여자가 이것을 말할 때 암시하는 것은 무엇인가: 

   W : You've never been here before, haven't you?

   Ⓐ 스페인어 DVD는 이용 불가능하다.
   Ⓑ 학생은 DVD를 대출할 수 없다.
   Ⓒ 학생은 미디어 센터를 이용했었어야 한다.
   Ⓓ 학생은 스페인어 DVD를 더 자주 봐야 한다.

02

여 : Ducharme 교수님, 미적분학 기말고사에 관해 잠깐 이야기 좀 나눌 수 있을까요?
남 : 그래, 무슨 일이지?
여 : 그게 말이죠, 제가 교수님 수업 시간에 그렇게 잘 하고 있지 못해요.
남 : 그래, 조금 더 좋은 성적을 받을 수도 있을 텐데 말이야.
여 : 어, 시험이 정말 죽정이에요. 아직 이해 못하는 부분이 너무 많아요. 기본 개념은 알겠는데, 문제를 풀다 보
    면 헤매게 되요. 시험은 2주 밖에 안 남았는데…
남 : 꾸준히 공부는 하고 있니?
여 : 네, 아무래도 미적분학에는 도무지 소질이 없나 봐요.
남 : 쉽게 포기하지 말아라! 이렇게 해보렴. 앞으로 2주간은 이 곳 연구실에 평소보다 더 자주 있을 거야. 약속을 정
    해 만나서 공부하는 것을 도와주도록 할게. 그리고 튜터링 센터에도 가서 대학원생들의 도움을 받도록 하렴.
여 : 교수님의 도움에 제가 얼마나 감사하게 생각하는지 모르실 거에요!
남 : 별것 아닌데 뭘. 여기 내 강의 스케줄이 있어.

어휘 calculus 미적분학 steadily 꾸준히 aptitude 적성, 소질 give up 포기하다

대화의 일부를 다시 들으시오. 그러고 나서 질문에 답하시오.

2. 남자가 이것을 말할 때 암시하는 것은 무엇인가: 

   M : Your grade could be a little better, yes.

   Ⓐ 학생이 잘 하고 있다고 생각한다.
   Ⓑ 학생이 좀 더 좋은 성적을 내기를 기대하고 있었다.
   Ⓒ 학생의 말에 동의하지 않는다.
   Ⓓ 학생이 낙제를 할 것이라는 걸 이미 알고 있다.

03

남 : 컨퍼런스를 개최하려고 하는데요, 캠퍼스 시설 담당자세요?
여 : 네, 맞습니다. 행사를 개최할 공간이 필요한가요?
남 : 네. 제가 시에라 클럽(미국의 자연 환경 보호 단체)의 캠퍼스 지부 회장인데요, 우리 학교에 지역 컨퍼런스를
    개최할 수 있는 공간이 있는지 알고 싶습니다.
여 : 언제로 계획하고 있나요?
남 : 연말 즈음이요. 11월이나 12월요.
여 : 아, 그럼 아직 시간이 많이 있네요. 캠퍼스 컨퍼런스 센터를 사용할 수도 있고, 가을 방학 기간에 컨퍼런스를
    개최한다면, 기조 연설을 위해 대강당을 사용할 수도 있어요.

남 : 사용료를 내야 하는 건가요?
여 : 다양해요. 이 사용료 스케줄을 참고하도록 하세요. 클럽 회원들과 상의한 후에 우리에게 알려주는 것이 어때요?
남 : 네, 그렇게 하겠습니다.

어휘 in charge of ~를 담당하고 있는 hold 개최하다 keynote speech 기조 연설

대화의 일부를 다시 들으시오. 그러고 나서 질문에 답하시오.

3. 여자가 이것을 말할 때 의미하는 것은 무엇인가? 
   W : It varies. Here's a copy of the fee schedule.
   Ⓐ 임대료가 보통 비싸다.
   Ⓑ 연초에는 사용료가 더 저렴하다.
   Ⓒ 가을 방학에는 무료이다.
   Ⓓ 사용료는 월마다 다르다.

04

여 : 안녕하세요, 제가 신청한 환불에 관해 여쭤보고 싶거든요? 제가 환불에 관해 이메일을 보냈는데, 아무런 연락이 없어서요.
남 : 무엇을 바꾸고 싶어했죠?
여 : 원래 하루에 세끼 모두 먹는 급식을 신청했는데요. 제가 강의 스케줄을 바꾸었어요, 그래서 이번 학기에 오전 수업은 안 들어요. 아침 식사 시간에도 잠을 잘 것 같아서, 아침 식사비를 낼 이유가 없어요. 하루에 2번만 먹는 급식으로 바꿔달라고 했어요.
남 : 언제 이메일을 보냈나요?
여 : 8월 말에요. 여기요, 카피를 해왔어요.
남 : 아. 그런 경우라면, 별 상관이 없겠네요. 약관에는 변경 사항에 대한 마감일도 적혀 있어요. 8월 15일 이후에 신청한 변경 사항에 대해서는 환불을 받을 수가 없습니다. 15일 이후에 이메일을 보냈기 때문에, 별 도리가 없겠네요.
여 : 그럼 먹지도 않을 아침 식사비도 내야 한다는 말씀이세요?
남 : 아무래도 그래야 할 것 같군요.

어휘 refund 환불 matter 중요하다

대화의 일부를 다시 들으시오. 그러고 나서 질문에 답하시오.

4. 남자가 이것을 말할 때 의미하는 것은 무엇인가? 
   M : I'm afraid so.
   Ⓐ 학생은 급식을 변경할 수 없다.
   Ⓑ 학생은 오전 수업을 꼭 들어야 한다.
   Ⓒ 학생은 돈을 일부 돌려 받을 것이다.
   Ⓓ 학생은 아침을 거르지 말아야 한다.

Lectures
1. 1. ⓒ 2. Ⓑ **2.** 1. ⓒ 2. Ⓑ 3. Ⓓ

Dictation: Lectures
1. 1. as destructive behavior 2. applicable to humans 3. attempting to flee from a threat 4. more prone to physical violence 5. arises from outside stimuli 6. at least partly inherited

2. 1. a risk of ext nction 2. without passing it on 3. being the official language 4. fewer native speakers 5. how many regional languages exist 6. are in rapid decline 7. to take into account 8. within a couple of generations

01 심리학 수업

P : 자, 오늘 강의의 마지막 주제는 공격성입니다. 심리학과 기타 사회 과학 분야에서는 공격성을 위해를 입히거나 고통을 야기하고, 재산을 파괴하는 의도로 나타나는 파괴적인 행동으로 정의 내립니다. Moyer(모이어) 분류법에 따르면 공격성은 7가지 다른 형태로 나타나며, 모두 인간에게도 적용될 수 있어요. 그렇다면, 이 7가지 형태는 무엇일까요?

S : 약탈적, 성별간, 두려움에서 생겨난 것, 짜증… 그리고, 그리고, 영역, 부모, 수단요!

P : 정말 잘했어요! 이들 중, 두려움에서 생겨난 공격성은 위협으로부터 도망치려고 할 때 생겨나는 일종의 보복 같은 것이죠. 그리고 부모로서의 공격성은 자식이 위협을 받는 상황에 처해 있을 때 생겨나는 것이고요. 그리고 수단적 공격성은 목표를 달성해야 하는 상황에서 볼 수 있는 형태죠. 우리가 살면서 이 모든 형태의 공격성을 겪어보았던 순간을 떠올려보는 것은 그리 어려운 일은 아니에요… 하지만 한꺼번에는 아니어야죠!
자, 이제 인간의 공격성에 영향을 주는 요인들을 살펴봅시다. 연구 결과에 따르면, 공격성의 정도가 다른 국가 출신의 사람들 사이에서 다르게 나타난다고 하죠. 누가 예를 한 번 들어보겠어요?

S : 음, 미국 남성이 일본 남성보다 신체적 폭력을 휘두르는 경향이 더 높다고 해요. 그리고 한 국가 내의 다른 지역에 사는 사람들 사이에서도 차이점이 드러난다고 해요. 미국에서는, 남부에 사는 백인 남성이 북부에 사는 백인 남성보다 더 공격적인 것으로 나타났어요.

P : 그래요, 이런 점으로 볼 때 문화는 공격성을 조절하는 중요한 요소죠. 공격성이 외부 자극으로부터 비롯되는 경우가 흔하지만, 과학자들은 내부적 요인 역시 공격성에 영향을 준다고 생각해요. 시상하부와 같은 뇌의 조절 부위가 관련이 있죠. 그리고 호르몬과… 유전적 요인도 있어요. 공격적인 경향은 부분적으로는 내재되어 있다고 말할 수 있죠, 그래서 "우리 부모님 때문이야"와 같은 방어기제가 생겨나는 것이고요.

어휘 aggression 공격성 define A as B A를 B로 정의 내리다 destructive 파괴적인 manifest 나타나다 intention 의도 property 재산 applicable to ~에 적용 가능한 predatory 약탈적 gender 성 induce 야기하다 irritable 짜증나는 territorial 영토의 parental 부모의 instrumental 수단의 retaliation 보복 flee 도망가다 offspring 자손 threaten 위협하다 southerner 남부주 사람 northerner 북부주 사람 arise from ~에서 생겨나다 genetics 유전적 특징 tendency 경향 inherited 내재되어 있는 give rise to ~를 발생시키다

강의의 일부를 다시 들으시오. 그러고 나서 질문에 답하시오.

1. 교수가 이것을 말할 때 의미하는 것은 무엇인가: 

    P : It is not hard to imagine examples in all our lives in which we have experienced all these forms of aggression... though not all at once, hopefully!

Ⓐ 사람들은 공격적인 행동을 하는 것을 피하도록 해야 한다.
Ⓑ 다른 형태의 공격성을 분류하는 것은 어렵지 않다.
Ⓒ 사람들이 공격성을 경험하는 것은 흔히 있는 일이다.
Ⓓ 공격성을 생각하는 것만으로도 공격성이 나타나게 할 수도 있다.

강의의 일부를 다시 들으시오. 그러고 나서 질문에 답하시오.

2. 교수가 이것을 말할 때 암시하는 것은 무엇인가: 
   P : A tendency towards aggression can be at least partly inherited, giving rise to the "I blame my parents" defense.
   Ⓐ 유전적 특징이 공격적인 행동을 유발하는 가장 중요한 원인이다.
   Ⓑ 사람들은 때때로 자신들의 행동에 대해 개인적인 책임을 지는 대신 유전적 성향을 탓한다.
   Ⓒ 공격적인 부모에게는 흔히 더 공격적인 자녀가 있다.
   Ⓓ 공격성에 직면할 때, 특히 부모로부터의 공격성에 직면할 때, 자기 방위 행위는 적절하다.

02 언어학 수업

P : 자, 이제 쉬는 시간이 끝났으니 오늘의 마지막 주제를 다뤄보도록 하죠, 바로 멸종 위기 언어입니다. 언어가 사라질 위기에 처해 있을 때 이 언어를 멸종 위기에 처해 있다고 합니다. 다시 말해서, 이 언어 사용자들이 모두 죽어서 더 이상 이 세상에 존재하지 않게 되는 경우죠. 영어나 스페인어, 만다린어(북경 관화) 같은 세계 주요 언어를 떠올려볼 때, 이 언어들의 사용 인구가 너무 적어서 다음 세대로 언어가 전해지지 않은 채 사라져 버릴 지도 모른다고 생각하기란 쉬운 일이 아니죠. 하지만 이런 일들이 실제로 일어난 적이 있고, 아직도 일어나고 있어요. 왜 그런 일들이 일어나게 될까요?

S : 일부 국가에서 공용어를 정하면 아이들이 학교에서 그 언어를 배워야 하기 때문이 아닐까요? 그 공용어가 그들의 토착어가 아니라 해도 말이에요.

P : 맞아요, 아주 잘 말해주었어요. 예를 한 번 들어보겠어요?

S : 프랑스요? 제가 프랑스어를 전공하고 있는데요, 프랑스에는 국가의 공용어로 프랑스어만을 사용해야 한다는 아주 엄격한 법이 있어요.

P : 맞아요. 브르타뉴어, 알사스어, 옥시타니아어와 같은 프랑스의 소수 언어들은 점차 사라지고 있어요. 이 언어를 사용하는 원어민의 수가 점점 줄어들고 있고, 아이들은 학교에서 이 언어를 배우고 있지 않아요. 전세계적으로 이런 일들이 일어나고 있어요. 카탈로니아어를 제외하고는, 스페인의 모든 지방 언어가 사라질 위기에 처해 있어요. 레온어, 아라곤어, 바스크어 모두 쇠퇴하고 있죠. 한 번 찾아보면, 전세계적으로 얼마나 많은 지역 언어가 있는지 놀라게 될 거에요. 북미와 남미, 아프리카와 호주에서도 비슷한 일들이 일어나고 있어요. 호주와 미국의 원주민 언어들이 급격한 퇴보 양상을 보이고 있죠. 다수의 아프리카 국가에서는 부족의 정략적 이해 관계에 의해 정부 구성원이 정해지고, 따라서 어떤 언어가 쓰일지 역시 그에 따라 결정되죠. 멸종 위기 언어에 대해 살펴볼 때는 이 언어를 유창하게 구사하는 사람들의 수와 그들의 평균 연령, 그리고 그 언어를 유창한 수준으로 말하는 아이들의 비율 등을 고려해야 해요. 수천 명의 사람들이 그 언어들을 사용하고 있을 수도 있지만, 오늘날 이 언어를 유창하게 사용할 수 있는 성인들이 아이들을 가르치지 않으면, 몇 년 내로는 이 언어들이 결국 사라지게 될 거에요. 이런 일들이 일어나게 될 대표적인 국가로 인도네시아가 자주 거론되고 있어요.

어휘 endangered 멸종 위기에 처한 risk 위험 extinction 멸종 die out 죽어 없어지다 pass on 전수하다 strict 엄격한 tribal 부족의 politics 정치 take A into account A를 고려하다 generation 세대 cite 언급하다

1. 강의에서 화자들은 주로 무엇에 관해 이야기 하고 있는가?
   Ⓐ 지역 언어의 수
   Ⓑ 소수 언어
   Ⓒ 언어의 멸종
   Ⓓ 각국의 공용어

2. 스페인의 지방 언어 중 멸종 위기 언어로 간주되지 않는 것은 무엇인가?
   Ⓐ 바스크어
   Ⓑ 카탈로니아어
   Ⓒ 레온어
   Ⓓ 아라곤어

강의의 일부를 다시 들으시오. 그러고 나서 질문에 답하시오.

3. 인도네시아에서 멸종 위기 언어의 보존과 관련하여, 교수가 이것을 말할 때 암시하는 것은 무엇인가? 
   P : Indonesia is often cited as an example of this scenario.
   Ⓐ 어린 학생들이 이러한 언어들을 배우는데 관심이 없다.
   Ⓑ 어른들이 아이들데게 언어를 가르칠만한 능력을 갖추고 있지 않다.
   Ⓒ 부모들은 자녀가 공용어를 사용하기를 원한다.
   Ⓓ 멸종 위기 언어어 대한 사람들의 관심이 부족하다.

Practice

[1-5] **1.** Ⓒ **2.** Ⓓ **3.** Mentioned – Ⓐ, Ⓑ, Ⓓ Not Mentioned – Ⓒ, Ⓔ **4.** Ⓓ **5.** Ⓐ
[6-11] **6.** Ⓑ **7.** Low-level waste – Ⓑ, Ⓓ, Ⓔ High-level waste – Ⓐ, Ⓒ **8.** Ⓐ **9.** Ⓒ **10.** Ⓒ
11. Ⓐ

[문제 1–5] Listen to part of a conversation between a student and a professor.

W : Thanks for letting me turn in the photo series today. Here they are. I saved them all on a USB drive. If you want to take a look, we can do that now.

M : Sure. Umm, I was busy yesterday when you asked if you could have an extension, and I didn't really catch what you said. What was going on?

W : I've been really swamped. I'm taking a heavy course load this semester. Among other things, I'm studying both Russian and Japanese, and I'm doing a language exchange with a couple of the international students. And I had a paper to write for my art history class, and...

M : And you have a part-time job, don't you?

W : That's right!

M : In other words, it's the usual student craziness.

W : Something like that. I honestly couldn't find the time to go downtown to take pictures until Sunday. I wanted to take pictures at different times of day, to capture the shadows and light. I also wanted to try a few long-exposure shots, to see how they'd turn out.

M : Well, can you show me the results?

W : Sure... See, here are the morning shots, just after sunrise. Then here's the batch from late morning, around lunchtime.

M : So they're in order? Late afternoon, early evening, sunset, night. These are very nice. I can tell you spent more time on this than a lot of your fellow students did. The composition's good, the focus is crisp and sharp, and you did a good job of capturing interesting color contrasts.

W : Thanks. To be honest, I also took plenty of bad ones, but I just deleted those.

M : Of course. That's part of being a photographer: you have to know which images to keep and which ones to throw away.

W : So I did all right? You like them?

M : 🎧 Yes. I won't take off any points because you only needed one extra day. 5. Just be sure you keep managing your time, all right? Don't take on more work than you can do.

W : I'll keep that in mind. Thanks again.

여 : 사진을 오늘까지 제출하게 해주셔서 감사합니다. 여기 사진이 있습니다. 모두 USB 드라이브에 저장해왔어요. 지금 보시고 싶으시면, 바로 보실 수 있어요.

남 : 그래. 아, 어제 네가 과제 제출을 연기할 수 있는지 물었을 때 내가 좀 바빠서 무슨 얘기였는지 제대로 못 들었단다. 무슨 일이었다고 했지?

여 : 제가 요즘 하는 일이 많아서 좀 정신이 없거든요. 이번 학기에는 수업도 빡빡하게 듣고 있어요. 무엇보다도, 러시아어와 일본어를 함께 공부하고 있는데다, 유학생들과 언어 교환 스터디도 하고 있어요. 그리고 미술사 수업 시간에 제출할 리포트도 작성해야 했고, 그리고…

남 : 아르바이트도 하겠지?

여 : 맞습니다!

남 : 결국 대부분의 학생들이 바쁜 것과 똑같구나.

여 : 그런 셈이죠. 솔직히 일요일 전까지는 다운타운에 나가서 사진을 찍을 시간이 없었어요. 전 시간대별로 사진을 찍어서 명암을 표현하고 싶었어요. 장시간 노출 사진도 찍어보고 싶었어요, 어떻게 나올지 보려고요.

남 : 그럼, 사진이 어떻게 나왔는지 좀 볼까?

여 : 네… 여기요, 해가 뜨자마자 찍은 아침 사진이에요. 이건 점심 시간 즈음에 찍은 늦은 아침 사진이에요.

남 : 그럼 시간 순서대로 정렬되어 있는 거니? 늦은 오후, 초저녁, 해질녘, 밤 순서구나. 정말 정리를 잘했구나. 다른 학생들보다 시간을 더 많이 들인 것 같구나. 구성도 괜찮고, 초점도 또렷하고 선명하고, 색대비도 잘 잡아냈고.

여 : 감사합니다. 솔직히 말씀 드리면, 잘 안 나온 사진도 많았는데, 모두 지워버렸어요

남 : 원래 그런 거란다. 그런 부분 역시 사진 기술의 일부라고 할 수 있지. 어떤 사진을 살리고 어떤 사진을 지워버려야 하는지를 알아야 하니까.

여 : 그럼 제가 잘 한 건가요? 제가 찍은 사진이 마음에 드세요?

남 : 그래. 과제물을 하루 늦게 제출했다고 해서 점수를 깎지는 않을 거야. 시간 관리를 잘 해야 한다는 것만 명심하도록 하렴, 알겠지? 감당할 수 있을 정도의 일만 해야 한단다.

여 : 명심하겠습니다. 다시 한 번 감사 드립니다.

어휘 save 저장하다 extension 연기, 연장 batch 한 묶음, 일단 crisp 또렷한

Topic: Turn in phctos 사진 제출

1. Turned in late 늦게 제출함
   – busy ← language, paper, part-time job 바빴음 ← 외국어 공부, 리포트, 아르바이트
2. Photos 사진
   – different times of day 다른 시간대에 찍음
   – long-exposure shots 장시간 노출 사진
   – good color contrast 색대비가 잘 되어 있음
3. Prof.'s advice 고수의 충고
   – Time management 시간 관리

1. 학생이 교수와 대화를 나누는 이유는 무엇인가?
   Ⓐ 수업에 여러 번 지각했다.
   Ⓑ 사진 프로젝트에 대한 피드백을 받고 싶어한다.
   Ⓒ 과제물을 늦게 제출해야 했다.
   Ⓓ 디지털 사진을 배우는 것에 관심이 있다.
   해설 학생은 사진 과제물을 기한보다 늦게 제출하고 있다. 전날 교수에게 허락을 받고 오늘 제출하러 온 것이다.
   정답 Ⓒ

2. 학생은 교수에게 사진 과제물을 어떻게 제출했는가?
   Ⓐ 이메일을 통해
   Ⓑ 노트북으로
   Ⓒ 사진을 인화해서
   Ⓓ 휴대용 장치로
   해설 학생은 사진 찍은 것을 USB 드라이브에 담아왔다. 이것은 휴대용 장치이다. 사진을 USB 드라이브에 저장
       해 온 후, 교수와 함께 그것을 컴퓨터로 연결하여 보고 있는 것이기 때문에 보기 Ⓑ는 오답이다.
   정답 Ⓓ

3. 대화에서, 학생은 요즘 무엇을 하느라 바쁜지 이유를 설명하고 있다. 아래 표의 각 보기가 이런 이유에 속하는지
   표시하시오. 각 보기에 맞는 칸에 클릭하시오.

	Mentioned	Not Mentioned
Ⓐ 캠퍼스에서 다른 학생들과 함께 외국어를 공부함		
Ⓑ 아르바이트를 하고 있음		
Ⓒ 그림 레슨을 밷음		
Ⓓ 다른 수업 시간에 제출할 리포트 작성		
Ⓔ 사진 클럽에 가입했음		

   해설 학생은 교수에게 과제물을 늦게 제출할 수 밖에 없었던 이유를 설명하고 있다. 유학생들과 외국어 공부를
       함께 하고 있고, 다른 수업 시간에 제출할 리포트도 작성해야 하고, 아르바이트도 해야 한다.
   정답 Mentioned – Ⓐ, Ⓑ, Ⓓ   Not Mentioned – Ⓒ, Ⓔ

4. 사진을 배열한 스타일로 볼 때 학생에 관해 추론할 수 있는 것은 무엇인가?
　　Ⓐ 게으른 사람이다.
　　Ⓑ 밤보다 아침을 더 좋아한다.
　　Ⓒ 교수가 좋아하는 학생 중 한 명이다.
　　Ⓓ 정리를 아주 잘한다.
　　해설 사진을 찍고 나서 컴퓨터에 시간대를 구분하여 사진을 정렬한 것으로 보아 학생은 정리를 잘 하는 사람일
　　　　것임을 미루어 알 수 있다. 교수가 사진을 체계적으로 정리했다고 학생을 칭찬하기는 하지만, 그렇다고 해서
　　　　교수가 평소에 학생을 마음에 들어 했는지는 알 수 없다. 따라서 보기 Ⓒ는 오답이다.
　　정답 Ⓓ

대화의 일부를 다시 들으시오. 그리고 나서 질문에 답하시오.

5. 교수가 이것을 말할 때 암시하는 것은 무엇인가: 
　　M : Just be sure you keep managing your time, all right? Don't take on more work than you
　　　　can do.
　　Ⓐ 교수가 다시는 학생의 편의를 봐주는 일이 없을 것이다.
　　Ⓑ 학생이 맡은 일을 제대로 해내고 있다.
　　Ⓒ 학생은 건강을 돌보아야 한다.
　　Ⓓ 교수는 학생이 과외 활동 시간을 줄여야 한다고 충고한다.
　　해설 교수는 학생에게 과제물을 하루 늦게 제출했다고 해서 점수를 깎지는 않겠지만 앞으로는 시간 관리를 잘
　　　　하고 너무 많은 일을 하지 말라고 충고하고 있다. 이를 통해 앞으로는 학생의 개인적인 사정 때문에 학생
　　　　의 상황을 봐주지는 않을 것임을 짐작할 수 있다. 시간 관리를 잘 하라는 말에 과외 활동 시간을 줄여야 한
　　　　다는 의미가 함축되어 있는 것은 아니므로 보기 Ⓓ는 오답이다.
　　정답 Ⓐ

[문제 6-11] Listen to part of a lecture in a physics class.

P(M) : Today we'll talk a little bit about radioactive waste. There are many sources of radioactive
　　　　waste. Can anyone give me an example or two?
S(W) : Leftover medical supplies? Like, from X-rays...
P : Very good. That's what we'd call low-level waste, meaning it doesn't emit large amounts of
　　radioactivity, and is low in intensity of radioactivity. The actual definition of radioactive waste
　　is waste that contains radioactive material for which there is no immediate practical use.
　　Protective shoe covers and clothing, gloves, replacement parts, filters, equipments and tools
　　tend to become contaminated with radioactive material after enough exposure to neutron
　　radiation. Those would be considered low-level waste. On the contrary, the highly radioactive
　　materials that are generated as a byproduct of the nuclear reactions are called high-level
　　waste. They take a form of either used reactor fuel or waste materials that remain after used
　　fuel is reprocessed. Used or spent nuclear fuel is of no use for producing electricity, but it is
　　still extremely hot and considerably radioactive.
　　Now, uh, we've discussed medicine, research institutions, and the nuclear industry. Believe it
　　or not, the oil industry produces a tremendous amount of radioactive waste, as well. Millions
　　of tons of it.
S : Is oil radioactive?

P : Not in its purest form, but certain types of oil shale and coal are. Oil shale may contain radium, and the water, oil, and gas that have been in contact with it may contain the radioactive gas radon. Coal contains tiny amounts of three different radioactive elements: uranium, barium, and thorium. When coal is burned, those elements are released into ash.

Now, radioactivity decreases over time. Every radioactive element has a half-life.

S : The amount of time it takes to lose half its radioactivity?

P : That's right. The waste products from nuclear reactors, like some of the plutonium isotopes, will be dangerous for hundreds of thousands, or millions, of years. Others have half-lives measuring only a few days and are therefore much easier to dispose of.

The goal for nuclear waste disposal is to do it in a way that protects people and the environment. To do that, we either have to shield it so well that there's almost no risk of accidental exposure, or have to dilute it so much that it becomes harmless.

There are a number of options for long-term storage. Generally, these storage facilities are 500-1000 meters below the surface of the Earth. A number of countries have chosen sites where the geology is most appropriate. For example, Canada is using rock formations below the Canadian Shield, which is a very stable formation. The batholiths below it don't have significant groundwater movement and aren't prone to earthquakes. Something similar has been done in Australia, the U.S., and some of the northern European countries. Disposal at sea, in a subduction zone that would gradually take the material back into the Earth's mantle, or under an abyssal plain, has been discussed, [11.]but there's a tricky legal issue and it's not one that countries are likely to agree on. No method is perfect, and they all have their pros and cons, but progress is definitely being made.

P : 오늘은 방사성 폐기물에 관해 이야기 해보겠어요. 방사성 폐기물이 배출되는 원인이 다양하죠. 누가 예를 들어보겠어요?

S : 의료용으로 사용하고 남은 것들이요? 가령 엑스레이 촬영시에 나오는 방사능 같은...

P : 그래요. 학생이 지금 말한 건 저준위 방사성 폐기물에 해당하는데, 많은 양의 방사능을 배출하지 않고 방사능의 세기가 낮은 것을 뜻해요. 방사성 폐기물이란 방사성 물질을 포함하고 있는 갖가지 폐기물로, 곧바로 사용할 수는 없는 상태에요. 방사선 작업시에 사용한 신발 커버와 작업복, 장갑, 교체부품, 필터, 각종 장비와 도구가 일정 시간 중성자 방사능에 노출되면 방사능에 오염되죠. 이런 것들은 저준위 방사성 폐기물이에요. 반대로, 핵반응이 일어나고 나서 그 부산물로 생기는 고준위 방사성 물질을 고준위 방사성 폐기물이라고 해요. 고준위 방사성 폐기물에는 사용후 연료나 이 사용후 연료가 재처리 되고 나서 남는 폐기물이 있어요. 사용후 연료는 더 이상 전기를 생산하는데 쓰이지 않지만, 온도가 매우 높고 많은 양의 방사능을 가지고 있어요.

자, 의료기관과 연구기관, 핵산업에서 발생되는 방사성 폐기물에 대해 알아봤는데요. 믿기 어렵겠지만, 석유 산업에서도 엄청난 양의 방사성 폐기물이 배출되고 있어요. 수백만 톤이 방출되죠.

S : 석유도 방사능 물질인가요?

P : 순수한 상태에서는 그렇지 않지만, 일부 유모혈암과 석탄은 그렇다고 할 수 있어요. 유모혈암에는 라듐이 들어있을 수도 있는데, 이것과 접촉하게 된 물, 석유, 가스에는 라듐의 방사성 붕괴로 생기는 방사성 가스인 라돈이 들어있죠. 석탄에는 세 가지 다른 종류의 방사능 원소가 소량 들어있는데, 바로 우라늄과 바륨, 토륨이에요. 석탄이 연소할 때, 이러한 원소들이 재로 방출되죠.

자, 방사능은 시간이 흐르면서 감소해요. 모든 방사능 원소는 반감기를 가지고 있어요.

S : 방사성 원소의 원자수가 붕괴되어 절반으로 줄 때까지 걸리는 시간이죠?

P : 맞아요. 플루토늄 동위원소처럼 원자로에서 방출되는 폐기물은 수십만 년, 아니 수백만 년 동안 아주 위험한 상태로 존재하죠. 반감기가 며칠 밖에 안 되는 원소들도 있는데, 이런 것들은 처리하기가 더 쉽죠.

핵폐기물 처리의 목표는 인간과 환경을 보호하면서 폐기물을 처리하는 겁니다. 그렇게 하기 위해서는, 폐기물을 밀봉하여 사고 누출의 위험을 제거하거나 잘 희석시켜서 무해한 물질로 변화시켜야 하죠.

폐기물을 장기간 저장 및 보관하는 방법은 다양해요. 일반적으로, 이런 저장 시설들은 지표면에서 500~1000 미터 아래의 지하 깊숙이 만들어져 있어요. 많은 국가에서 지질학상으로 이런 시설을 세울 최적의 장소를 선정했어요. 예를 들어, 캐나다는 캐나다 순상지 밑의 암석층을 이용하고 있는데, 아주 안정적인 구조를 갖추고 있어요. 순상지 아래의 저반(底盤)은 지하수의 흐름이 적고 지진이 일어날 가능성도 적죠. 호주와 미국, 북유럽의 일부 국가에서도 이와 유사한 방식을 채택하고 있죠. 해구퇴적물이 지구의 상부 맨틀로 끌려들어가는 대륙 연변의 해구지역인 해양 침입대나 심해평원에서 폐기물을 처리하는 방법 역시 논의되어왔지만, 미묘한 법적 문제가 있어서 이에 동의할 국가는 거의 없어요. 완벽한 방법이란 것이 없고, 모두 찬반양론이 존재하지만, 폐기물 처리 방식을 두고 상당한 진전이 이루어지고 있어요.

어휘 radioactive waste 방사성 폐기물 radioactivity 방사능 intensity 세기, 강도 practical 실용적인 contaminate 오염시키다 exposure 노출 on the contrary 반대로 byproduct 부산물 release 방출하다 ash 재 element 원소 dispose of 처리하다, 처분하다 shield 보호하다 dilute 희석시키다 long-term 장기간의 be prone to ~하기 쉽다 abyssal 심해의 pros and cons 찬반양론

Note-taking

Topic: Radioactive waste 방사성 폐기물

1. Low-level waste 저준위 방사성 폐기물
   - medical supply 의료기관
   - small amounts of radioactivity 적은 양의 방사능
   - low in intensity 세기가 낮음
   - protective clothing,etc. become contaminated after exposure to neutron radiation
     보호복 등이 중성자 방사능에 노출된 후에 방사능 오염됨
2. High-level waste 고준위 방사성 폐기물
   - used reactor fuel/waste after used fuel's reprocessed
     사용후 연료/사용후 연료가 재처리 되고 나서 남는 폐기물
   - hot and radioactive 뜨겁고 많은 양의 방사능이 들어있음
3. Oil industry produces waste 석유 산업에서도 방사성 폐기물이 나옴
   - oil shale: radium 유모혈암: 라듐
   - coal: uranium, barium, thorium 석탄: 우라늄, 바륨, 토륨
4. Half-life 반감기
   - The amount of time to lose half its radioactivity 방사능이 절반으로 줄어드는데 걸리는 시간
   - waste from nuclear reactor: dangerous for huge amounts of time
     원자로에서 방출되는 폐기물: 아주 오랜 시간 위험한 상태
5. Long-term storage 장기간 저장
   - deep underground 땅속 깊이
     :e.g. Canada 예. 캐나다
   - disposal at sea: legal issue/not likely 바다에서 처리: 법적 문제/이용될 것 같지 않음

6. 이 강의의 주제는 무엇인가?
   Ⓐ 방사능의 세기
   Ⓑ 방사성 폐기물의 종류와 저장
   Ⓒ 핵폐기물 처리
   Ⓓ 핵반응의 목적
   해설 크게 방사성 폐기물의 두 종류와 저장 방식에 관해 강의가 진행되고 있다. 보기 Ⓐ의 방사능의 세기는 방사
       성 폐기물을 분류하는 기준이고, 보기 Ⓒ의 핵폐기물 처리는 잠깐 언급되었기 때문에 강의 전체의 주제가
       될 수 없다.
   정답 Ⓑ

7. 강의에서, 교수는 저준위 방사성 폐기물과 고준위 방사성 폐기물을 설명하고 있다. 아래 표의 각 보기가 어떤 종
   류의 특징인지 표시하시오. 각 보기에 맞는 칸에 클릭하시오.

	Low-level waste	High-level waste
Ⓐ 핵반응이 일어날 때 생성됨		
Ⓑ 중성자 방사능어 노출된 후 방사능에 오염됨		
Ⓒ 매우 뜨겁고 많은 양의 방사능을 가지고 있음		
Ⓓ 보호장비를 방사능 오염시킴		
Ⓔ 적은 양의 방사능을 방출함		

   해설 방사능의 세기에 따라 저준위와 고준위 방사성 폐기물로 나뉜다. 저준위 방사성 폐기물은 방사선 작업시에
       착용한 보호장비가 중성자 방사능에 노출되어 오염된 것이다. 방사능 배출량이 많지는 않다. 반면, 고준위
       방사성 폐기물은 핵반응이 일어나고 나서 부산물로 생기는 물질로, 온도가 매우 높고 많은 양의 방사능을
       가지고 있다. 따라서 저준위 방사성 폐기물의 특징에 해당하는 것은 보기 Ⓑ, Ⓓ, Ⓔ고, 고준위 방사성 폐
       기물의 특징어 해당하는 것은 보기 Ⓐ, Ⓒ이다.
   정답 Low-level waste – Ⓑ, Ⓓ, Ⓔ High-level waste – Ⓐ, Ⓒ

8. 다음 중 저준위 방사성 폐기물 배출원에 해당하는 것은 무엇인가?
   Ⓐ 병원
   Ⓑ 지하수
   Ⓒ 우라늄 광산
   Ⓓ 순수한 상태으 석유
   해설 대화의 도입부에서 의료기관에서 발생되는 방사성 폐기물은 저준위 방사성 폐기물에 속한다고 하였다.
   정답 Ⓐ

9. 다음 중 석탄에 들어있는 방사성 원소가 아닌 것은 무엇인가?
   Ⓐ 토륨
   Ⓑ 우라늄
   Ⓒ 라듐
   Ⓓ 바륨
   해설 보기 Ⓒ의 라듐은 석탄이 아니라 유모혈암에 들어있다.
   정답 Ⓒ

10. 방사성 물질의 반감기란 무엇인가?

Ⓐ 모든 물질의 방사능이 안전한 수준까지 감소하는데 걸리는 시간

Ⓑ 생물체가 방사능의 영향에서 벗어나는데 걸리는 시간

Ⓒ 방사능 물질의 방사능이 절반으로 붕괴하는데 걸리는 시간

Ⓓ 생물체가 방사능을 띠게 되는데 걸리는 시간

해설 교수가 모든 방사능 원소는 반감기를 가지고 있다고 하자 학생이 반감기란 방사성 원소의 원자수가 붕괴되어 절반으로 줄 때까지 걸리는 시간이라고 대답했다. 보기 Ⓐ는 '안전한 수준'이란 말의 의미가 애매모호하다.

정답 Ⓒ

강의의 일부를 다시 들으시오. 그러고 나서 질문에 답하시오.

11. 교수가 이것을 말할 때 암시하는 것은 무엇인가: 

P : but it's a tricky legal issue and not one that countries are likely to agree on.

Ⓐ 가까운 장래에 폐기물을 해양 침입대에서 처리하는 일은 일어나지 않을 것이다.

Ⓑ 폐기물을 바다에서 처리하는 것이 가장 안전한 방법이다.

Ⓒ 방사성 폐기물 처리에 진전이 있다.

Ⓓ 폐기물 처리에 심해평원을 이용하는 것이 해양 침입대를 이용하는 것보다 더 낫다.

해설 해양 침입대나 심해평원에서 방사성 폐기물을 처리하는 방식에 대해 논의가 이루어져왔지만 미묘한 법적 문제가 있어서 이러한 처리 방식에 동의할 국가가 거의 없다고 하였다. 이를 통해 당분간은 이런 처리방식이 실제로 채택되는 일은 보기 힘들 것이다.

정답 Ⓐ

Actual Test

1. Ⓑ   2. Ⓓ   3. Mentioned – Ⓐ, Ⓑ, Ⓓ   Not Mentioned – Ⓒ, Ⓔ   4. Ⓓ   5. Ⓑ   6. Ⓒ

7. Ⓑ   8. Mentioned – Ⓐ, Ⓑ, Ⓒ   Not Mentioned – Ⓓ, Ⓔ   9. Ⓐ, Ⓓ   10. Ⓐ   11. Ⓑ

12. Ⓑ   13. Ⓐ   14. Ⓒ   15. Ⓓ   16. Ⓓ   17. Mentioned – Ⓒ, Ⓓ, Ⓔ   Not Mentioned – Ⓐ, Ⓑ

[문제 1–5] Listen to part of a conversation between a student and a professor.

W : Hi, Professor? Ah, do you remember me? I'm in your first-year sociology course.

M : Ah, yes, of course. You must be Sharon.

W : Yes, that's me. I've actually come to speak to you about my marks.

M : Oh, what seems to be the problem?

W : It's just that I missed some classes and...

M : You know that participation is part of your final grade.

W : I know, but I, um, well...

M : What happened?

W : You see, about last week, I came down with a really bad case of the flu and had to be hospitalized. They had me on some pretty strong medication and I couldn't come to class for several days. Unfortunately, I also missed class on Thursday.

M : So, you missed your final presentation.

W : I know. I asked your teacher's assistant if I could present it next week, but he said it was too late. Then he told me to talk to you about the situation. I guess he was sympathetic, but just following the rules.

M : Yes, John knows procedure. Sharon, I'm terribly sorry about your illness and I hope you are feeling better now. But, the problem is that we've covered a lot of ground during the last few seminars. So, I don't want you spending your time preparing for a presentation; catching up on your reading is more important. To be honest, I'm not sure that your presentation topic - I think you said you were going to talk about the Chicago School of Thought and Henry Rouseau? It just wouldn't be all that relevant anymore. Most students have already completed their reading on the subject. Besides, I don't think we can afford the extra class time.

W : What are my options then?

M : How are you doing on the rest of your assignments?

W : I scored well on the last mid-term and I've been keeping up with my other assignments. But, the presentation is worth 20 percent of the final, so...

M : 4·Well, we have to come up with an alternative. Would you consider doing an oral examination? I have a few minutes right now.

W : Is it possible that we could do it tomorrow at the same time? I just need a little time to prepare.

M : That's totally understandable. OK, let's meet tomorrow and we can do it then. Um, one more thing.

W : Yes, sir?

M : It's university policy that I need to see a doctor's note for the classes that you missed. It's the only way that I'm allowed to treat your situation differently than any other student. I don't want to make this any more difficult than it already is, but I, uh, you don't have any other choice.

W : That's totally fair. Listen, I'll stop by the clinic tomorrow before I come to meet you. Is that ok?

M : That's great.

여 : 교수님, 안녕하세요? 절 기억하세요? 교수님의 1학년 사회학 강좌를 듣고 있어요.

남 : 아, 그래. Sharon이구나.

여 : 네, 맞아요. 실은 제 점수에 관해 드릴 말씀이 있어서 왔어요.

남 : 무슨 문제가 있니?

여 : 제가 수업을 몇 번 결석해서……

남 : 참여도 최종 성적에 포함된다는 건 알겠지.

여 : 알고 있습니다, 그런데, 음……

남 : 무슨 일이 있었니?

여 : 지난 주에 제가 정말 심한 독감에 걸려서 병원에 입원해야 했어요. 병원에서 상당히 강한 약물 치료를 해서 며칠 간 수업에 출석할 수가 없었어요. 안타깝게도, 목요일 수업도 빠지게 되었죠.

남 : 그래서 기말 프리젠테이션을 못했구나.

여 : 네. 다음 주에 프리젠테이션을 할 수 있을지 TA에게 물어봤는데요, 너무 늦었다고 말하더군요. 그리고 교수님께 상황을 설명 드리라고 말해주었어요. TA가 동점심은 있었던 것 같은데 규정을 지키려는 것 같아요.

남 : 그래, John은 절차를 알고 있지. Sharon, 네가 아팠다니 정말 유감이란다. 그리고 지금은 좀 나아졌기를 바란단다. 하지만 문제는 지난 몇 번의 세미나 동안에 많은 분야를 다루었어. 그래서 네가 프리젠테이션을 준비하는 데 시간을 들이지 않으면 좋겠구나. 읽기 자료를 다 읽어보는 것이 더 중요하단다. 솔직히 말하자면, 네가 정한 프리젠테이션 토픽, 네가 시카고 학파와 Henry Rouseau에 관해 이야기 하고 싶다고 했던 것 같은데? 그런데

더 이상 그리 상관이 있을지 모르겠구나. 대부분의 학생들이 이미 그 주제에 관해 읽기 자료를 다 읽었단다. 그리고 우리가 보충 수업 시간을 가질 여유가 있는지 모르겠다.

여 : 그럼 전 어떡해야 하죠?

남 : 남은 과제물은 어떻게 하고 있니?

여 : 지난 중간고사에서는 좋은 점수를 받았고 다른 과제물도 잘 진행시키고 있어요. 그렇지만 프리젠테이션이 기말 성적의 20%를 차지해서요……

남 : 음, 대안을 생각해보아야겠구나. 구두 시험을 치를 생각은 있니? 지금 몇 분 정도 시간을 낼 수 있는데.

여 : 저, 내일 이 시간에 뵐 수 있을까요? 준비할 시간이 좀 필요하거든요.

남 : 그렇게 하려무나. 그럼 내일 만나서 이야기하도록 하자. 아, 한 가지 더 있구나.

여 : 네?

남 : 대학의 정책에 따라 결석한 수업 사유가 되는 의사의 진단서를 확인하고 싶구나. 그게 다른 학생과 다르게 너의 상황을 처리해줄 수 있는 유일한 방법이란다. 지금보다 일을 더 어렵게 만들고 싶지는 않지만, 이 방법 밖에는 없는 것 같구나.

여 : 정말 공정하시네요. 그럼 내일 교수님을 뵈러 오기 전에 병원에 들를게요. 괜찮은가요?

남 : 그렇게 하렴.

어휘 come down with ~ 병에 걸리다 hospitalize 입원시키다

[문제 6-11] Listen to part of a lecture in an ecology class.

P(M) : All right, before I wrap things up today, does anyone have any questions?

S(W) : Yeah, um, well, you see, I'm thinking of doing my paper on the desert. I want to compare two different classes of living things, which are animals and plants, and see how they adapt to the climate in a similar way. But, I'm not exactly sure which direction to take.

P : Well! That paper isn't due for another two weeks. You must be working ahead. Good planning. So, um, let me go over some of the major adaptations that you might see. Ah, perhaps it's best if I use specific organisms as examples. Well, let's look at the camel first. It's ah, it's a four-legged ungulate - these are a kind of herbivores, like goats and sheep. Um, well I don't need to go into their characteristics. But, basically the camel is a desert-dwelling beast and, as such, must be able to cope with the extreme heat and lack of water. As a result, the camel has adapted a special internal compartment that retains moisture for a long period of time. It also recycles water through its urine. Like, um, human urine contains a lot of liquid, but for the camels, theirs is more like syrup, so they don't actually lose much water. They have also developed a way to manage the desert sun and what many people don't realize is that the desert also gets quite cool at night. So, the camel has a wide range of normal temperatures that it must deal with. Like, in the morning, it may be, oh 10 degrees, but by the afternoon, it is well over 40.

So, their regular body temperature can actually change to accommodate to this shift in external temperatures. Consider this; a human must keep a temperature of about 37 degrees. If we go up, we have a fever and this means we're sick; if we go down, we may experience hypothermia and die. Camels, on the other hand, have evolved their range as an adaptation, so it doesn't harm them.

But, also, camels have another trait - they sweat. Now, you might not think this is very interesting because humans can also sweat, but it is pretty rare in the animal kingdom.

Sweating is a much more efficient cooling system than panting, which is what dogs and cats do, because essential moisture is less lost in the process. They also have course body hair to protect against direct sun, and, well, I'll let you do the rest of the research yourself.

S : Then, what about a plant? There are plenty of plants that live in the desert even though we usually think of it as a barren landscape.

P : OK. Why don't I give you an example of the cactus? It can thrive in the desert and uses much the same adaptations as camels. I mean, camels can drink almost 100 liters of water at a time without becoming intoxicated. The cactus, well, when it rains, it quickly sucks up as much water as possible into its succulent stem system, a feat that would cause most plants to seriously damage their cellular walls, but not the cactus.

Now, the cactus can minimize its water loss through evaporation because it has evolved these really thin, spiny leaves, kind of like pine needles. Not only do they help to screen the plant from the hot sun, but they also don't lose water in the same way that a broad-leaf would. Oh, and they also have this waxy coat that seals the moisture inside the plant so it doesn't ooze out.

S : But I'm still curious, though. How does the cactus practice photosynthesis if it doesn't have leaves?

P : 🎧 You mean because it has those pointy spines instead? Ah, well, the cactus has evolved this really fascinating ability to open up its pores quite wide - these are called stomata - and this helps it absorb all of the carbon dioxide it needs to perform photosynthesis. Um, I should mention it does this at night when it's not exposed to sunlight. Then, during the day, it just needs to get a little sun on its stem. [11.]But, I think this process is something that you can look up on your own. You will also want to research its stem system, which is a pretty important feature as well.

S : So, let me just clarify; water and heat are the big issues for desert species. Now, a plant gets its food from soil and water. But, how does the camel get food?

P : Well, you know that hump on its back? That's a big lump of fat that it can use when it's hungry. When it has plants available to consume, it will eat a lot and fill up its hump. Then, it can go for weeks consuming this stored energy. Kind of like a plant that takes in a lot of water and swells out; then, it shrivels as it uses up the water. They both have great storage capacities.

P : 자, 오늘 수업을 마무리하기 전에 질문 있는 사람 있어요?

S : 네, 음, 제가 사막에 관해 리포트를 작성할까 하는데요. 다른 두 생명체, 즉 동물과 식물을 비교하고 그런 것들이 어떻게 비슷한 방식으로 기후에 적응해가는지를 알아보고 싶어요. 그런데 방향을 어느 쪽으로 잡아야 할지 잘 모르겠습니다.

P : 음! 그 리포트는 아직 2주나 더 남았잖아요. 미리미리 해 놓으려고 하는 모양이군요. 좋은 계획이에요. 음, 그럼 몇 가지 주요 적응 형태에 관해 복습을 해 볼까요? 구체적으로 예를 들어주는 것이 좋을 것 같군요. 먼저 낙타를 살펴보죠. 낙타는 네 발 달린 유제 동물입니다. 염소와 양처럼 일종의 초식 동물이죠. 음, 낙타의 특징까지 이야기 할 필요는 없을 것 같군요. 하지만 기본적으로 낙타는 사막에 살고 있는 짐승이고 따라서 극도의 더위와 수분 부족을 견뎌내야만 합니다. 그 결과 낙타는 오랜 기간 동안 수분을 간직하고 있는 특별한 신체 내부 기능을 가지고 있죠. 또한 소변을 통해 물을 재활용합니다. 인간의 소변에는 많은 액체가 들어있지만, 낙타의 경우에는 뭐랄까 더 시럽과 같아서 수분을 많이 손실하지는 않아요.

낙타는 또한 사막의 태양을 견뎌내는 방법을 발전시켰는데, 많은 사람들이 모르고 있는 사실은 사막이 밤에는 매우 서늘해진다는 것입니다. 따라서 낙타가 이겨내야 할 평온은 광범위하죠. 오전에는 10도 정도이지만 오후가 되면 40도가 넘어가는 거죠. 그래서 낙타의 일반 체온은 외부 온도의 변화에 맞추어 바뀌게 됩니다. 다음의 경우를 생각해봐요. 인간의 몸은 37도 정도의 체온을 유지해야 합니다. 그 이상 온도가 오르면 열이 나고 아프게 되죠. 그 아래로 온도가 내려가면 저체온증 현상이 일어나고 사망하게 될 수도 있어요. 반면에 낙타는 온도 변화를 환경 적응 구조의 일부로 발달시켰기 때문에 별 다른 해가 없는 것이죠.

또한 낙타에게는 다른 특징도 있는데, 바로 땀을 흘린다는 것입니다. 음, 인간도 땀을 흘리기 때문에 이 점이 별로 흥미롭지 않게 보일 수도 있지만, 동물의 세계에서는 아주 드문 일이에요. 땀을 흘리는 것은 개와 고양이가 헐떡거리는 것 보다 훨씬 더 효율적인 냉각 방식인데, 땀을 흘리면 필수적인 수분이 덜 손실되기 때문이죠. 낙타에게는 또한 결이 거친 체모가 있어서 직접적인 태양으로부터 낙타를 보호해주는데, 음, 이 이상의 연구는 여러분이 직접 하도록 해요.

S : 그럼, 식물은 어떻죠? 보통 사막을 황량한 곳이라고 생각하지만 사막에 살고 있는 식물이 많이 있잖아요.

P : 좋아요. 선인장을 예로 들어볼까요? 선인장은 사막에서 아주 잘 서식하고 낙타와 같은 방식의 적응 구조를 이용해요. 낙타는 중독되는 일 없이 한 번에 거의 100리터 가량의 물을 마실 수 있어요. 비가 내리면 선인장은 가능한 한 많은 양의 물을 다육 다즙 조직을 가진 줄기로 빨리 흡수하는데, 이 경우 대부분의 식물은 세포벽에 심각한 손상을 입게 되지만 선인장은 그렇지 않죠. 선인장은 솔잎과 같은 아주 가늘고 가시가 많은 잎을 가지고 있기 때문에 증발 작용을 통한 수분 손실을 최소화 할 수 있어요. 이 잎은 뜨거운 태양을 가려줄 뿐만 아니라 넓은 잎을 가진 식물이 수분을 손실하는 것처럼 수분을 손실하지는 않아요. 또한 식물 내부에 수분을 가두어두는 납질의 막이 있어서 수분이 새어나오지 않아요.

S : 그런데 아직 궁금한 것이 있어요. 선인장에 잎이 없으면 어떻게 광합성을 하는 거죠?

P : 선인장에 뾰족한 가시가 있기 때문에 그렇게 생각하는 것이죠? 음, 선인장은 stomata라고 불리는 기공을 아주 넓게 여는 멋진 능력을 가지고 있는데, 이것을 통해 선인장은 광합성을 하기 위해 필요한 이산화탄소를 흡수해요. 이런 작용을 햇볕에 노출될 염려가 없는 밤에 한다는 것도 말해줘야 할 것 같군요. 그리고 낮 동안에는 줄기에 햇볕을 흡수하면 되는 것이죠. 음, 이 과정은 여러분이 직접 찾아봐야 할 것 같군요. 또한 선인장의 줄기도 연구해봐야 할 거에요. 매우 중요한 특징이니까요.

S : 음, 이 점만 명확하게 하고 넘어갈게요. 사막에 사는 생물에게는 물과 더위가 큰 문제가 되요. 식물은 토양과 물을 통해 양분을 얻잖아요. 그럼 낙타는 어떻게 양분을 얻죠?

P : 낙타의 등에 있는 혹을 알죠? 이 혹은 낙타가 배가 고플 때 이용하는 큰 지방 덩어리에요. 먹을만한 식물을 구할 수 있을 때 많이 먹어두고 이 혹을 채워둬요. 그런 다음 저장해 놓은 이 에너지를 소비하며 몇 주 동안 지낼 수 있죠. 물을 많이 흡수하면 부풀어 오르고 물을 다 써버리면 오그라드는 식물과 같은 거죠. 낙타와 선인장 모두 훌륭한 저장 능력을 갖고 있어요.

어휘 adaptation 적응, 적응 구조 ungulate 유제 동물(발굽을 가진 동물) cope with ~에 대처하다 retain 유지하다, 간직하다 urine 오줌, 소변 accommodate 적응하다, 조절하다 external 외부의 hypothermia 저체온증 coarse 결이 거친, 굵은, 조잡한 intoxicate 중독시키다 succulent 다육 다즙 조직의 minimize 최소화하다 spiny 가시투성이의 seal 봉하다, 닫다 waxy 납질(蠟質)의 ooze 스며나오다, 새어나오다 pore 기공 hump 혹 shrivel 오그라들다, 시들다

[문제 12-17] Listen to part of a lecture in an architecture class.

P(M) : So, the colonists who arrived in the Unites States around the seventeenth century were mostly of English origin. And, with them they brought a lot of their traditional culture, including their architectural styles. Specifically, they tended to model their homes after the middle class half-timbered houses that were popular in Europe at the time. These became known as Cape Cod cottages because the area was probably one of the first settled.

  ALL ABOUT JUNIOR TOEFL

🎧 But, you know, the Cape Cod was perfectly suited for the New England climate, which was exactly like the Old Country. It was wet and stormy. [13.]You get the idea. So, everything had to be modeled to suit this. But, also, the house needed to be built with material available in the region. And as a result, there were a few modifications that had to be made. Also, they added some features as time went on to suit the changing fashion and needs of the American family.

But, the Cape Cod house as we know it today is actually a revival of this style. It became quite popular in the 1930s because it was economical, easy to construct, and could be mass produced using one simple floor plan. Um, you could say that these were some of the first houses built to meet the development needs of the suburban communities across the States and the style has been widely used for houses in the twentieth century. Of course, it still maintains the charm of its 17th century prototype. Besides, these one-and-a-half story homes symbolized the pioneering spirit of early American immigrants.

So, um, the features. Well, first of all, each house was built to withstand the violent wind that plagued the region throughout most of the winter. As such, the windows were designed to keep out the rain and prevent wind from blowing into the interior. Now, keep in mind, these houses were originally built during a time when the price of glass was astronomical. So, a lot of the time, they did not actually have panes in the windows. Instead, they had dormers and shutters that could be closed when it got cold or wet outside.

Of course, the revival homes all have glass windows, but they've kept the dormers and shutters as decorative pieces. It's simply the style. Many can't even really be shut. Oh, I should also mention that they have a door in the center of the front wall and one window on either side, making a kind of symmetrical feel to the structure.

Well, let's go back to the wind part here. Cape Cod houses were built low to the ground to minimize winter wind resistance. This was not one of the coldest regions of the United States, but still chilly enough to warrant protection from the elements. This is also why they are not complete two-stories as I mentioned before. The Cape Cods were almost always built facing the South. Why? To be exposed to as much sunlight in winter as possible to help heat up the house.

They were also built in rectangular shapes with a central chimney so that it could be linked to a fireplace in each of the corners. This could heat up the whole house evenly, but reduce the risk of fires. Ah, there were usually four rooms on the main floor, each with one of those fireplaces, and a couple of smaller rooms upstairs.

The rooftops, well, these were pretty steep. You can imagine, with all of this rain, the architects wanted to minimize the amount of residual water on the roof in order to prevent cave-ins. So, any precipitation easily slid off these angled tops and water was caught, along with debris, in overhanging eaves. It was then funneled toward a main drop point and then it usually was collected in a large receptacle.

You know, I really just want to stress that the entire facade of a Cape Cod is really quite simple. It's austere and has little ornamentation. Everything was designed for a purpose, at least originally. That's probably why the style persisted for so long.

자, 17세기경에 미국으로 건너온 식민지 이주자들은 대부분 영국 출신이었어요. 그들은 자신들의 건축 양식과 같은 많은 전통 문화를 함께 들여왔죠. 구체적으로 말하자면, 이 건축 양식은 당시에 유럽에서 유행했던 중산층의 반 목조 양식을 본뜬 것이었죠. 이 양식은 Cape Cod cottages로 알려지게 되었는데, 이 지역이 식민지 이주자들이 정착한 최초의 지역 중 한 곳이었기 때문일 겁니다. Cape Cod 양식은 New England 지역의 기후에 완벽하게 맞아떨어졌는데, 바로 본국의 기후와 비슷했던 것이죠. 비가 자주 내리고 비바람이 몰아치고, 그리고도 비가 많이 내렸죠. 어떤 상황이었는지 알겠죠. 그래서 모든 것이 이런 환경에 맞게 지어졌어요. 하지만 또한 집이란 그 지역에서 구할 수 있는 자재로 지어져야 했지요. 그 결과로 몇 가지 변형이 생겨났어요. 또한 시간이 지나면서 미국 가정의 바뀌는 유행과 필요사항에 맞추기 위해 몇몇 새로운 특징이 생겨났죠.

하지만 오늘날 우리가 알고 있는 Cape Cod 양식의 주택은 사실상 이런 스타일의 부흥이라고 할 수 있어요. Cape Cod 양식은 경제적이고 건축하기가 쉽고 하나의 평면도로 여러 채의 집을 대량으로 지을 수 있었기 때문에 1930년대에 상당히 인기가 높았어요. 이 양식은 미국 전역의 교외 지역의 개발 필요성을 충족시키기 위해 지어진 최초의 집이라고 할 수도 있고 20세기에 지어진 주택에 널리 이용되었어요. 물론 17세기 원형의 매력을 계속 간직하고 있죠. 또한 이 1.5층짜리 주택은 초기 미국 이민자들의 개척 정신을 상징했죠.

자, 그럼 Cape Cod 양식의 특징을 알아볼까요. 먼저 각 주택은 겨울 내내 기승을 부렸던 세찬 바람을 막아내도록 지어졌어요. 창문은 비가 들이치지 않고 바람이 실내로 들어오지 못하도록 설계되었죠. 이 부분을 잘 알아두어야 하는데, 이 Cape Cod 양식의 주택은 원래 유리 가격이 매우 비쌀 때 지어졌어요. 그래서 상당수의 집에는 창문에 창유리가 없죠. 대신 추울 때나 비가 내릴 때 닫을 수 있는 지붕창과 겉창이 있었어요. 물론 최근에 이 양식을 본떠 새로 지어진 주택은 모두 유리 창문을 갖추고 있지만 장식용으로 지붕창과 겉창을 계속 가지고 있죠. 단지 스타일일 뿐이에요. 상당수가 실제로 닫히지도 않고요. 아, 그리고 이 양식의 주택에는 주택 앞면의 중앙에 문이 있고 그 양쪽으로 창문이 하나씩 있어서 대칭적인 느낌을 주고 있어요.

자, 그럼 다시 바람에 관한 이야기로 돌아가 볼까요. Cape Cod 주택은 겨울에 불어오는 바람에 대한 저항을 최소화하도록 낮게 지어졌습니다. 미국에서 가장 추운 지역에 속하는 것은 아니었지만 그래도 여전히 쌀쌀한 편이라 폭풍우에 대비해야 했으니까요. 바로 이 점이 또한 아까 말한 것처럼 완전한 2층 주택이 아닌 이유입니다. Cape Cod 주택은 거의 모두 남향으로 지어졌는데요. 왜 그럴까요? 집 안을 난방 하기 위해 겨울에 가능한 한 많은 햇볕에 노출되도록 하기 위해서였지요. 또한 중앙에 굴뚝이 있는 직사각형의 구조를 가지고 있었는데, 이 중앙 굴뚝은 구석구석에 있는 벽난로에 연결될 수 있도록 하는 것이었죠. 집안 전체를 균일하게 따뜻하게 하지만 화재 위험은 줄일 수 있었어요. 1층에는 대개 4개의 방이 있었는데, 각 방에는 벽난로가 있었고, 위 층에는 2개 정도의 더 작은 방이 있었어요.

지붕은 매우 가파르죠. 그렇게 비가 많이 내리면 건축가는 함몰을 예방하기 위해 지붕에 남아있는 물의 양을 최소화하고 싶어한다는 걸 쉽게 짐작할 수 있잖아요. 따라서 빗물은 이 각진 지붕을 타고 쉽게 내려오고 물은 파편과 함께 처마에 닿죠. 그 후에 물이 떨어지는 곳으로 흘러 내려가 큰 용기에 모아지죠.

음, Cape Cod 주택의 전체적인 외관은 매우 단순하다는 걸 강조하고 싶군요. 간소하고 장식이 거의 없어요. 모든 것은 목적에 맞게 설계되었죠, 적어도 원래는 말이에요. 그 점이 바로 이 양식이 오랜 시간 동안 지속된 이유겠죠.

어휘 old country 본국 revival 부흥 economical 경제적인 floor plan 평면도 prototype 원형 immigrant 이주자 plague 괴롭히다, 귀찮게 하다 withstand 견디어 내다, 버티다 astronomical 숫자가 천문학적인 pane 판유리, 창유리 dormer 지붕창 shutter 겉창, 덧문 symmetrical 대칭적인 resistance 저항 rectangular 직사각형의 chimney 굴뚝 rooftop 지붕, 옥상 residual 남은, 나머지의 cave-in 함몰 precipitation 강수, 강수량 eaves 처마 funnel 붓다, 쏟다, 흘리다 receptacle 용기 facade 겉보기, 외관, 정면 austere 간소한, 꾸밈없는 ornamentation 장식 persist 지속하다, 잔존하다

Book List 반석 도서목록

TOEFL

ALL ABOUT JUNIOR iBT TOEFL Listening 시리즈
L1 Pre-intermediate Naomi Kim, Alan Hahn / 4×6배판 / 208쪽
(Answer Keys 포함) / 12,000원 (mp3용 CD 포함)
L2 Intermediate Naomi Kim, Alan Hahn / 4×6배판 / 240쪽
(Answer Keys 포함) / 12,000원 mp3용 CD 포함
L3 Advanced Naomi Kim, Alan Hahn / 4×6배판 / 260쪽
(Answer Keys 포함) / 12,000원 (mp3용 CD 포함)

본 교재는 크게 영어 발음과 영어 리듬 원리를 공부하는 Part I과 유형별로 토플 문제를 공략하는 Part II로 구성되어 있다. Part I에서는 혼동하기 쉬운 영어 발음을 구분하고 영어의 리듬에 적응하여 청취력을 향상시키는 훈련을 한다. Part II에서는 리스닝 섹션의 출제경향을 철저히 분석하여 각 문제 유형별로 최적의 전략과 학습방법을 제시하고 있다. 또한 시험에 실제로 자주 출제되는 대화 상황과 강의 주제를 중심으로 지문을 제작하여 실전 시험과의 유사성을 높였으며, 학습 효과를 극대화 하기위해 난이도가 높은 문제들을 뒤쪽에 배치하였다.

ALL ABOUT JUNIOR iBT TOEFL Reading 시리즈
R1 Pre-intermediate Naomi Kim, Alar Hahn / 4×6배판 / 216쪽 / 12,000원
R2 Intermediate Naomi Kim, Alan Hahn / 4×6배판 / 232쪽 / 12,000원
R3 Advanced Naomi Kim, Alan Hahn / 4×6배판 / 268쪽 / 12,000원

All About Junior TOEFL 시리즈는 토플을 전반적으로 다루고 섹션마다 모든 문제형식을 훈련시킨다. 최신 출제경향을 반영한 본 시리즈는 학습자들을 토플 학습에 자신감을 갖게 하고 고득점에 필요한 모든 것을 제공한다. Reading, Listening, Speaking, Writing 섹션은 수준별로 각 초급, 중급, 고급이 있다.

TOEFL myself Reading (Advanced Course)
Steven Oh, Michael Nolan, Richard Owell, Kevin Heiser / 국배판 / 376쪽 / 22,000원

iBT 시대를 알리는 최초의 iBT Reading 대비 교재. Reading 부분만 20회를 엮고 별권으로 해답과 해설을 실었다. 이 책의 특징은 전체가 영문으로만 되어 있다는 것. advanced reader들에게 필독서가 될 것이다.

TOEFL myself Listening (Advanced Course)
Steven Oh, Michael Nolan, Richard Owell, Kevin Heiser / 국배판 / 440쪽
(Answer Keys 포함) / 29,000원 (mp3용 CD 포함)

ETS에서 제시된 규정에 따라 편집되어 실제 시험과 같은 조건에서 자기 실력을 평가할 수 있도록 하였다. 본서는 12회분의 iBT Listening 문제를 제시하고 별권인 해설서에는 정답과 영문 해설이 들어 있다. 약간 높은 수준으로 만들어졌기 때문에 실제 시험에서는 더욱 좋은 결과를 얻을 수 있을 것이다.

iBT TOEFL myself Reading (Regular Course)
Steven Oh, Michael Nolan, Richard Owell, Kevin Heiser / 국배판 / 336쪽
(Answer Keys 포함) / 22,000원

iBT 토플을 준비하는 수험생을 위한 Reading 실전문제집. 본서는 ETS에서 제시하는 요구사항의 형식과 유형에 충실한 최상의 수험서로서, 실제 TOEFL 시험과 똑같은 환경에서 시험을 치르게 된다. 어휘를 넓히고 모든 문제에 대한 이해력을 높여주기 위해 제시문에 대해 정답 및 한글 해설을 꼼꼼히 달았으며 정답부문에 Summary를 첨부했다. 본서는 20회분의 iBT Reading 문제 및 별책인 해설서로 구성되었다.

iBT TOEFL myself Listening (Regular Course)
Jessica Jung / 국배판 / 416쪽 (Answer Keys 포함) / 25,000원 (mp3용 CD 포함)

iBT 토플을 준비하는 수험생을 위한 Listening 실전문제집. 12회분의 iBT Listening 문제 및 별책인 해설서로 구성되었다. 새로운 iBT TOEFL 형식에 더 익숙해질 수 있도록 실제 미국 대학 강의내용 수준이나 학구적인 내용에 바탕을 두고 있으며 수험생의 어휘를 넓혀주고 모든 문제에 대한 이해력을 높여주기 위해 제시문에 대해 정답 및 한글 해설을 꼼꼼히 달았다. 뿐만 아니라, 지문에 대한 내용 이해를 돕기 위해 정답부문에 Summary(지문요약)를 첨부했다.

iBT TOEFL Reading (Prep-Advanced Course)
Steven Oh, Michael Nolan, Richard Owell, Kevin Heiser / 4×6배판 / 316쪽
(Answer Keys 포함) / 21,000원 (mp3용 CD 포함)

iBT에 출제되는 지문은 역사적, 과학적, 사회적 사실이 대부분이므로 여러 번 응시하면 내용이 비슷한 것을 만나게 된다. 따라서 영역별로 가장 많이 등장하는 내용을 엄선하였으므로 청취학습을 겸들이면 학습효과가 배가된다. 난이도는 고급자를 목표로 하는 중급자 수준에 맞추었다.

TOEFL Vocabulary & Reading
오규상 / 4×6배판 / 624면 / 19,800원 (mp3 파일 무료제공)

어휘와 독해를 묶은 회심의 역작. 모든 어휘를 테마별로 분류하고 독해지문 100편을 수록했다. 특히 34편에 달하는 미국 역사는 역사 교과서 한 권을 읽는 효과를 준다. 동의어 찾기 문제해설은 英英韓사전 방식으로 되어 많은 동의어를 익히는데 큰 도움이 된다.

Find TOEFL Vocabulary 1 · 2 with Listening & Reading
Steven Oh / 국배판 / 424쪽(1권), 432쪽(2권) / 각권 15,000원 (mp3용 CD 포함)

iBT TOEFL의 어휘, 청취, 독해를 한 권으로 마스터하려는 학습자를 위한 교재. 영역별로 실전에 가장 빈번히 등장하는 중요 어휘와 5천여 개의 어구를 모두 영영한 사전 방식으로 해설하였고 어휘학습 후 청취 문제를 접합으로써 청취 실력을 향상시킬 수 있다. 한 테마에 어휘와 그에 해당하는 다양한 독해를 수록하였으며 독해 지문을 청취와 병행하여 청취 실력을 동시에 올리는 학습효과를 누릴 수 있다.

Essential TOEFL WORDS 5000
임 공 / 신국판 / 432쪽 / 12,000원 (테이프 포함 : 15,900원)

토플 리스닝과 리딩에서 갈수록 비중이 높아져 가는 Lecture 분야를 공략하기 위한 필수어휘서다. 리스닝과 리딩에서 질문하는 토픽이 동일하다는 점에 착안하여 리스닝과 리딩 점수를 동시에 향상시킬 수 있도록 Lecture 빈출지문 40개를 엄선하고, 각 빈출지문을 청취하거나 독해할 때 반드시 알아 두어야 할 핵심문장과 핵심어휘를 정리하였다.

iBT Find TOEFL Reading
Steven Oh / 4×6배판 / 600쪽 (Answer Keys 포함) / 22,000원 (mp3용 CD 포함)

iBT 토플에서 단기간에 고득점을 올릴 수 있도록 테마별 학습이 가능하도록 하였다. 지문별로 중요하거나 어려운 어휘는 영영한 사전식의 설명이 되어 있고, 원어민이 녹음한 mp3 파일이 제공되어 청취를 병행한 입체적 학습이 가능하다. 권말에는 Actual Test를 통해 실전 감각을 키울 수 있도록 하였다.

iBT Find TOEFL Listening
Rebecca Hardy, Naomi Kim / 4×6배판 / 368쪽 / 19,000원 (mp3용 CD 포함)

iBT Listening 출제경향을 분석하고 고득점을 얻을 수 있는 최적의 전략과 학습 방법을 제시하고 있다. 실질적인 청취력 향상을 위하여 Dictation 훈련에 중점을 두고 있다. 긴 지문 중 밑줄로 듣기 능력을 테스트해 나아가 보면 점점 자신감이 높아지는 걸 느낄 수 있다.

iBT Find TOEFL Speaking
Rebecca Hardy, Naomi Kim / 4×6배판 / 379쪽 / 15,000원 (mp3용 CD 포함)

본서는 iBT TOEFL Speaking 섹션의 출제경향을 철저히 분석한 후 고득점을 얻을 수 있는 최적의 전략과 학습 방법을 제시하고 있다. 다양한 출제 예상문제와 대화 상황, 강의 주제를 다루고 있으며, 문제의 이해와 답변 제시 등의 과정을 실제 시험 상황과 동일하게 훈련할 수 있도록 체계적으로 구성되었다. 4주 또는 6주간의 계획에 맞춰 학습하도록 하였고 권말에는 Actual Test를 수록하여 최종 점검이 가능하도록 하였다.

iBT Find TOEFL Writing
Jack Betts, Naomi Kim / 4×6배판 / 332쪽 / 15,000원 (mp3용 CD 포함)

iBT 체제로 바뀐 토플 Writing 섹션의 출제경향을 철저히 분석하고 고득점을 얻을 수 있는 최적의 전략과 학습 방법을 제시하고 있다. 다양한 출제 예상문제와 대화 상황, 강의 주제를 다루고 있으며, 시험을 단계적으로 공략할 수 있도록 난이도를 조정하였다. 자신의 생각을 명확하게 표현할 수 있도록 문제의 이해와 답변 제시 등의 과정을 실제 시험 상황과 동일하게 훈련할 수 있도록 체계적으로 구성하였다.

SAT & IELTS

SAT WORDS 2400
SATWorld / 크라운판 변형 / 303쪽 / 12,000원 (mp3용 CD 포함)

이 책은 CollegeBoard의 Official Guide 및 SAT기출문제(총 35회분)를 분석했기 때문에 Sentence Completion에 출제되는 어휘의 90% 이상을 해결할 수 있다고 확신한다. 비단 SC뿐만 아니라 다른 Reading이나 Writing 섹션의 문제 해결에도 커다란 도움을 줄 것이다.

ALL ABOUT IELTS 실전문제집 1 (Listening)
이수영, Liam Heppleston / 4×6배판 / 232쪽 / 13,000원 (mp3 CD 포함)

IELTS의 전반적인 이해를 돕기 위해 IELTS의 시험제도와 각종 정보(영역별 시험시간, 시험 평가와 방법 등)와 전반적인 리스닝 섹션의 특징을 설명했다. 그리고 리스닝 실력을 향상시키기 위해 절대적으로 필요한 각종 리스닝 스킬을 예제와 함께 간략하게 살펴볼 수 있도록 했다. 섹션별로 출제되는 문제유형과 관련 팁들은 학생들에게 감초 같은 역할을 할 것이다.

ALL ABOUT IELTS 실전문제집 2 (Speaking)
이수영, Liam Heppleston / 4×6배판 / 240쪽 / 13,000원 (mp3용 CD 포함)

본 책은 IELTS 스피킹 10회분의 문제와 해설을 수록한 최종 마무리 테스트용 교재이다. 각 1회분은 파트 1(5~6 Questions), 파트 2(1 Task Card), 파트 3(5~6 Questions)으로 구성되었고, 실제 시험과 비슷한 최신의 출제경향과 문제형태를 반영했다. 특히, 파트별로 실제 시험에 출제되었던 질문을 응용하여 만들었기 때문에 실전감각을 익히는 데 많은 도움이 된다. 영어가 모국어인 사람들에게도 면접관과 1대 1로 진행되는 인터뷰는 수월한 일이 아니다. 더군다나 영어가 비모국어인 수험생들에게는 상당한 노력과 연습이 필요하다. 하지만 사전에 각 파트별 예상 질문과 모범 답변을 충분히 숙지한다면 자신이 원하는 점수를 효과적으로 획득할 것이다.

ALL ABOUT IELTS 실전문제집 3 (Reading–General module)

이수영, Julie Tolsma / 4×6판 / 256쪽 / 13,000원

본 책은 IELTS Reading TEST (General Module) 5회분의 문제와 해설을 수록한 최종 마무리 테스트용 교재이다. 각각의 1회분은 42문항(4개 지문)으로 구성되었고, 실제 시험과 비슷한 최신의 출제경향과 문제형태를 반영했다. 특히, 섹션별로 다양한 지문(6주제)과 문제유형(7형태)을 제공하여 실전감각을 익히는 데 많은 도움이 된다.

TOEIC

토익채널 60 (RC 비법서)

강성호, 김정훈 / 4×6배변형판 / 517쪽 / 13,900원 (부록/알맹이 어휘집 포함)

본 교재는 900점 이상의 고득점자를 위한 책이 아닌 토익시험에 반드시 출제되는 비법과 정보를 한데 모아 짧은 시간 안에 RC를 해결할 수 있는 솔루션을 제공해주는 토익초중급자를 대상으로 하는 RC비법서이다. 획일적인 페이지 배치방식을 지양하고 추가적인 설명이 많은 부분에는 많은 설명을 제공하고, 반대로 간략하게 요점만 정리해야 할 부분에는 필요한 만큼의 설명을 제공하면서 비합리적인 구성을 피했다. 또한, 각 섹션의 특징이 모두 다르기 때문에 교재구성과 진행방식을 탄력적으로 조정했다.

토익채널 41 (LC 비법서)

임동찬 / 4×6배변형판 / 280쪽 / 13,000원 (mp3용 CD 포함)

본 교재는 900점 이상의 고득점자를 위한 책이 아닌 토익시험에 반드시 출제되는 비법과 정보를 한데 모아 짧은 시간 안에 LC를 해결할 수 있는 솔루션을 제공해주는 토익초중급자를 대상으로 하는 LC비법서이다. 비법별 구성으로 하루에 비법을 1개씩 공부하여 2달 안에 마무리할 수 있게 꾸몄다. LC의 모든 내용을 41개의 비법으로 나누어, 비법의 체득이 본 시험장에서 바로 적용이 가능하다. 〈채널비법제시 – 채널비법해설 – 기출표현정리 – 채널예제 – 채널문제〉로 이어지는 구성과 딕테이션과 의미구별 해석을 통해 LC 실력을 탄탄하게 키울 수 있다.

처음부터 다시 시작하는 토익은 내밥 RC 입문편

Pat Jeon / 4×6배판 / 432쪽 / 13,800원

본서는 TOEIC Part 5, 6, 7을 위한 입문서로 기획된 책이다. 어휘력과 문법 실력을 동시에 공략할 수 있도록 하였으며 TOEIC 독해를 위한 전략비법 70, 1~2초 안에 정답 고르기 공략법 등으로 구성되었다. 강의용 및 독습자를 위해 강의식 해설이 수록되었고 실전모의고사 10회분 체험하기 프로그램이 포함되어 있다.

처음부터 다시 시작하는 토익은 내밥 LC 입문편

김형주 / 4×6배판 / 456쪽 / 15,800원 (테이프 포함 : 25,000원)

TOEIC Part 1, 2, 3, 4를 위한 입문서로 기획된 책이다. 뉴토익의 경향에 맞춰 각 파트별 문제 유형을 data화하여 분석하였고 각각에 대한 대비책을 제시하여, 수험생들이 실제 시험에 대한 적응력을 높이고 고득점을 얻을 수 있도록 하였다. 각 파트마다 실전 테스트가 수록되었으며 미국인과 영국인 네이티브 발음으로 녹음된 MP3 파일이 제공된다.

뉴토익은 내밥1 LC 실전문제집

Jason Kim, Jay Lee / 국배판 / 256쪽 (별책 146쪽) / 15,000원 (테이프 포함 : 25,000원)

뉴토익 수험자의 최종 마무리 테스트용, 네이티브의 말하기 스피드에 적응력을 기르는데 주안점을 두었으며 680점 이상의 중고급자에게 뉴토익 LC의 파트별 공략법을 제시한다. 10회분의 미니테스트인 Pretest가 있고 10회분의 정식 Actual Test가 수록되어 있다.

뉴토익은 내밥2 RC 실전문제집

남재조, 박영광 / 국배판 / 400쪽 (별책 128쪽) / 16,000원 (별책 포함)

최근 토익 RC 문제를 심층 분석하여 적중률 높은 문제를 엄선하여 12회로 구성하였다. 특히 종합적 사고를 기를 수 있도록 출제하였고 혼자서도 공부할 수 있도록 문제의 흐름을 상세히 설명하였다. Part 5, 6에 다채로운 테마의 지문을 수록하였으며, Part 7 장문 독해를 강화하였다.

토익은 내밥 Basic LC

김학용 / 4×6배판 / 446쪽 / 16,800원 (mp3 파일 무료제공)

New TOEIC LC Section, 즉 Part Ⅰ, Ⅱ, Ⅲ, Ⅳ별로 최신 출제유형과 경향을 분석하였고 문제별 핵심을 파악하는 핵심 포인트를 제시했다. 철저한 출제유형 해부에 따른 파트별 공략법이 제시되었으며 실전을 대비한 Model Test와 Actual Test를 통해 실제 시험에 대한 적응력을 키울 수 있다.

토익은 내밥 Basic RC

김학용 / 4×6배판 / 618쪽 (별책 103쪽) / 16,800원

어휘 문법 독해를 일망타진하는 책! New TOEIC의 출제 유형을 철저히 분석하였으며 그에 따른 내용을 충실히 전달하고자 파트별 출제빈도와 그 유형을 표시해두었다. 어휘편에선 고득점으로 인도하는 토익 어휘 공략법을, 문법편에선 문장을 분석하는 문법 지식을 탄탄히 쌓을 수 있도록 하였으며, 독해편에선 지문에 관련된 문제의 핵심을 파악하는 훈련이 가능하도록 하였다.

토익은 내밥 Xpeed 700 RC

김영진, 이희연 / 4×6배판 / 624쪽 / 16,500원

New TOEIC RC 단기 완성용 특강 교재. TOEIC 초급~중급자들이 단기간에 Part 5, 6, 7에서 고득점을 거둘 수 있도록 기획된 책이다. 각 파트별 출제유형과 출제경향에 대한 철저한 분석을 바탕으로, 단순히 문제풀이 요령을 익히는데 그치지 않고 기초 실력 배양까지 가능하도록 12주에 걸쳐 학습하도록 구성되었다.

토익은 내밥 Xpeed 700 LC

이희연, 김영진 / 4×6배판 / 464쪽 / 16,500원 (테이프 포함 : 25,000원)

New TOEIC LC 단기 완성용 특강 교재. TOEIC 초급~중급자들이 단기간에 Part 1, 2, 3, 4에서 고득점을 할 수 있도록 기획된 책이다. 각 파트별 출제 유형의 철저한 분석과 더불어, 토익시험이 선호하는 단어와 중요 표현에 대한 반복 청취 훈련과 확인 학습을 할 수 있도록 구성되어 있다.

즉석 토익 VOCA

김학용 / A5 / 432쪽 / 12,000원

파트별로 유용한 어휘를 충분히 연습하도록 구성했고 파트1에서는 사진 문제의 핵심을 파악하는 연습을 시킨다. L/C와 R/C편의 어휘를 종합적으로 공부할 수 있도록 각 Part별로 출제 빈도가 높은 어휘를 실었기 때문에 어휘력 향상에 큰 도움이 될 것이다.

JUNIOR TOEIC RC

도성자 / 4×6배판 / 440쪽 / 15,000원

TOEIC을 처음 치르는 주니어들이 시험 준비 첫걸음을 디딜 수 있도록 구성되었다. 토익의 기본 유형 뿐만 아니라 저자 고유의 〈문장 분석의 해법〉을 통해 영어 독해 전반에 대한 기본실력을 쌓을 수 있도록 하였다. 또 반드시 극복해야 할 문법과 독해 공략법을 꼼꼼한 〈강의식 해설〉로 구성하였다.

독해 · 어휘 · 문법 · 작문

기본 중학영어 (상,하)

방정인 / 국배변형판 / 상권 128쪽, 하권 128쪽 / 각권 8,000원

〈STEP BY STEP 기본 중학 영어〉는 중학교 2학년 영어 교과서를 종합, 분석하여 해당학년 수준의 기본 문형을 모두 다루었으며, 더 나아가 중학 문법의 기본을 전부 수록하였다. 이 두 권의 책이 중학영어의 확실한 기초가 될 것이다.

기초영문법 (상,하)

방정인 / 국배변형판 / 상권 204쪽, 하권 208쪽 / 각권 10,000원

〈STEP BY STEP 기초영문법〉은 누구나 단어에 대해 부담 이 공부해 나갈 수 있도록 기초단어 700여개로 문장을 구성하였고, 문법 내용은 중학교 교과과정부터 고등학교 전 과정의 모든 문법을 다루었다. 그리고 본서는 문법항목이 나올 때마다 PATTERN PRACTICE(문형연습)를 많이 수록하여 같은 내용의 문법을 여러 번 되풀이함으로써 그 문법의 항목만큼은 완벽하게 터득하도록 편집되었다. Exercise(연습문제)도 주로 주관식 문제로 구성하였다.

New Start Voca (뉴스타트보카)

김학용 / 4×6배변형판 / 560쪽 / 17,000원

본서는 필수적인 동의어, 파생어를 제시하여 사전을 찾는 수고를 덜도록 배려하고 있으며 접두어의 의미를 오래 기억할 수 있는 보조설명하고 있고 단어학습의 결과를 평가해 볼 수 있는 충실한 평가문제를 수록하였다. 어려운 어근을 쉽게 익히도록 의미를 나타내는 단어로 표현하고 있으며 하나의 어원을 가지고 최대한 많은 단어를 익힐 수 있도록 편집하였다. 또한 어휘와 더불어 숙어를 익힐 수 있도록 권말에 제시하였다.

스토리 보카

신재현 / 4×6배변형판 / 304쪽 / 9,800원

본서는 그림과 함께 각 유닛의 재미있는 단어 탄생이야기로 자연스럽게 어휘를 익히도록 하였다. 단어의 뜻과 동의어, 파생어, 반의어 등을 읽어보고 본문에서는 다루지 못했지만, 반드시 알고 넘어가야할 고급 어휘들을 읽어서 기억된 단어들을 간단한 연습문제에서 체크하도록 고급 어휘들을 수록하였으며 유닛 중간 중간에 있는 재미있는 '쉼터이야기'에서 다양한 이야기들로 구성하였다.

3일만에 끝내는 Super 영문독해 핵심전략

오규상 / 4×6배변형판 / 312쪽 / 9,500원

이 책은 영문 독해의 핵심 전략적인 비법을 제공한다. 우선 Reading Skill과 Reading Material에서 독해의 기본구조를 바로 잡고 꼼꼼히 기초를 다진다. 실전문제를 통해 자신감을 배양하며, 학습자에게 부담 없이 꾸며져 있어 읽다보면 독해실력을 검증해볼 수 있다. Part·4에서는 구문과 문법사항을 확인하며 술술 읽을 수 있게 꾸몄다.

3일만에 끝내는 Super 영문법

Ueda Ichizo / 4×6배변형판 / 339쪽 / 9,500원

본서는 문법을 처음부터 끝까지 배우는 것이 아니라 문법의 중요사항을 엮어 단기간에 문법 전체의 핵심을 짚을 수 있도록 도와주는 기획서이다. 그리고 영작문 연습과 각종 숙어, 구문별 뉘앙스 설명으로 영어 실력을 특별히 한 단계 업그레이드시킬 수 있다.

3일만에 끝내는 Super 영작문

Hironobu Takeoka / 4X6배변형판 / 272쪽 / 9,500원

영작을 쉽고 빠르게 마스터할 수 있도록 구성된 영작문 기본서. 영작을 위해 꼭 필요한 58가지 법칙과 빈출패턴 67문형을 제시함으로써 영작의 기본을 다질 수 있으며 자연스럽게 영작 실력을 업그레이드 할 수 있다

영어원론

김건태 / 4×6배판 / 540쪽 / 25,000원

영어 독해에 어느 정도 자신이 있는 중상급 이상의 영어 학습자를 위한 기획서. 이 책은 친절하고 풍부한 해설을 담고 있으며 문장을 설명하면서 그 문장이 왜 틀렸는지 알기 쉽게 설명해준다. 부자연스러운 문장과 좋은 문장을 나란히 비교하고 차이를 설명한 것을 꾸준히 읽음으로서 조금씩 영어를 보는 안목이 넓어질 수 있도록 도와준다.

반석 영문독해 ❶ 사회과학편

편집부 / 4×6배판 / 352쪽 / 10,000원

TOEFL, 대학원, 국가고시 등에 고정적으로 인용되는 텍스트들을 사회과학 분야(경제학 · 경제사상, 사회학 · 사회사상, 정치학 · 정치사상)별로 엄선, 체계적으로 엮었다.

반석 영문독해 ❷ 인문과학편

편집부 / 4×6배판 / 348쪽 / 10,000원

TOEFL, 대학원, 국가고시 등에 고정적으로 인용되는 텍스트들을 인문과학 분야(문학, 문학이론, 역사, 역사인식, 철학, 철학인식)별로 엄선하여 체계적으로 엮어놓았다.

반석 영문독해 ❸ 자연과학편

편집부 / 4×6배판 / 368쪽 / 10,000원

TOEFL, 대학원, 국가고시 등에 고정적으로 인용되는 텍스트들을 자연과학 분야(과학기술의 현단계, 과학과 사회, 과학철학)별로 엄선, 체계적으로 구성하였다.

즉석 영단어 3000

오규상 / 국반판 / 496쪽 / 8,900원 (mp3용 CD 포함)

본서는 TOEFL, TOEIC, 공무원 시험 등 각종 시험게 출제되는 많은 어휘들 가운데 시험에 꼭 나오는 핵심어휘들만 모아 동의어, 반의어, 파생어와 함께 예문들을 엮어 놓았다. 이러한 단어만 확실히 익혀둔다면 시험에 나오는 어떤 독해지문이라도 읽어나가는데 어려움이 없을 것이다.

즉석 영숙어 900

편집부 / 국반판 / 464쪽 / 8,900원 (mp3용 CD 포함)

본서는 영어를 읽고 구사하는데 필요한 900개의 필수 숙어와 2,000개의 각종 시험 대비 기출 숙어로 구성되었다. 필수 숙어는 모두 Q&A의 짧은 대화로 이루어진 상황과 함께 제시되며, 토플, 토익이나 여타 시험에 자주 출제되는 문제를 수록하여 새로운 어휘를 확장할 수 있도록 편집했다.

와신상담 공무원영어 9급 (독해·어휘편)

박기혁 / 4×6배판 / 448쪽 / 15,000원

각종 공무원 및 공사시험을 위한 강의식 어휘·독해 교재. 어휘와 독해를 단번에 정복할 수 있도록 기출 유형을 철저하게 분석하였으며, 셀프체크에서 문제 해결 비법을 제시하여 문제 풀이 능력을 업그레이드 할 수 있도록 했다.

와신상담 공무원영어 9급 (문법편)

박기혁 / 4×6배판 / 472쪽 / 15,000원

독학용 강의식 수험 영문법 교재로서 어떤 유형의 공무원 시험이라도 적용할 수 있는 기초적인 영문법을 총망라하였으며, 각종 수험 영어의 실전에 대비할 수 있도록 문법사항마다 문제 풀이 비법과 영문법의 출제 원리를 체계적으로 분석한 기획서이다.

로그인 1318 영문법

윤상범 / 4×6변형판 / 328쪽 / 12,000원 (Tape 2개 포함)

필요없는 문법은 과감히 생략하고 수능 독해에 꼭 필요한 알짜 문법만을 구어체로 서술하였다. 반복하여 읽다보면 문장과 문법이 자연스럽게 습득되며, 각 장의 끝에 연습문제를 통해 자신의 문법과 독해실력을 평가해 볼 수 있다.

초급 Junior Vocabulary

이홍배·김덕중·서석봉 / 4×6배판 / 300쪽 / 8,000원

TOEFL·TOEIC을 비롯한 각종 영어시험 빈출 어휘 3,000개와 매 과마다 9가지 이상의 상이한 응용문제를 수록하였다.

중급 College Vocabulary

이홍배, 김덕중 / 4×6배판 / 494쪽 / 10,000원

TOEFL·TOEIC을 비롯한 각종 영어시험 빈출 어휘 5,000개를 엄선하여 수록하였고 매과 시작전에 어휘력 측정시험(Pretest)을 실시함으로써 자신의 어휘력 수준을 진단할 수 있다.

시험에 잘 나오는 영어문법

선맹수 / 4×6배판 / 508쪽 / 15,800원

본서는 공무원을 비롯하여 대학원, 편입, 각종 저격시험 따위에 빈출되는 TOEFL 유형을 토대로 기획 및 구성되었으며, 어떤 유형의 시험어서라도 고득점을 올릴 수 있도록 영문법의 기초적인 원리와 개념을 실전적으로 접목

아주 쉽게 배우는 영문법

최희 / 4×6배판 / 431쪽 / 10,000원

문법을 알기 쉽게 설명했고, 예문을 회화와 실용영어 중심으로 구성하여 '회화·작문·독해'를 처음부터 끝까지 이 책 하나로 끝낼 수 있다.

처음 시작하는 영작 기술

간종현 / 4×6배판 / 304쪽 / 9,500원

누구나 만들 수 있는 짧고 간단한 문장으로 숨이 찰 만큼 길고 복잡한 문장을 어떻게 수월하게 만들 수 있는가를 보여주고 훈련시켜 준다. 간단한 문장을 확장과 연장의 과정을 통해 자유자재로 원하는 문장을 만들 수 있는 수준까지 끌어올릴 수 있다.

즉석 기초 영작문

장승재 / 4×6배판 / 348쪽 / 10,000원

어렵게만 느껴졌던 영작문을 초보 학습자들도 쉽게 다가갈 수 있도록 구성한 영작문 교재. 영작을 위한 핵심 문법을 근간으로 하여 쉬운 것부터 점진적이며 반복적인 연습을 통해 영어식 사고 방식을 체득할 수 있다.

회화 · 일반

팝콘 영어 (동사편, 명사 · 형용사편)

이수영, Liam Heppleston / 4×6배변형판 / 동사편 208쪽, 명사 · 형용사편 221쪽 / 각권 9,800원 (mp3용 CD 포함)

본서는 사전과 비슷하지만 유사어를 기준으로 묶여져 있기 때문에 필요한 단어를 스스로 찾고 혼자서도 공부할 수 있게 만들었다. 이 책은 전2권으로 만들어져 1권은 영어를 공부하는 학생들이 반드시 알아야 할 동사 70개를, 2권에는 형용사, 명사 70개를 실었다. 각 페이지에는 하나의 중심어(Key Word)가 있으며 그 단어와 관련된 유사 의미를 지닌 4개에서 8개의 단어들이 있다. 각 유사어에는 그 의미가 영어로 설명되어 있어서 그 단어의 뜻을 명확하게 알 수 있으며 간단한 예문을 통해 문장 내에서 그 단어를 어떻게 사용해야 할지 알게 된다. 주어진 예문의 문장을 읽고 학생들이 이해한 단어의 뜻을 확인하도록 퀴즈 형식으로 꾸몄다.

램 영어회화

김형주 / 4×6배변형판 / 240쪽 / 12,000원 (mp3용 CD 포함)

본서는 5스텝, 레벨업 영어회화구문과 해설하였으며 영어회화를 확장시키는 응용표현 수록

하였다. 효과적인 영어회화 공부방법 제시하고 원어민 녹음 MP3 파일 제공하였다.

거침없는 영어를 위한 스피킹 툴 (상,하)

소피아 리 / 크라운판 / 상권 225쪽, 하권 221쪽 / 각권 9,500원

본서는 우리말을 영어로 바꿔 말하는 능력을 향상시켜주는 영어회화 교재이다. 영어로 유창하게 말을 하기 위해서는 먼저 영어식 사고에 익숙해져야 한다. 이를 위해 한글문장을 의미 단위(청크)로 구분하여 영어로 쉽게 말을 할 수 있는 장치를 마련했다. 처음에는 어색하더라도 반복해서 읽다보면 영어식 사고가 저절로 체득될 것이다. 또한 영어의 발음법칙과 현상 등을 친절하게 설명해주며 원어민의 발음에 비교적 근사치의 음가를 한글로 표기하여 유창한 영어회화를 가능하게 한다.

즉석에서 바로바로 활용하는 비즈니스 레터 & 이메일 사전

편집부 편저 / 4×6배판 / 608쪽 / 19,800원

본서는 비즈니스 레터와 이메일 230여 개 수록했다. 실제 영문 무역서신 사례를 바탕으로 해당 어구, 풀이, 해석 등을 인용해 설득력 있는 비즈니스 서신을 실전에 응용할 수 있도록 자세하게 설명하고 있다. 무역, 상업용 서신(이메일)을 아주 쉽게 작성할 수 있게 도와주는 최고의 가이드 북이다.

영어수업이 즐거워지는 메이킷 교실영어

정한석 / 국판 / 483쪽 / 15,000원 (테이프 포함 : 19,000원)

본서는 국제중, 특목고, 민사고 완벽 대비서로서 중, 고등학생들이 교실이나 집에서 영어로 의사소통을 할 때 필요한 대화와 표현을 담았다. 특히 영어수업을 위해 반드시 필요한 기본 표현들과 대화들을 상황별로 수록한 본격 〈교실영어 회화교재〉이다. 영어의 4가지 영역인 듣기, 말하기, 읽기, 쓰기를 골고루 다루었고 특히, 자신의 생각을 효과적으로 전달하기 위해서 반드시 알아야 할 문장패턴 강화훈련을 제공하며 영어식 사고를 길러준다.

즉석 비즈니스 영어회화 사전

이수영, 줄리 톨스마 저 / 크라운 변형판 / 216쪽 / 12,000원 (mp3용 CD 포함)

국내외 다국적 기업에 근무하거나 세계화 경제에 발맞춰 국제시장에서 활약하는 전문 기업인들을 위한 Daily Business 영어 회화 교재. 본문은 모두 11개의 단원으로 이루어져 있으며 각 단원은 주제에 따라 국제업무 환경에서 기업업무를 수행하는데 흔히 접할 수 있는 상황을 중심으로 한 다양한 대화로 구성되어 있다.

즉석 영어 회화 패턴 900

김수진 / A5 / 432쪽 / 10,000원 (mp3 파일 제공) 테이프 포함 : 15,000원)

본서는 상황별 영어회화를 토대로 기초적인 표현에서부터 각종 질의응답의 요령까지 Basic Expressions를 통하여 영어회화에 자신감 있게 접근할 수 있도록 구성하였다. 본서는 60개 주제와 900개의 기본 문형으로서 기본적인 문장구조와 회화에 많이 쓰이는 어휘를 모두 실었다.

즉석 일본어 회화 900

봉영아 / A5 / 440쪽 / 10,000원 (mp3 파일 제공) (테이프 포함 : 15,000원)

본서는 주제별, 상황별, 장면별 일본어 회화를 토대로 기초적인 표현에서부터 각종 질의응답의 요령까지 Basic Expression을 통하여 일본어 회화에 자신감 있게 접근할 수 있도록 구성하였다. 실용 일본어에서 빈출되는 900개의 패턴문형을 중점적으로 반복 훈련하여 일본어 회화를 정복해 보자. 본서의 기획 핵심은 Pattern Drill에 나오는 대체형 반복연습으로 聞取り (청해) 실력을 비약적으로 향상시키는 것과 여기 나오는 다양한 표현을 회화에서 직접 응용할 수 있도록 하는 것이다.

즉석 중국어 회화 900

김현철, 조길 / A5 / 439쪽 / 10,000원 (mp3 파일 제공) (테이프 포함 : 15,000원)

본서는 주제별, 상황별, 장면별 회화를 토대로, 일상생활에서 겪는 기초적인 회화에서부터 비즈니스나 해외여행에 필요한 상황이나 장면에 적용할 수 있는 중국어 회화 표현 900문형 이상을 수록하였다. 총 60 Unit으로 구성되었으며, Basic Expression과 Pattern Drill에서 빈출 핵심 패턴문형, 묻고 답하는 요령에 의한 어휘력과 표현력 확장, 문형변화까지 폭넓게 다루었다. 또한 중국인 네이티브 스피커의 목소리로 녹음된 MP3 파일을 제공함으로써 중국 현지인들의 발음과 성조에 익숙해지도록 하였다.

즉석 일상 영어

이국호 / 국판 / 351쪽 / 9,500원 (mp3 파일 무료제공) (테이프 포함: 12,500원)

이 책은 영어 기초 정도의 실력을 가지고 회화를 막 시작하려는 학습자를 대상으로 하여 일상생활, 여행 등에 기본적으로 쓰일 수 있는 회화 표현을 중심으로 엮었다. 어떤 장면이나 상황에서도 영어 회화를 가능한 정확하고 다양하게 익힐 수 있도록 체계적으로 구성하였으며, 영어 초보자도 쉽게 접근할 수 있도록 한글로 영어발음을 표기하였다.

즉석 일상 일본어

이화승 / 국판 / 351쪽 / 9,500원 (mp3 파일 무료제공) (테이프 포함 : 12,500원)

이 책은 일본어 기초 정도의 실력을 가지고 회화를 막 시작하려는 학습자를 대상으로 하여 일상생활, 여행 등에 기본적으로 쓰일 수 있는 회화 표현을 중심으로 엮었다. 어떤 장면이나 상황에서도 일본어 회화를 가능한 정확하고 다양하게 익힐 수 있도록 체계적으로 구성하였으며, 일본어 초보자도 쉽게 접근할 수 있도록 한글로 일본어발음을 표기하였다.

즉석 일상 중국어

이춘호 / 국판 / 351쪽 / 9,500원 (mp3 파일 무료제공) (테이프 포함 : 12,500원)

이 책은 중국어 기초 정도의 실력을 가지고 회화를 막 시작하려는 학습자를 대상으로 하여 일상생활, 여행 등에 기본적으로 쓰일 수 있는 회화 표현을 중심으로 엮었다. 어떤 장면이나 상황에서도 중국어 회화를 가능한 정확하고 다양하게 익힐 수 있도록 체계적으로 구성하였으며, 중국어 초보자도 쉽게 접근할 수 있도록 한글로 중국어발음을 표기하였다.

넘버원 여행영어

이국호 / 4×6판 / 208쪽 / 7,000원

영어에 서툰 여행자가 해외여행을 자유롭게 즐길 수 있도록 도와주는 본격 Spoken Travel English 회화교재. 여행 시에 일어날 수 있는 수많은 돌발 상황들에 대처하기 위해 늘 휴대할 수 있도록 포켓북 사이즈로 제작하였으며, 영어에 서툰 여행자라도 자연스럽게 영어를 구사할 수 있도록 원어민 발음법에 따라 우리말로 표기를 달아두었다.

즉석 여행 영어

이국호 / 4×6판 / 336쪽 / 7,500원 (mp3 파일 무료제공)

현지에서 바로바로 활용이 가능하도록 원어민의 발음에 가깝게 한글 발음을 병기하였고, 상황별로 필요한 영어 표현은 물론 각종 정보가 가득한 여행 가이드북이다. 또한 네이티브의 정확한 발음을 익힐 수 있도록 CD가 포함되어 있으며 자료실에서 책 전문을 mp3 파일로 다운받을 수 있다.

즉석 여행 일본어

이화승 / 4×6판 / 336쪽 / 7,500원 (mp3 파일 무료제공)

현지에서 바로바로 활용이 가능하도록 원어민의 발음에 가깝게 한글 발음을 병기하였고, 상황별로 필요한 일어 표현은 물론 각종 정보가 가득한 여행 가이드북이다.

즉석 여행 중국어

송준호 / 4×6판 / 336쪽 / 7,500원 (mp3 파일 무료제공)

현지에서 바로바로 활용이 가능하도록 원어민의 발음에 가깝게 한글 발음을 병기하였고, 상황별로 필요한 중국어 표현은 물론 각종 정보가 가득한 여행 가이드북이다.

그들만의 영어표현 아주 쉽게 따라잡기

홍성은 / 크라운판 / 330쪽 / 11,000원 (mp3용 CD 포함)

미국의 초등학생은 잘 알지만 한국의 영문과 학생들은 잘 모르는 표현을 위주로 엮은 독특한 내용의 회화책. 재미있는 일러스트와 재치 있는 설명이 가득하고 슬랭ъ도 과감하게 소개했다. 원어민들의 솔직한 표현과 헐리웃 영화를 제대로 이해하고 싶다면 일독을 권한다.

프리토킹에 강해지는 즉석 영어 회화

이국호 / 국판 / 560쪽 / 18,500원 (mp3용 CD 포함)

영어회화를 약간 해본 사람이 원어민과 자유로운 대화가 가능하도록 다양한 표현을 담아 영어 회화사전식 구성을 취했다. 즉석에서 활용할 수 있는 필수적인 표현을 엄선했고 6,000개 이상의 방대한 회화 표현이 나오며 다양한 주제의 실용 회화가 가능하다.

프리토킹에 강해지는 즉석 일본어 회화

泉勇吉 · 村上二郎 / 국판 / 656쪽 / 18,500원 (CD 포함)

이 책은 자연스러운 일본어 회화를 위해 언제 어디서나 즉석에서 사전처럼 바로 활용할 수 있도록 만들어진 기획서이다. 기본 회화, 실용 회화, 필수 문형의 세 파트로 구성되어 있으며 유창하고 자연스러운 회화를 위해 필수적인 관용적 표현 25,000문장을 수록하여 체계적으로 일본어 프리토킹에 대비할 수 있다.

프리토킹에 강해지는 즉석 중국어 회화

조요섭 · 김형준 / 국판 / 480쪽 / 15,000원 (mp3 파일 무료제공)

본서는 중국어 회화를 본격적으로 시작하려는 학습자를 대상으로 하며, 기본어법, 기본회화, 실용회화로 나누어 중국어 회화에 대한 모든 것을 총망라한 학습서이다. 어떤 장면이나 상황에서도 중국어 회화를 가능한 정확하고 다양하게 익힐 수 있도록 사전식으로 구성하였으며 즉석에서 바로바로 활용할 수 있도록 국내 최대의 중국어 8,000여 표현을 수록하였다.

캐티리의 병원 영어회화 첫걸음

캐티리 / 신국판 / 293쪽 / 10,000원 (테이프 2개 포함)

영어권 국가로의 이민, 여행, 유학, 출장 중 위급하게 병원을 찾았을 때, 자신의 증상을 쉽게 표현하고 병원 의료진과의 대화를 보다 원활하게 할 수 있는 가이드 북으로, 실제 병원에서 일어날 수 있는 모든 상황들을 거의 다 수록했다.

대한민국 1% 영어고수로 가는 영어공부법

John Park / 신국판 / 256쪽 / 7,900원

본서는 영어를 잘 하고 싶은 한국인들을 위해 쓴 책이다. 오랜 세월 영어를 공부했음에도 불구하고, 영어가 잘 안되는 한국인들에게 정말 영어를 잘 할 수 있는 방법과 길을 제시해준다. 그리고 영어의 초급자부터 영어의 고수를 목표로 삼고 있는 중급자나 고급자까지를 대상으로 한다. 또한 현장에서 영어교육을 담당하고 있는 모든 분에게도 유용하도록 하였다. 이 책은 그냥 물고기를 주는 것이 아니라, 물고기를 잡는 방법을 알려주고 있다.

청소년이 꼭 읽어야 할 세계의 위대한 인물 사전

편집부 / 신국판 / 526쪽 / 13,500원

초 · 중 · 고생을 위한 세계위인 백과사전으로 사상가, 정치인, 예술가, 문학가, 경제인 등 일반인에게 잘 알려진 위인들의 숨겨진 비화나 성장과정에서의 역경이 잘 나타나 있다. 이 책에는 인류 역사에 큰 영향을 끼치고 독창적인 개성으로 깊은 감동을 선사했던 101명의 위인들이 엄선되어 있으며, 지금까지 교양이나 지식 차원에서 알고 있던 내용도 포함되어 있을 수도 있겠지만 청소년들의 입장에서 꼭 알아두어야 할 인물들에 관한 개별적 정보도 얻을 수 있다.

영어비결

장승원 / 신국판 / 253쪽 / 8,900원

국내 최연소 토플 만점자 장승원의 영어공부 방법서이다. 토익보다 어렵다는 토플에서 만점을 받고 외고에 입학하기까지의 모든 과정을 14살이던 중학교 2학년 시절의 기억을 되살려 솔직담백하게 풀어썼다.

즉석에서 바로바로 활용하는 Make it 일어회화 사전

이화승 / 4×6판 / 512쪽 / 12,000원(mp3용 CD 포함), 15,000원(테이프 4개+mp3용 CD 포함)

본서는 일본 현지에서 사용하는 정통 일본어 표현의 다양성을 만끽할 수 있으며, 여기서 익힌 표현을 상황에 따라 활용할 수 있도록 뉘앙스를 고려하여 기획된 일본어회화 사전이다. 누구나 쉽게 일본어회화를 익힐 수 있도록 기본표현부터 빈출 패턴 문형, 관용표현까지 핵심표현을 폭넓게 실었다. 작은 판형으로 일상생활에서 일어나는 모든 주제의 대화를 수록하고 있다.

즉석에서 바로바로 활용하는 Make it 영어회화 사전

Steven Oh / 4×6판 / 496쪽 / 12,000원(mp3용 CD 포함), 15,000원(테이프 4개+mp3용 CD 포함)

본서는 미국 현지에서 네이티브들이 사용하는 정통 영어 표현의 다양성을 만끽할 수 있으며,

여기서 익힌 표현을 상황에 따라 활용할 수 있도록 뉘앙스를 고려하여 기획된 영어회화사전이다. 누구나 쉽게 영어회화를 익힐 수 있도록 기본표현부터 빈출 패턴 문형, 관용표현까지 핵심표현을 폭넓게 실었다.

즉석에서 바로바로 활용하는 Make it 중국어 회화 사전

김현철, 김춘희 / 4×6판 / 511쪽 / 12,000원(mp3용 CD 포함), 15,000원(테이프 4개+mp3용 CD 포함)

중국 현지에서 사용하는 표현을 상황에 따라 활용할 수 있도록 뉘앙스를 고려하여 기획된 중국어회화사전이다. 기본표현부터 빈출 패턴 문형, 관용표현까지 핵심표현을 폭넓게 실었다. 독자들이 정확한 발음으로 자신감 있게 학습할 수 있도록 mp3용 CD를 제공하고 있으며, 사이즈를 크게 줄여 휴대하기에 편리하도록 배려하였다.

어린왕자

앙투안 생텍쥐페리 / 이화승 역 / A5 / 한글판 136쪽, 영어판 136쪽 / 각권 5,000원 합본 9,500원

이 책은 묘한 매력이 있어서 본래 '어른을 위한 동화'지만, 어린이가 읽으면 동화가 되고 어른이 읽으면 어른과 사회에 대한 비판이 된다. 그리고 작가가 이 책을 쓴 시대(1942년 경)를 더듬어 보고 비행사로서 작가의 인생관을 생각하면 이야기 내면에는 깊은 철학이 감춰진 것을 알 수 있다.

동물농장

조지 오웰 / 조혜정 역 / A5 / 한글판 120쪽, 영어판 160쪽 / 각권 5,000원 합본 9,500원

스탈린 치하의 소비에트 전체주의에 대한 풍자소설. 현대 사회의 전체주의적 경향이 도달하게 될 종말을 묘사한 조지오웰의 대표작으로서, 정치적인 면을 배제하고 우화로서 읽더라도 훌륭한 작품이다. 유명한 정치소설이라 난해한 소설이라고 생각하기 쉬우나 단순한 스토리에 분량도 짧아 쉽게 읽을 수 있는 책이다.

위대한 개츠비

스콧 피츠제럴드 / 이화승 역 / A5 / 한글판 271쪽, 영어판 143쪽 / 각권 5,000원 합본 9,500원

20세기 최고의 미국 소설이라는 명성 덕분에 국내 대학 영문과 교재로 오래 사랑받아온 작품. 완벽한 번역과 이해를 돕는 배경지도, 인물 분석을 더했다. 본서는 지금까지 나온 어떤 번역본보다 오류가 적다는 점을 자부한다.

안네의 일기

안네 프랑크 / A5 / 한글판 140쪽, 영어판 156쪽 / 각권 5,000원 합본 9,500원

꿈 많은 문학소녀가 남긴 생생한 감동. 안네는 아빠가 열세 살 생일선물로 준 일기장에 친한 친구를 대하듯 속마음을 털어놓는다. 유태인 탄압이 극심해지면서 8명의 '은신' 생활이 시작된다. 안네는 게쉬타포에 발각될 때까지 2년 여의 힘겨운 생활을 기록으로 남긴다.

변신

프란츠 카프카 / A5 / 한글판 104쪽, 영어판 112쪽 / 각권 5,000원 합본 9,500원

그 어떤 소설보다도 더 충격적인 묘사로 이야기는 시작된다. 평범한 월급쟁이 그레고르 잠자는 흉측한 벌레가 되어 누워 있는 자신을 발견한다. 그의 모습을 본 사람들은 모두 혼비백산하지만 가족들은 '혹시 그가 인간으로 돌아오지 않을까' 하는 기대를 품고 동거를 시작한다.

포우 단편선

에드가 앨런 포우 / A5 / 한글판 128쪽, 영어판 152쪽 / 각권 5,000원 합본 9,500원

〈검은 고양이〉는 인간의 잔혹성과 두려움의 전형을 보여준다. 최초의 추리소설 〈모르그 가의 살인사건〉에서는 독특한 구성과 분석을 구사하였다. 〈도둑맞은 편지〉는 포우의 뛰어난 지성이 드러난 작품이다. 일반적 추리소설과 달리 사건의 범인을 알려주고 이야기를 풀어가는 추리의 묘미와 재치가 흥미롭다.

기타

세계 유명인사들의 명연설문

편집부 편저 / A5 / 한글판 168쪽, 영어판 183쪽 / 각권 5,000원, 합본 9,500원

본서는 미국 민주당의 유력 대선 주자인 버락 오바마(일리노이) 상원의원을 비롯하여 세계적인 기업 마이크로소프트사의 전 회장인 빌 게이츠, 프레젠테이션의 귀재인 스티브 잡스 등의 기업가와 토크쇼의 여왕 오프라 윈프리 등 각 분야에서 세계적인 리더들로 평가받는 15인의 명사들이 대학교 졸업을 앞두고 사회에 진출하려는 젊은이들에게 전하는 희망메세지가 실려 있다.

반석수학 시리즈 초등 수학비타민 A~E

Hisakazu Kato저 / 4×6배변형판 / 각권 112쪽 / 각권 8,500원

본서는 만화로 초등학교 수학의 핵심 원리를 친근하게 배울 수 있다. 어린이들이 수학에서 특히 어려워하는 부분을 그림으로 재미있게 해설하고 있으며 학생들이 실제로 많이 틀리는 계산 과정까지 친절하게 보여주고 일상을 통해 수학의 도형과 그래프, 길이 · 부피 · 무게의 단위를 배운다. 중간 쉬는 페이지에서는 역사적인 수학자들의 이야기가 나오고 수학을 잘하는 학생들의 비결이나 수학이 실생활에 어떻게 쓰이는지 배운다. 만화 뒷부분에 본문에서 배운 내용을 확인하는 문제 및 정답 수록되어 있다.

귀뻥 선생의 리스닝 특별훈련 30

강홍식 / 4×6배변형판 / 284쪽 / 12,000원 (mp3용 CD 포함)

본서는 초중급자들을 위한 단계별 리스닝 프로그램으로 구성되어 하루에 한 UNIT씩 5단계별 구성을 따라가다 보면 어느덧 초급에서 중급으로, 중급에서 고급으로 레벨업된 자신을 발견할 수 있다. 귀가 뚫리지 않는 이유 30가지를 설명하고 해결책을 제시했다. 발음기호로도 설명할 수 없는 어색한 발음들을 한글로 알기 쉽게 써놓아 발음상의 취약점을 잡아냈다. 미국식 영어뿐 아니라 영국식 영어도 수록하여 영국발음과 함께 현지표현을 학습할 수 있다.

아들에게 보내는 아버지의 편지 (Letters To His Son)

필립 체스터필드 / A5 / 한글판 120 쪽, 영문판 144쪽 / 각권 5,000원, 합본 9,500원

본서는 교양인이 되기 위해 꼭 알아야 할 처세술 17가지를 제시하고 있다. 원제는 〈Letters to His Son 아들에게 보내는 편지〉이며, 저자인 필립 체스터필드가 네덜란드 대사로서 헤이그에 주재 중 얻은 아들에게 보낸 편지글을 엮은 것이다. 그의 편지는 재치와 품위로 포장된 빈틈없는 충고이며 실리적이며, 출세지향적인 철학을 담고 있다. 문학적 가치도 뛰어나지만 만인이 알아야 할 처세술을 담은 책으로도 유명하다.